Few construction projects of the twentieth century match the building of the Alaska Highway for drama, setting, and engineering challenge. From the authorization for highway construction in February 1942 until the completion of the pioneer road through the harsh northern landscape, scarcely eight months passed. The struggle of "man and machine against the wilderness" conducted under the pressures of war captured the imagination of the North American public. The annual flood of tourists along the "Route of '42" suggests that this sense of drama and fascination is still alive.

In recognition of the 40th anniversary of this episode in Canadian-American cooperation, a symposium was held at Fort St. John, one of several communities that were, and still are, profoundly affected by the building of the road. The papers presented at this interdisciplinary gathering of international scholars of the Canadian and American norths illustrate the significance of the highway in such diverse spheres as Canadian-American relations, British Columbia politics, American military history, and the evolution of the northern society.

American military planners to push the road through as a wartime project. Surveying, building, maintaining, and operating the highway are the subjects of the following papers, while the next two deal with the postwar administration of the road by Canada.

The remaining papers discuss the impact of the highway on Canadian-United States wartime relations and on the economy and society of the region — including its effects on the native population and wildlife resources — and on the eclipse of Dawson City as the administrative and economic centre of the Yukon Territory.

With much new information and insight, this book makes an original and important contribution to twentieth-century Canadian history. It will be of interest not only to historians specializing in northern studies but also to local history buffs who inhabit the region traversed by the highway.

KENNETH COATES is an assistant professor of history at Brandon University.

THE ALASKA HIGHWAY

THE
ALASKA HIGHWAY

PAPERS OF THE
40TH ANNIVERSARY SYMPOSIUM

Edited by
KENNETH COATES

University of British Columbia Press
Vancouver
1985

The Alaska Highway
Papers of the 40th Anniversary Symposium

© The University of British Columbia Press 1985
All rights reserved

This book has been published with the help of a grant from the Social Science Federation of Canada, using funds provided by the Social Sciences and Humanities Research Council of Canada, and a grant from The Canada Council.

Canadian Cataloguing in Publication Data
Main entry under title:

The Alaska Highway

Papers presented at the Alaska Highway 40th
　　Anniversary Symposium, held June 1982 at Northern
　　Lights College.
ISBN 0-7748-0229-4

1. Alaska Highway — History — Congresses.
I. Coates, Kenneth, 1956-　　II. Alaska Highway
40th Anniversary Symposium (1982: Northern Lights
College)
HE356.A4A42 1982　　388.1'09798　　C85-091325-X

International Standard Book Number 0-7748-0229-4
Printed in Canada

Contents

List of Illustrations	*vii*
Preface	*ix*
Acknowledgments	*xvii*

SECTION 1: PLANNING THE HIGHWAY

1. The Latent Fear: Canadian-American Relations and Early Proposals for a Highway to Alaska — DAVID REMLEY … 1
2. T.D. Pattullo and the British Columbia to Alaska Highway — ROBIN FISHER … 9
3. The Realities of Strategic Planning: The Decision to Build the Alaska Highway — M. V. BEZEAU … 25

SECTION 2: BUILDING THE HIGHWAY

4. General Bill Hoge and the Alaska Highway — JOHN T. GREENWOOD … 39
5. Cut, Fill and Straighten: The Role of the Public Roads Administration in the Building of the Alaska Highway — HEATH TWICHELL … 54
6. The Army Medical Department and the Construction of the Alaska Highway — DWIGHT D. OLAND … 65
7. Surveying the Line: The Canadian Participation — DON W. THOMSON … 75

SECTION 3: CANADIAN SOVEREIGNTY AND THE ALASKA HIGHWAY

8. The Army of Occupation: Malcolm MacDonald and U.S. Military Involvement in the Canadian Northwest — CURTIS R. NORDMAN … 83

Appendix: Note on Developments in North-Western Canada … 95

9. The Alaska Highway in Canada-United States Relations   102
RICHARD J. DIUBALDO

SECTION 4: THE POSTWAR HIGHWAY

10. "Really a Defile Throughout its Length": The Defence of the Alaska Highway in Peacetime   119
STEPHEN J. HARRIS
11. The Civilian Highway: Public Works Canada and the Alaska Highway, 1964-83   133
KENNETH COATES

SECTION 5: THE IMPACT OF THE ALASKA HIGHWAY

12. The Alaska Highway and the Indians of the Southern Yukon, 1942-50: A Study of Native Adaptation to Northern Development   151
KENNETH COATES
13. The Gravel Magnet: Some Social Impacts of the Alaska Highway on Yukon Indians   172
JULIE CRUIKSHANK
14. The Impact of the Alaska Highway on Dawson City   188
RICHARD STUART

Index   205

Illustrations
following page 116

1. Signing the documents to begin construction
2. T.D. Pattullo
3. Survey crews laying out the highway route
4. Mule train on the Alaska Highway
5. Improving the pioneer road
6. William Hoge inspecting road construction
7. Ditch digging on the Army road
8. Workers along the highway
9. The meeting of the "cats"
10. Army trucks travelling the highway
11. An Army 6 x 6 truck on the road
12. General William Hoge
13. Improving the highway east of Teslin Lake
14. Resurfacing crew on highway
15. Workers and equipment on the northern road
16. The 341st Engineers, Company F
17. Inspecting a difficult section of the road
18. Pontoon bridge over the Donjek River
19. The permanent bridge over the Donjek River
20. The first convoy on the Alaska Highway
21. Construction camp at the south end of Kluane Lake
22. Camp life on the highway
23. Camp Americanada
24. The Whitehorse camp of the 18th Engineer regiment
25. Supplies for the army workers
26. An isolated construction camp
27. Milepost "0" at Dawson Creek
28. The official opening of the Alaska Highway
29. Flood damage on the Alaska Highway
30. Inspecting flood damage
31. Washout on the highway
32. Bridge damage
33. The Northwest Highway System headquarters
34. Signposts at Watson Lake
35. The Beaver Creek church on the highway
36. Whitehorse in 1942
37. Modern Whitehorse
38. The Alaska Highway at Jakes Corner

PHOTO CREDITS

The following institutions and individuals have supplied the illustrations indicated:
Government of the Yukon: 34, 35, 37, 38
Phyllis Church: 4, 10, 14, 23
Provincial Archives of British Columbia: 2
Public Archives of Canada: 1, 3, 5, 8, 15, 22, 25, 26
Public Works Canada: 7, 11, 17, 29, 30, 31, 32, 33
U.S. Army: 6, 9, 12, 13, 28
Yukon Territorial Archives: 16, 18, 19, 20, 21, 24, 27, 36

Preface

Few construction projects of the twentieth century match the building of the Alaska Highway from 1942 to 1945 for drama, setting, and engineering challenge. From the authorization of highway construction in February 1942, until the completion of a pioneer road through the forbidding northern landscape, scarcely eight months had passed. This struggle of "man and machine against the wilderness," conducted under the pressures of war and seemingly imminent Japanese attack, captured the imagination of the North American public. The annual flood of tourists along the "Route of '42" suggests that the sense of drama and fascination has hardly abated, even after forty years.

In June 1982, in recognition of the 40th anniversary of this episode in Canadian-American co-operation, military enterprise, and northern development, Northern Lights College of Fort St. John, British Columbia, hosted an interdisciplinary and international gathering of scholars of the Canadian and American norths. Modelled after the successful Arctic Islands Centenary held two years earlier in Yellowknife, the conference sought to bring academics together to reflect on the issues, personalities, and effects of the construction of the Alaska Highway. Well-attended and enthusiastically received, the meeting ably reflected the efforts and commitment of its organizer, Curtis Nordman.

Mention must be made of conference participants whose work is not part of this collection. Richard Finnie, northern author and filmmaker, started the conference off on the right foot. His film record and reminiscences gave a unique insight into the building of the highway. Dr. Stan Thomson, professor of Civil Engineering at the University of Alberta, provided a most entertaining illustrated lecture on postwar maintenance difficulties along the highway. Frank Duerden's contribution on the demographic implications of highway construction, and Robert Page's analysis of the collapse of the Alaska Highway natural gas pipeline proposal provided further evidence of the wide-ranging impact of the highway on the north. At the end of the conference, representatives from British Columbia Hydro and Public Works Canada helped place our historical deliberations in a contemporary context through short presentations on current plans for highway redevelopment. A special note of appreciation is due former Governor General Edward

Schreyer, whose keen interest in the north led him to accept an invitation to be the conference's keynote speaker.

The essays collected here, presented at the conference by leading authorities in their fields, document the breadth and originality of the proceedings. The papers illustrate the significance of the highway in such diverse themes as Canadian-American relations, British Columbia politics, American military history, and the evolution of northern society. This volume, however, does not seek to provide a comprehensive summary of the construction of the Alaska Highway. Further study is needed of southern perceptions of the highway, postwar implications for northern development, the organization of labour and private contractors, and many other subjects. The conference and, therefore, this anthology, were designed to stimulate further professional research on the Alaska Highway.

The essays are presented in five sections. Section 1 examines the rationale for and fate of early proposals for a highway to Alaska. The idea of expanding existing transportation networks to the far north was hardly original to the 1940's. Beginning with the Klondike gold rush (1896-1904), numerous suggestions for trails, railways, and roads surfaced. Each one, from the Mackenzie and Mann railway of the early 1900's to T. D. Pattullo's dream of a northern highway, fell victim to cautious governments or reluctant bankers. Lacking political and economic power, the north relied on southern promoters to develop transportation links with "outside" markets. As the essays in this section demonstrate, the decision to build a highway was permanently outside northern control. Instead, the authority lay with southern politicians, Canadian and American, national and regional, who alone could raise the funds and justify the risk of the massive and expensive venture. The construction of the Alaska Highway was dependent upon southern priorities, not northern realities.

David Remley, a professor of English at the University of New Mexico and author of *Crooked Road: The Story of the Alaska Highway,* offers an assessment of the failure of several early highway proposals. Remley argues that Canadian-American tensions, particularly Canadian fears of American military encroachment, defeated the projects. During the 1930's, British Columbia premier Thomas Dufferin Pattullo suggested a federal-provincial highway to the north and, when that failed, proposed a joint project with American authorities. Throughout, Remley argues, Pattullo's plans foundered amidst public and government concern that the highway served American economic and strategic interests and hence threatened Canadian sovereignty. This "latent fear" proved sufficient to kill all peacetime proposals for a highway to Alaska.

Currently preparing a biography of Thomas "Duff" Pattullo, Robin Fisher of Simon Fraser University offers a markedly different interpretation of the same proposals. To Fisher, the northern highway was another of Pattullo's public works projects designed to alleviate the devastating impact of the depression. Pattullo's solution to prevailing economic chaos, however, clashed with those of his Liberal counterpart in Ottawa, Prime Minister William Lyon Mackenzie King. The ever-cautious King rejected Pattullo's grandiose plans, rebuffed his requests for financial assistance, and tried to counter the B.C. premier's efforts to secure American backing. Contrary to Remley, Fisher argues that the failure of Pattullo's northern vision reflected not Canadian-American tensions, but rather an ongoing federal-provincial dispute over government spending and public works.

Captain M. V. Bezeau of the Directorate of History, Department of National Defence, moves ahead a decade to examine the 1942 decision to proceed with construction. His provocative essay rejects conventional wisdom by challenging the often repeated assertion that the Alaska Highway was built after careful consideration of the strategic requirements for such a route. Examining the tortuous decision-making processes of the United States' military and civilian bureaucracy. Bezeau concludes the highway "was a magnificent achievement, carried out as a military project in time of war, but it was not needed for defence. The highway was actually planned and built for other reasons."

Section 2 offers a variety of perspectives on the personalities and issues of the actual construction of the Alaska Highway. In so doing, these essays flesh out the rather shallow images of the work of soldiers and civilian labourers in the north. What emerges is an illustration of the importance of co-operative ventures, both between government departments and between countries. Also evident are the frequent departures from that co-operative spirit, the consequences of limited preplanning, and the role of key individuals in expediting the project. Together, the essays provide a greater appreciation of the logistical challenge facing the engineers and construction workers during their push northward.

The first essay is a detailed study of the northern career of General Bill Hoge by John Greenwood, chief of the historical division of the U.S. Army Corps of Engineers. As commander of the northern sector of the Alaska Highway project, Hoge faced a formidable task. He located sections of the route, organized his engineering units, co-ordinated his activities with those of the Public Roads Administration (P.R.A.) and wrestled with the difficult technical challenges posed by muskeg and permafrost. Greenwood's examination provides an incisive glimpse into the operational difficulties faced by army personnel and, more importantly, into the internal disputes caused by differing perspectives of the construction plan and process. Hoge repeatedly ran afoul of the P.R.A., finding their preoccupation with highway standards incompatible with his orders to hasten construction. Hoge's seeming disregard for internal politics proved his undoing, and he was relieved of his duties in August 1942. Greenwood ascribes Hoge's dismissal to the reputation of General Sommervell, Hoge's superior, for "pomp, show and grand designs" and to Hoge's disregard for such ceremonial niceties. Hoge's subsequent success as a tank commander in Europe and his eventual promotion to Commander-in-Chief, United States Army in Europe supports the author's contention.

The second paper, Heath Twitchell's assessment of the work of the Public Roads Administration, offers a much needed corrective to existing images of the construction phase. In Alaska Highway lore, the U.S. Army engineers receive the credit for pushing the road through under exacting conditions. While correct, this perspective ignores the role of the P.R.A. in turning the rustic, often poorly located pioneer trail into a usable military highway. As Twitchell documents, the P.R.A. had the difficult and low-profile task of cutting, filling, and straightening. These duties lacked the drama of the engineers' bulldozers pushing through the night to meet at Soldier's Summit, but they were essential in converting the Alaska Highway into a viable and lasting transportation link.

The third essay examines the intricacies of construction in even more detail. Sewers, slit-trenches, and socks seldom receive much historical mention, but Dwight Oland's essay on the activities of the United States Army Medical Corps provides important insights into the medical side of the highway project. The potential for disease, injury and suffering during construction of the highway was great, given climatic conditions, often inadequate supplies, and isolation from proper hospital facilities. To overcome anticipated problems with sanitation, infectious disease, poor nutrition, frostbite and other maladies, the Medical Corps established an elaborate preventive medicine programme. By enforcing strict standards, co-operating with Canadian medical authorities, and treating local inhabitants, the medical detachments successfully controlled the level of suffering attending Alaska Highway construction.

In the final essay in this section, Don W. Thomson, author of *Men and Meridians: The History of Surveying and Mapping in Canada,* cautions against the assumption that the Alaska Highway project was an exclusively American undertaking. Examining the role of several Canadian surveyors, most notably Knox F. McCusker of the Dominion Land Survey, Thomson illustrates how Canadian specialists played a key role in the location of the southern segments of the highway. These surveyors had been active in the area before the Second World War, particularly in locating the airfields of the Northwest Staging Route. These earlier activities, and some joint ventures with American personnel in the spring of 1942, were crucial, Thomson suggests, for permitting the rapid commencement of construction in the summer of that year.

In Section 3, the emphasis shifts from the highway itself to Canadian government attitudes towards the north. Historians have long acknowledged that from the decline of the Klondike gold fields in the early twentieth century to 1945, the federal government expressed little interest in its northern territories. Scientific missions by V. Stefansson and the Canadian Arctic Expedition and flag-waving journeys by the Royal Canadian Mounted Police and Captain Bernier constituted little more than symbolical assertions of sovereignty. The two essays in this section illustrate the importance of the Alaska Highway and related defence projects in awakening government interest in the north.

The first paper, by Curtis R. Nordman of Northern Lights College, revolves around the irony that this new federal interest originated in the activities of Malcom MacDonald, British High Commissioner in Ottawa. In both 1942 and 1943, MacDonald travelled through the north, examining defence projects and visiting northern communities. He returned gravely concerned. The district appeared to be a United States territory and MacDonald was worried that the Americans might stay. He carried his fears directly to the federal cabinet, arguing for firm measures to prevent an American takeover. MacDonald was not without supporters, for a small group of Ottawa-based government officials, self-styled "Northern Nationalists," shared his concern. The government responded quickly to Macdonald's strongly worded memorandum, appointing a special commissioner to oversee construction activities and attempting to establish a more formal presence in the north. MacDonald's noted memorandum on the northern defence projects is included as an appendix.

Richard J. Diubaldo of Concordia University places the question of sovereignty in a somewhat larger context. Focusing on the Alaska Highway and the associated Canol Project, Diubaldo demonstrates that the Canadian government feared further American involvement on Canadian soil. Extracting the nation from the potential dispute over sovereignty proved difficult, however, as the interests of the two countries in continental defence and northern development remained intertwined. The warnings of Malcom MacDonald and a heightened awareness of the potential value of the north convinced the Canadian government to act decisively. Canada moved to assert its claims to the north and to deny any attempted American incursions. The government also reluctantly agreed to maintain the Alaska Highway after the war, thus allaying American fears about the potential loss of a valuable and expensive defence asset while guaranteeing a permanent Canadian presence along the highway.

Section 4 examines aspects of highway responsibility after the Second World War. The federal government felt compelled to maintain the highway, even though there was little economic justification for the expense and reluctance to fund the necessary reconstruction. With the official transfer of the road to Canada on 1 April 1946, the Canadian government was left to determine the future of the Alaska Highway. Military authorities argued that the route was of questionable military value, but politicians decided to maintain the highway as a defence measure, if only to justify the massive wartime and postwar expenditures. Federal hesitation, however, clashed with the attitudes of northern residents and businessmen who clamoured for the immediate opening of the route to civilian travel and the rapid upgrading of the highway to encourage tourist and commercial traffic. The government attempted to balance these requests against the impressive cost of reconstruction. The result has been that from 1946 to the present, two federal departments, the Department of National Defense and Public Works Canada, have administered the highway without a clear federal commitment to the road's future.

Steven J. Harris, historian with the Directorate of History of the Department of National Defence, assesses the army's handling of the Alaska Highway. Initially, the army saw the road as an important defence responsibility and a potential training ground for Canadian armed forces. Such maneuvers as Operation Sweetbriar soon illustrated the futility of defending the route given limited troop commitments. The postwar development of intercontinental ballistic missiles also rendered such frontline defence substantially redundant. Harris argues that the army had been given a responsibility it did not want and, delegated the task, the Department of National Defence consistently found itself without the necessary resources either to defend or improve the highway.

The frustrations evident during the Department of National Defence's tenure did not end with the transfer of the highway to the Department of Public Works (later Public Works Canada) on 1 April 1964. Kenneth Coates of Brandon University summarizes the department's attempt to reconstruct the highway in the face of conflicting jurisdictions, vociferous public demands and federal government reticence. Recognizing the low priority ascribed the highway by the national government and responding to the cautious recommendations of the 1966 Stanford Institute study, Public Works Canada (P.W.C.) implemented a limited development programme. Unable to justify the massive expenditures necessary for a complete renovation, the department sought instead to proceed on a piecemeal basis, repairing badly damaged or poorly sited sections, systematically replacing bridges and paving the highway near settled areas. Despite continued public demands, P.W.C. adhered to its programme as funds and government priorities permitted. Like the Department of National Defence a somewhat reluctant player, Public Works Canada has been caught between the conflicting priorities of federal, provincial and territorial governments, an on-going problem that has thwarted the department's attempts to delegate responsibility for the road to other levels of government.

Section 5, consisting of three essays on the highway's impact on the Yukon Territory, deals with subjects given little coverage in other studies of the Alaska Highway. Despite the persistent image of men and machines crossing a northern wilderness, the route did not traverse a wasteland. Many natives inhabited the districts opened by the highway; their life patterns and conditions changed noticeably as a result of the construction. As well, the Yukon had a small society based on the extraction of mineral resources and seasonal river travel. The Alaska Highway altered life in the north. New districts were opened for potential development, contact with the "outside" improved, and existing economic, social and political structures faced major challenges. There were other changes as well. The awakened federal interest in the north, combined with improved access to southern districts, led to expanded government programmes for natives, subsidized economic development, and increased social planning. The Alaska Highway both instigated and came to symbolize the establishment of a new territorial order.

The first paper, by Kenneth Coates, examines the impact of the highway on the natives of the southern Yukon. Placing the developments from 1942 to 1950 in the context of previous native-white relations in the territory, Coates argues that the changes were more quantitative than qualitative. Owing to the continued vitality of the fur trade, the natives remained as before, on the margins of the territorial economic and social order. The highway proved disruptive in other ways. It served as a conduit for disease, which had a devastating effect on the local natives. The opening of the Alaska Highway coincided with other developments in native-white relations, such as the introduction of family allowances, a major depression in the fur trade beginning in 1949, and increased federal intervention in Indian affairs. Coates suggests that these latter developments, as much as the actual construction of the highway, were responsible for the major alterations in native lifestyle so evident in the 1950's.

Anthropologist Julie Cruikshank, of the Yukon Native Languages Project in Whitehorse, offers a somewhat different and broader perspective on the question of native response to the highway. Tracing changes in native values and lifestyles from aboriginal times to the present, Cruickshank suggests that the Alaska Highway and postwar developments significantly undermined existing Indian customs and migratory patterns. Based largely on an extensive series of interviews with natives of the southern Yukon, this essay illustrates the decisive shift in native attitudes evident in the 1950's and thereafter. Most importantly, it documents how the Alaska Highway came to serve as the natives' symbol for this reordering of their way of life.

Richard Stuart, a historian for Parks Canada, examines a different transformation attending the construction of the Alaska Highway. Before 1942, the territorial economic and political system revolved around Dawson City, centre of the Klondike gold fields. At that time, Whitehorse was little more than a way station on the route to Dawson City, although it was the important junction of the White Pass and Yukon Route railway and the company's sternwheelers operating along the Yukon River. With the completion of the highway, population, power, and business opportunity shifted south to Whitehorse. The territorial and federal governments acknowledged the change by shifting several key departments and a large number of government personnel to the southern centre. The politicians and businessmen of Dawson fought to prevent a total loss of influence, arguing in particular for an extension of the highway system to their community. Buttressed by its role as the service centre for the Alaska Highway, Whitehorse's claim to economic and political preeminence in the territory proved unassailable. Recognizing the fundamental reordering brought on by the construction of the Alaska Highway, the federal government made Whitehorse the capital of the Yukon Territory in 1953.

Individually, the essays in this volume provide new, often challenging insights into the personalities, issues and effects of the construction of the Alaska Highway; collectively, they point to the need to continue the reexamination of the history of this important event. This volume is not intended to provide the final word on the construction of the Alaska Highway. As mentioned earlier, a great deal of work remains to be done. The arguments, approaches and issues mentioned here will perhaps suggest the possibilities of carrying the study much further. If this collection has accomplished this much, it will serve as an appropriate symbol of the Alaska Highway 40th Anniversary Symposium.

A volume of this type is very much a collective effort, and I would be remiss if I did not acknowledge the assistance provided to me. Though personal commitments prevented Curtis Nordman from continuing the editorial work on this collection, the conference and this book reflect his inspired leadership and dedication. Those at the conference recorded their thanks to Curtis for his magnificent efforts; I would like to add my personal appreciation for his continued support and encouragement. Dr. Jane Fredeman of the University of British Columbia Press attended the conference, shared the participants' enthusiasm and provided every possible assistance to ensure the publication of the proceedings. I must also thank Dr. Peter Hordern, Dean of Arts at Brandon University, for his encouragement, and Janice Mahoney, Sherry Hayward and especially Joan Thiessen of the Arts Typing Pool for their patient and painstaking attention to the numerous drafts of this book. Finally, I would like to acknowledge the financial assistance of the Social Sciences and Humanities Research Council of Canada, whose grant in aid of publication made production of this volume possible.

Kenneth S. Coates
Brandon University

Acknowledgements

The idea for the Alaska Highway Symposium came to me shortly after I moved up to live along what my five year old son Trevor mistakenly, but perhaps not inappropriately, referred to as the "Elastic Highway." The conference, however, was the product of many people and many sponsors. As is always the case, the contributions made really deserve much more than a passing reference in an acknowledgement.

Nevertheless, mention must be made of the generous support provided by B.C. Hydro; the City of Fort St. John; the Directorate of History of the Department of National Defence; the Government of British Columbia; Northern Lights College; the Peace River Liard Regional District; Public Works Canada; and Westcoast Transmission. Of special note was the funding received from the Social Sciences and Humanities Research Council and the Employment and Development Branch of Employment and Immigration Canada.

The last mentioned grant allowed the hiring of Penny Kary, Norma Graham, Wendy Culling, and Andrea Keen, without whose hard work the conference would not have been the success it was. Others owed a note of gratitude include: Forrest Hutchinson, Gert Babcock, Sue Popesku, Marg Cleaveley, Brian Palmer, and Michael Puttonen.

Finally, I would like to thank the two people responsible for ensuring the publication of the proceedings. First, my thanks to Dr. Jane Fredeman, the Senior Editor of UBC Press, who not only recognized the worth of the papers, but continued to press for publication when the tumultuous politics of British Columbia tended to divert me from my commitment. And, lastly, I'd like to thank Dr. Kenneth Coates who salvaged the project when Operation Solidarity claimed the final ounces of energy that I should have been directing to this worthy task.

Curtis R. Nordman
Conference Chairperson

SECTION 1:

Planning the Highway

1

The Latent Fear: Canadian-American Relations and Early Proposals for a Highway to Alaska

DAVID REMLEY

Throughout the 1930's, citizens of both the United States and Canada tried to begin construction of a highway to Alaska across British Columbia and the Yukon. Their efforts were continually stalled, however, by problems which seemed largely beyond their control. Not until the attack on Pearl Harbor did both national governments, apparently realizing the military need for the international highway, put aside their fears and get on with the colossal construction job.

One aspect of the complicated struggle was that two British Columbian premiers, Simon Fraser Tolmie in the early 1930's and Thomas Dufferin Pattullo in the later part of the decade, looked to the American government for aid when it seemed apparent that the Dominion had little intention of committing money and effort to the planning and construction of the highway. Pattullo's efforts particularly illustrate that often expressed view that the dominion government has traditionally overlooked the needs of the western provinces. There have been a number of economic and political reasons for this neglect. One of the reasons in the 1930's seems to have been a fear of American economic and military domination. If indeed the dominion government did overlook the west in the 1930's, it drove the western premiers to imaginative and, in Pattullo's instance, somewhat irregular methods to achieve their objectives.

In February 1938, Premier Pattullo announced that his province stood on the threshold of an era of economic expansion which would end unemployment in British Columbia. This promising forecast, the Vancouver *Sun* reported, was based upon a "program" for construction of the Alaska Highway which would employ "thousands" of local citizens, "hundreds" of graders, tractors, and trucks, open up the "untold potential wealth ... from the vast northern hinterland" and bring in romantic, dollar-spending North American tourists. "The 600 miles of road" to Hazelton "already constructed," said the *Sun* of the Premier's plans, would "be the contribution of this province, with the Dominion and United States jointly arranging the remainder."[1] What evidence Pattullo or the *Sun* staff may have had that the federal and provincial governments were about to work out some arrangement for the building of the more than one thousand miles of road from Hazelton to Alaska remains a mystery. There is in fact no evidence that the dominion government was willing at that time to help with the project.

Aware of this unwillingness in Ottawa, Premier Pattullo went to Washington in April 1938 to see if he could get American funds for construction. He called upon various important officials, including Ernest Gruening, director of the Interior Department's Division of Territories and Island Possessions, and Delegate Anthony J. Dimond of Alaska, both long interested in the proposed international highway. Gruening was pleased to hear of Pattullo's interest. But his statement that the premier's activity was "the most hopeful reaction ... we have yet had from the Canadian side" revealed his naiveté about politics across the border.[2] Pattullo's efforts were, in fact, causing consternation in Ottawa. Some Canadian leaders seemed offended by the premier's initiative. Besides, there was the sticky question of funding. If Pattullo had had Canadian sources of money, things might have gone well. But he had no money at home and could find none.

Dr. O. D. Skelton of the Canadian Department of External Affairs was furious. He wrote angrily to Prime Minister King about Pattullo's trip to Washington, complaining that his statement that the American government might loan British Columbia fifteen million dollars for constructing the highway across Canada represented "surely ... a high water mark [or a low water mark] in provincial diplomacy."[3] Two weeks before Skelton wrote to King, Pattullo had discussed the proposed highway with the prime minister himself. King had been in no position to offer financial aid from the Dominion, nor had he, apparently, been prepared at the time for Pattullo's approach to the American government for help. King had simply noted after the conference that the matter should be thought of as strictly a provincial problem, one that might be "undertaken by a private company." He had added that his government might "on appropriate terms" consider turning the Yukon over to British Columbia, "in which event all parts of the highway would be within the control of the Province."[4] And indeed, Pattullo reportedly announced in a speech at home in May that when he spoke to King about the highway, the prime minister told him: "You are going to take over the Yukon — why don't you see what you can do about it."⁵ The provincial and federal Liberal leaders remained at odds.

When, on 25 April, Premier Pattullo called the Canadian Department of External Affairs after his visit to Washington, he seemed, as Dr. Skelton phrased it, "at a loose end." He said that his state visit had been "cordial" and "entirely unofficial." Having learned of American assistance for the PanAmerican Highway and of a plan to lend money to American towns and cities for public works, Pattullo told Skelton he had "put forward" in Washington "the suggestion, which all present accepted, for Congressional authorization to the President to lend or expend a sum not exceeding $15,000,000 for the construction" of the road across British Columbia. Pattullo added that he thought "there would be little difficulty in getting Congressional assent to a sum which would be a flea bite to the United States." Questioned by Skelton, the premier said he and the Americans had talked over the actual terms of the loan, that it would be interest free, and that the Americans themselves had suggested that the principal might be repaid at the rate of $300,000 a year for fifty years. Having concluded, he said, that British Columbia could neither borrow money on the market nor obtain any aid from the Dominion, he saw no way out but "to accept the friendly offer of the United States."⁶

Skelton was flabbergasted. His memorandum to Prime Minister King sparkled with indignation. Pattullo's programme, he wrote, "amounted ... to regarding Canada or British Columbia as a subdivision of the United States. However free the United States was in spending money at home," Skelton said, "it was certainly not going to spend money abroad without a very definite *quid pro quo*" which would be "an understanding" that the U.S. could use the highway in the event of war with Japan, whether or not Canada went to war. Skelton wrote that to accept the money "would be mortgaging our independence," that he did not see how the money could be repaid since the premier had admitted that "any tolls they could levy would not meet the cost of maintaining the road ... much less provide any amount for either principal or interest," and that it seemed "as if we might be putting ourselves under a double obligation to the United States — getting the money from them in the first place, and defaulting on repayment in the second."⁷ The comment King pencilled on Skelton's memo suggests the strength of his own reaction to the news. If realized, he scrawled, Pattullo's proposal would be in the nature of "financial penetration if not financial invasion of a foreign power."⁸

In succeeding days and weeks, Pattullo talked with the prime minister himself. King told him "there would be serious objection to any proposal that the United States Government should lend money to the Province of British Columbia." Pattullo then suggested borrowing from an "international corporation" funded by the Americans. King apparently did not object at first. The premier then proposed to go back to Washington to discuss this new formula with his contacts there. In the meantime, he phoned Dr. Gruening and told him about the "difficulties" that had developed in Ottawa, to which Gruening replied that he was not surprised. Dr. Skelton himself was no happier about this new scheme than about the proposal for a direct loan. "I told him," Skelton wrote, "I could not myself see any difference between a direct loan . . . and a loan through a dummy corporation."[9]

Dominion officials continued to mull over the problem throughout the summer and fall of 1938. In September, Pattullo and his ministers went to Ottawa for a meeting in the prime minister's office. King was absent, but several of his ministers, including T. A. Crerar, I. Mackenzie, C. D. Howe, and J. L. Ilsley, were present. The U.S. Congress had passed, and the president had signed into law, the act to create the Alaskan International Highway Commission, a board of Americans to study the possible construction of an international highway. Now Premier Pattullo suggested that a similar Canadian commission be appointed. He said that there was a great deal of "enthusiasm" in British Columbia, that the construction would solve the provincial unemployment problem, and that the highway was "ardently desired" by the American government. Indeed, he thought the Americans were so "thoroughly in favour of the scheme" that they would be "prepared to finance the road" if necessary, though he would prefer its being financed entirely by Canada. Since that was not to be so, he believed the dominion government "should not stand in the way of the alternative." Mr. Wismer, also representing British Columbia, added that the highway was the "livest issue" in B.C. politics and that if it were not built, the citizens of his province "would place the whole blame upon the Dominion government."

Crerar and Ilsley both raised the issue of American military domination, arguing that Canada might well lose her independence if she made a major financial arrangement with the U.S. to construct the highway. Mackenzie thought, on the other hand, that such worries were unimportant, for he believed that Canada would have little choice but to fight side by side with the Americans in the west if war were declared against Japan. The ministers also discussed the problem of all-Canadian funding, and Ilsley reminded Pattullo that he had admitted that the people of British Columbia would oppose any rise in the national income tax.[10]

A few weeks after the meeting in Ottawa, Premier Pattullo released a statement to the press, noting that Prime Minister King had told him "the Dominion Government would appoint a Canadian Commission to co-operate with the U.S. Commission as a fact finding body, without any commitment as to the construction of the road."[11] Inquiries about this statement revealed that King had indeed made that promise to Pattullo at Laurier House in late September or in October.[12] Pattullo's constant pressure had paid off, and subsequently the Canadian commission was appointed.

Some Canadian officials and newspaper editors were sensitive to the possibility of American military and economic control. In general, there was strong support for the Alaskan highway in British Columbia, except among members of the Conservative Party. In the Dewdney by-election of 20 May 1938, for example, local Conservatives argued that the highway was not only an impractical dream as there was no money, but also that the construction, if funded by the United States, would endanger Canada's neutrality and sovereignty.[13] The conservative Vancouver *Daily Province* even editorialized that American Assistant Secretary of War Louis Johnson's proposed trip to Alaska to consider, among other issues, plans for the highway, revealed the true military motives for the construction. The involvement of the war department "tears away the camouflage," cried the editorialist, that the highway was to be constructed for its economic benefits to the north.[14]

More important than the negative attitude on the part of Conservatives in British Columbia, however, was the stalling of dominion officials in Ottawa. And their stalling on the highway was based in part on a desire not to be dominated economically or militarily by their neighbour. Both Prime Minister King and Dr. Skelton revealed their fear of American control, and one finds manifestations elsewhere among the officials in Ottawa.

Among military leaders it was particularly striking. Gen. Ashton, chief of the Canadian general staff, had warned Dr. Skelton in 1935 that the United States' primary interest in the highway construction was military. "In fact," Ashton told Skelton, "the proposed highway is primarily a military project engendered by the U.S. fear of Japanese aggression." He also made it clear he had no doubt that the U.S. would even "disregard Canadian neutrality" if they thought it necessary.[15] Maj.-Gen. C. F. Constantine, Commodore Percy W. Nelles, and Air-Commodore G. M. Croil all signed a confidential statement early in 1938 warning that if Canada wanted to remain independent "of decisions in the matter of peace and war with Japan it would appear to be essential that the cost of the construction of this highway should not be assumed in any way by the United States Government."[15] Finally, a memorandum for Prime Minister King of June 1938 referred to the recent House and Senate Bills authorizing President Roosevelt to appoint an Alaska Highway Study Commission. It stated that both House and Senate committees had spoken of the defensive value of the highway and closed with a warning to Mr. King: "Although these are the first official acknowledgements of the military purpose behind the United States proposal, they are not by any means the first occasions upon which this feature of the proposed construction has been publicly noted....They can hardly be ignored if Canada is approached with an official request for cooperation."[17]

Ironically, the Canadian fear of American military domination had no foundation whatever in the American War Department's actual defence plans for the west coast and Alaska in the 1930's. Until the mid-summer of 1941, in fact, American military officials did more than the leaders of any other agency of the government to block the construction of the Alaska Highway. Throughout the depression years, the War Department consistently opposed all House and Senate bills to build the road, on the grounds that it would be of little military value, even in a war with Japan.[18] When the announcement of Assistant Secretary of War Louis Johnson's trip to Alaska caused a stir, Ruth Hampton, acting director of the Department of the Interior, wrote in a memo: "News releases from Canada indicate that military involvement is one of the chief fears which retards negotiations for the highway .... Never as far as I know has the military feature of this highway been proposed as one of its major justifications."[19] And Premier Pattullo himself said that in his several discussions with the officials in Washington "the military importance of the road had not been so much as mentioned."[20]

Several different forces worked to keep some powerful Canadians afraid of American domination during this period of political tangle over the proposed highway. Since the early 1930's, Seattle businessmen and west coast politicians had not been sufficiently sensitive to the effects of their energies upon the Canadian mind and heart. A Seattle based group had tried early in the decade to fund the construction of the highway with American dollars, since it seemed apparent to them that Canada could not or would not put up the money. This group had proposed to build the road across Canada in exchange for the gasoline and hotel concessions. When this news hit the papers, it seemed to Canadians to threaten economic sovereignty.

Another instance of American insensitivity was the 1933 report of the Alaskan highway "study" commission appointed by President Hoover. The report had concluded that the highway, if it were built, would cost America two million and Canada twelve million dollars. The Hoover Commission had made their study without the official co-operation of Canada, and the figures were their own. The statement that Canada would have to put up twelve million dollars for a project desired by the Americans angered Canadian citizens, politicians, and editors.[21]

And finally, there were the political activities between 1938 and late 1941 of the American Alaskan International Highway Commission.[22] Chaired by Congressman Warren Magnuson, the commissioners seemed especially interested in the commercial prospects of a highway following a route from near Seattle up the inside of the western coastal mountain range. Such a route would obviously have favoured west coast business enterprise, and it would also have made possible the construction of feeder roads into isolated Alaskan coastal towns and cities. The commissioners, led by the vigorous Magnuson, talked and wrote widely, however, of the military benefits of their favourite route. Magnuson's strategy seemed aimed at convincing American army officials that they should support the proposed highway and especially the western route. The army, of course, had never supported the highway and had consistently denied its military value. Now, as the world tensed for war, it was deemed necessary to gain military allegiance. In addition, the project required the approval of the Canadian-American Permanent Joint Board on Defence. The American army delegation to this board, as representatives of the U.S. War Department, would simply have to be convinced that the highway had real strategic value. But even though Magnuson and the commissioners approached such important persons and important centres of power as the Department of External Affairs, the Permanent Joint Board on Defence, the American State Department, the U.S. War Department, and President Roosevelt himself, their dreams came to nothing. They were able to convince neither the civilian leaders nor the military planners. But there is little doubt that their widespread publicity and unceasing efforts to promote the military value of the international highway helped to keep Canadian fears alive. It was the fear Bruce Hutchison defined in 1939 in the Vancouver *Sun* as "this latent fear — the vague feeling that Canada must . . . keep free of the military policies of the United States and of all other nations." It was that fear, Hutchison continued, that "made the Canadian Government cold towards the whole scheme at the start."[23] "An American financed highway," he wrote, "could be nothing less than a military highway, which, by tying us to American foreign policy would, forever, prevent our being masters in our own house."[24]

Notes

1. "Canada and U.S. May Link Up B.C. Highway with Alaska-Yukon Road," Vancouver *Sun,* 9 February 1938. See also "Pattullo, F. D. Talk Highway," Vancouver *Sun,* 15 October 1937. This article notes that Pattullo visited Franklin D. Roosevelt at Hyde Park and discussed the importance of the highway. Previously, Roosevelt had visited Victoria where Pattullo had been one of the hosts. See also "The Alaska Highway," Vancouver *Sun,* 6 May 1938.
2. For information about Pattullo's visit to Washington and his correspondence with officials there, see NARS, SERD, box 372, file 9-1-55. For the Gruening quotations see "Memorandum for the Secretary," 20 April 1938.
3. William Lyon Mackenzie King Papers, PAC, MG 26, J4, vol. 171, 23 April 1938.
4. Ibid., 7 April 1938.
5. John K. Davis, American consul general, Vancouver, B.C., "The Alaska Highway Proposal Becomes Increasingly Involved in British Columbia Provincial Politics," 26 May 1938. Consular report in "State Department and Consular Despatches," NARS, SERD.
6. King Papers, 25 April 1938.
7. Ibid.
8. Ibid. King's pencilled note was dated 26 April 1938.
9. All quotations and information in this paragraph are taken from memorandum from O. D. Skelton to the prime minister, 28 April 1938, ibid.
10. For the important meeting in Ottawa between Pattullo and his ministers and King's ministers see ibid., 26 September 1938.

11. Ibid., 9 November 1938.
12. Ibid., 26 October 1938. "Mr. King ... stated that *he had told Mr. Pattullo, at Laurier House, that the Dominion Government would appoint representatives to meet the Americans.* Apparently, therefore, the Government is obligated and the Commission must be appointed." [Italics in memo to Dr. Skelton from H. L. Keenleyside.]
13. Davis, "The Alaska Highway," 26 May 1938.
14. Vancouver *Daily Province,* 5 August 1938. The editorialist alleged that the road was to be purely a military highway for the benefit of the U.S. and that its construction would necessarily ally Canada to the U.S.
15. "Alaska-B.C. Highway," King Papers, n.d. This document is a summary of General Ashton's memorandum which, the summary states, was submitted to Dr. Skelton on 24 August 1935.
16. "Confidential, The Minister," 5 April 1938, ibid.
17. "Memorandum for the Prime Minister," 1 June 1938, ibid.
18. See for instance, Secretary of War Stimson's letter setting forth the reasons why the war department strongly opposed the highway project. The letter was written to Chairman Cartwright of the U.S. House Roads Committee, 2 August 1940. This letter is typical of war department reactions to the subject in the 1930's. In "Authorizing the Construction of a Highway to Alaska," A204[2], "Alaskan International Highway Commission," NARS, DFLB, BB.
19. Memorandum to Secretary Burlew by Ruth Hampton, acting director, U.S. Department of the Interior, 4 August 1938, NARS, SERD, box 372, file 9-1-55. Hampton also cited two articles which appeared in the Washington *Herald,* 13 August 1938, and which purported to uncover the true military significance of the proposed highway. "Both of these articles," Hampton wrote, "play on the military importance of the Proposed International Highway to such an extent that I feel some alarm over the repercussions."
20. King Papers, 26 September 1938. Pattullo made this statement at the meeting with King's ministers in Ottawa.
21. For these early efforts to promote the highway, see David A. Remley, *Crooked Road: The Story of the Alaska Highway* (New York: McGraw Hill, 1976), pp. 233-34, notes to ch. 13.
22. For the efforts of Warren Magnuson and the Alaskan International Highway Commission, see ibid., pp. 235-36, notes to ch. 13 and pp. 239-40, notes to ch. 14.
23. Bruce Hutchison, "Uncle Sam Doesn't Want Military Road to Alaska," Vancouver *Sun,* 31 January 1939. See also Hutchison, "Pattullo Denies Highway Contains Seeds of War," ibid., 9 May 1939. One of the points Hutchison made in these articles is that the U.S. military establishment opposed the highway project.
24. Vancouver *Daily Province,* 12 May 1938.

2

T.D. Pattullo and the British Columbia to Alaska Highway*

ROBIN FISHER

When the Alaska Highway was "opened" at Soldier's Summit on 20 November 1942, the Canadian government was represented by the British Columbia member of the federal cabinet, Ian Mackenzie. In his speech, Mackenzie quoted some "words of a former Prime Minister of British Columbia" appropriate to the occasion, referring to the common interests and hopes of Canada and the United States.[1] But the British Columbian who had pushed most vigorously for the building of the highway was absent from the ceremony, and all the talk of international brotherhood was not without some irony.

Thomas Dufferin Pattullo first asserted the need for a transportation link with the Yukon in the winter of 1897. As secretary to the newly appointed commissioner for the Yukon Territory, Pattullo, in December 1897, was cooling his heels in sixty below weather near the junction of the Big Salmon and Yukon rivers. In spite of the conditions, he had, since crossing the Chilkoot Pass two months before, been quickly impressed with the potential of the north. Characteristically, he was not slow to suggest ways in which that potential could be tapped. Pattullo described his initial reactions to the area in a series of letters written for publication in his family's newspaper the *Woodstock Sentinel* and syndicated in a number of other eastern papers. While he allowed that government policy concerning the north would be made by the powers that be, the young Pattullo repeatedly stressed the importance of building an all-Canadian transportation link to the Yukon. If this were accomplished, Pattullo wrote, the development of the territory in the next few years "should, and I think will, astonish the world." But, he added in a subsequent letter, "development cannot proceed without the means thereof."[2] It was a theme that Pattullo returned to frequently during his political career.

As a local politician in Dawson City and Prince Rupert, and, after 1916, as the minister of lands in British Columbia's Liberal government, Pattullo continued to be a persistent booster of the north. The potential of northern British Columbia and the Yukon seemed as boundless as his own optimism. All that was required to break loose the wealth of the area was the appropriate policies, implemented, of course, by the right government. Therefore, for partisan reasons Pattullo opposed the efforts of the Conservative premier of British Columbia, Simon Fraser Tolmie, to get work on the Alaska highway going in the early 1930's.

Tolmie saw a highway to Alaska largely as a means of bringing American tourists to British Columbia. When Prime Minister William Lyon Mackenzie King was in Victoria in November 1929, Tolmie tried to interest him in the highway scheme. The premier followed up with a letter to King drawing his attention to the potential mineral wealth of the area through which the road would pass. But Tolmie emphasized that the greatest source of revenue from the road would be tourism. American tourists, he claimed, were "fed up" with the Grand Canyon and Yellowstone Park and would jump at the chance to visit the "Land of the Midnight Sun."[3] King was unmoved by such enthusiasm. In Victoria, he tried to "sidestep the issue in every way," and in subsequent correspondence, he was non-committal while pointing out the "far reaching international considerations of such a proposal."[4]

Making little progress with the federal government, Tolmie continued to try to drum up local support for the project. In 1930, he led a caravan of Canadian and American officials and some private citizens to Hazleton, where the road north was to begin. The following year, during a visit to Olympia, Washington, he presented a picture display of the caravan trip to a packed state legislature. In his own legislative assembly, Tolmie spoke annually and enthusiastically in support of the highway, but the response was always muted. As a member of his own party laconically noted while Tolmie was in the midst of one of these speeches, "no one is kicking his desk over in frenzied excitement."[5] In the private sector, Tolmie tried to interest the president of British Pacific Properties Ltd. in the highway.[6] All of Tolmie's efforts produced some publicity for the project, but few concrete results. In 1930, the United States government appointed a board of commissioners to study the proposed highway, and three Canadians were associated with it. The commission reported in 1932 on the feasibility and cost of the highway. The report emphasized the benefits to the United States but said nothing about the benefits to Canada.[7] So, while Tolmie remained convinced that in British Columbia "the great mass of the people are thoroughly behind the project,"⁸ those with the power to make decisions were more restrained.

With Tolmie in power, Pattullo, as leader of the opposition, opposed without restraint. He did not doubt the desirability of building the Alaska road but, even before the crash of October 1929, he argued that any suggestion that the project was possible under present economic conditions was "simply foolish."⁹ As the depression deepened, Pattullo became more forthright. He scorned Tolmie's continued talk of the highway, "notwithstanding the innumerable practical matters requiring attention," as merely an effort to divert attention away from government blunders.¹⁰ Such statements did not, however, inhibit Pattullo in any way after he became premier himself in 1933.

Pattullo's first administration was vigorous and innovative in adopting liberal reform policies to deal with the depression, shore up the capitalist system, and meet the growing political threat from the left. Pattullo had always believed that private enterprise should be supplemented by public spending. A major part of his strategy for reducing the impact of the depression involved large-scale government expenditure on public works projects that would provide employment and stimulate development. But provincial resources were limited, and Pattullo was not very successful in his efforts to convince the federal government to increase spending in British Columbia. When it could raise the money itself, and when federal jurisdiction was too weak to be an impediment, the province proceeded alone. Thus, amidst a storm of controversy, the best known monument to his premiership, the Pattullo bridge across the Fraser river, was built during his first term of office. In the thick of this and other political battles, Pattullo took no more than a casual interest in the Alaska Highway project until 1937.

Others, meanwhile, kept the idea simmering. In 1935, the United States government passed an act appropriating $2,000,000 for the construction of a highway in Alaska, authorizing the president to discuss with Canada the possibility of building a road through British Columbia and the Yukon, and urging the beginning of survey work to determine the best possible route. The British Columbia government was asked, in a roundabout way through the lieutenant-governor, if it had "any observations to offer" on this American initiative.¹¹ A lukewarm resolution was passed in the legislative assembly indicating that it would be willing to facilitate the Alaska Highway project if and when other governments submitted proposals.¹² At the same time, Pattullo twice rebuked maverick Liberal M.L.A. George Murray for his over-zealous support of the highway project.¹³ Then, in the summer of 1936, Pattullo renewed his acquaintance with the north. He travelled by air to northern British Columbia and on to Dawson City, and the experience of flying over the land that he had walked as a younger man set Pattullo's mind turning once more on the potential of the north.

In 1937, the Pattullo government was to face the people again, but much of the reformist enthusiasm of the early years had faded, and Pattullo was turning to more conventional policies. Early in 1936, he had raised with Mackenzie King the possibility that British Columbia might take over the administration of the Yukon.[14] This was a matter that he wanted to bring to fruition before any election, so he pressed the federal government to discuss the idea. By March 1937, he had reached a tentative agreement on conditions under which Ottawa would transfer the administration of the territory to Victoria.[15] With the election a little over a month away, Pattullo, perhaps prematurely, made the agreement public and thereby succeeded in stirring up opposition and protest from a number of quarters. British Columbians were concerned about the possible cost to the provincial taxpayer of the acquisition of the Yukon, and Yukoners seemed to be unanimously opposed to the notion of being governed from Victoria. Yukon mining interests lobbied against the imposition of British Columbia's mining laws, and the transfer of jurisdiction also promised to raise the vexed question of separate schools.[16] By October, the two governments had agreed to shelve the whole matter pending the report of the Royal Commission on Dominion-Provincial Relations.[17] In the meantime, Pattullo had returned to an old idea as a means of dealing with new problems.

At the same time as the federal cabinet was considering British Columbia's proposal to take over the Yukon, Pattullo broached the question of the Alaska Highway. In a letter to King, he noted that he had already corresponded with the federal government and some American interests on the matter, and he indicated the willingness of his government to co-operate in an effort to get work started. "I believe," he concluded, "this to be a matter of much importance."[18] The highway had become important to Pattullo because the fundamental problems of the depression had not been solved. The British Columbia government had improved its financial position somewhat by 1937, but the level of unemployment in the province was still too high. Even with his own party back in power, Pattullo had not been able to convince the federal government to fund a "broad gauge" public works programme in British Columbia. The Pattullo bridge was almost completed and so a new project was needed to capture the public's imagination. For the premier, the British Columbia to Alaska highway was to be a means of providing employment and opening up new parts of the province for development, as well as being an attraction for American tourists.[19]

For his part, Mackenzie King remained impervious. He was still unimpressed by arguments in favour of the highway and, at this stage, overwhelmingly concerned about the cost of such a venture. While he was quite sure that there was great interest in the proposal on the Pacific coast, King pointed out that a definite solution to the financial problem had not yet been found.[20] British Columbia lacked the resources to fund the project, and the federal government under King remained unwilling to co-operate. But in the fall of 1937, Pattullo met with a kindred spirit.

Duff Pattullo and Franklin D. Roosevelt not only advocated similar policies to deal with the depression, they also had personality characteristics in common. In contrast to the tight, introspective King, Pattullo and Roosevelt were both optimistic and outgoing. It is not surprising that they got on well when the American president paid an informal visit to Victoria in September 1937. They agreed on the importance of building a highway to Alaska, and they arranged to meet at Hyde Park to discuss the question further when Pattullo visited New York the following month.

While Pattullo received a sympathetic hearing in the United States, he still made no progress in Ottawa, where opponents continued to count the probable cost of building the road. Soon after his visit to Hyde Park, Pattullo met King at the Château Laurier to discuss the matter. After the meeting, King noted in his diary that Pattullo wanted to build an Alaska Highway with "no thought of the cost to the people." The prime minister added the revealing comment that "I sometimes wish I could take my public duties with the free & easy assurance some of these men do. But I cannot be lighthearted."[21] The American president, meanwhile, had instructed his minister in Ottawa, Norman Armour, to write to the Canadian government to suggest the appointment of a commission to study the feasibility of building the road.[22] King consulted his officials at the Department of External Affairs and was advised that there was some objection to the highway on the grounds that the United States might use it for military purposes, which could pose a threat to Canadian sovereignty. But since this argument appeared to operate against all development in northern British Columbia, the department felt that discussions should be confined to the economic aspects, unless the United States suggested that it might pay for part of the Canadian section. At that point, the military implications would have to be raised.[23] Accordingly, King wrote to Armour to say that until the problem of financing had been solved, Canada could not enter negotiations with a view to completing the project. King was prepared for Canada to take part in a commission of inquiry as long as it implied no commitment to building the road. At the same time, he reminded the United States representative that a joint commission had met in Victoria in 1931 and concluded that, although the highway was feasible from an engineering standpoint, the financial difficulties were immense. On the advice of his officials, King did not close off the matter completely, but he probably thought that he had found an immovable obstacle to the project.[24]

While Pattullo may not have been an irresistible force, he was not so easily deterred and continued to press the matter at every opportunity. In March 1938, he wrote similar letters to both Roosevelt and King to make some more specific suggestions. The Americans favoured a westerly route through British Columbia close to the Alaska panhandle. Pattullo, on the advice of the surveyor-general of British Columbia, now advocated a more easterly route from Prince George through the Rocky Mountain trench and via the Pelly River to Dawson City. The cost of construction on this route would be less than the more difficult "coastal" route and, because the snowfall was lower, the cost of maintaining the road would also be reduced. The eastern route particularly appealed to Pattullo because feeder roads could be built to open up the Peace River country where there seemed to be a good possibility of finding oil and gas.[25] Roosevelt replied that Pattullo's suggestions would be given "careful consideration" and, mindful of the need for diplomacy, noted with pleasure that the premier intended to discuss the matter with King in Ottawa the next month.[26]

Pattullo did go to Ottawa in April, but he then went on to Washington and returned to Ottawa with a possible solution to the financial problem. In the American capital, Pattullo discussed the highway with Anthony J. Dimond, the congressional delegate from Alaska, and Harold L. Ickes, the secretary of the interior, along with other interested officials. He made the suggestion, which seemed to be accepted, that the Americans finance the building of the highway. The idea was that congressional authorization would be given to the president to loan or expend up to $15,000,000 for the construction of the highway.[27] Getting nowhere in Ottawa, Pattullo had simply turned to the United States for both support and funding for the highway. Ottawa, however, responded with another set of objections.

Pattullo constantly emphasized the "informal" nature of his discussions in Washington, but these extra-curricular activities certainly ruffled feathers in Ottawa, especially at the Department of External Affairs. When O.D. Skelton, King's under-secretary at external affairs, learned through despatches of Pattullo's talks and the possibility that the United States might finance the highway, he could scarcely believe it. Ever concerned about Canada's independence and the power of the federal government, it is not surprising that Skelton should object to this "high water mark ... in provincial diplomacy."[28] King and Skelton were very close, but they did not agree on all things, and King responded, officially at least, with more equanimity. He knew that there could be no agreement with the government of the United States on the financing of the road unless the Canadian government approved, and so he presumably saw less need to get excited about Pattullo's initiatives. King could also be more magnanimous because he had taken the precaution of checking out Pattullo's activities through the Canadian legation in Washington and had been reassured that, as far as the State Department in the United States was concerned, "nothing in the nature of negotiations" had taken place between Pattullo and Roosevelt.[29] The premier of British Columbia went to Washington again in late May to meet with Roosevelt and to lobby for the passage of legislation to provide financing for the highway. Again there were ripples of consternation in Ottawa. The leader of the opposition, R.B. Bennett, made some sarcastic comments in the House of Commons and later told Pattullo that he wholly disagreed both with his views on the Alaska Highway and with his action in dealing with a matter of national importance in a foreign capital.[30] The trips to Washington were also criticized by the Conservative press in British Columbia.[31] Pattullo wrote to King that he was "not insensible to the fact that some little umbrage exists at my activities," but he asserted that British Columbia had a primary interest in the highway proposal and that he had acted "entirely informally." Furthermore, he added in a characteristic statement, "one need not be deflected from a sound proposal by a news voracious press, an irresponsible opposition, or other frailties of human nature."[32] In a letter, King replied smoothly that he was not aware that any exception had been taken to his actions, while writing in his diary that Pattullo "like a fool, has been telling the Americans what to do to get under way with public works in Canada."[33]

Pattullo's unorthodox methods created a bit of a stir in Ottawa, but much more important were the objections to the substance of the deal that he had worked out in Washington. It was clear from the beginning that the federal government did not want to make any major financial commitment to the Alaska Highway. Apparently, the project was acceptable in Ottawa if the road were built by a private company authorized by the provincial government. Thus, at one point in the discussions, King felt that the solution to the problem was to have the Yukon made a part of British Columbia, thereby placing the entire route under provincial control.[34] The proposal that the Canadian part of the highway be built largely with money provided by a foreign government was, however, quite unacceptable. This was Skelton's immediate reaction when he first heard of the idea, and it was also the unanimous view of the federal cabinet when it met to consider the question. King's summary of the cabinet discussion ended with the note that "it would be, as Lapointe phrased it, a matter of financial invasion, or, as I termed it, financial penetration." When King conveyed the cabinet's decision to Pattullo later the same day, the premier suggested that the American government might funnel the money for the highway project through a private corporation, but King thought that notion to be "more fanciful than anything I have ever heard."[35] He confirmed in writing that if the United States government were proposing to fund a road through Canada, it would communicate with the Canadian government which would then indicate its objections. "This would be the case," wrote King, "whether the funds were advanced direct or through a private corporation."[36]

Ottawa's objections to the American government financing the Canadian part of the highway were based on the fear that the money would not come without strings attached. The major concern was that the United States wanted to build the road because of its military and strategic value and therefore, in the event of a war between America and Japan, Canada would be involved automatically. To accept American funding would, in Skelton's words, "be mortgaging our independence."[37] Pattullo was quite unimpressed with this view and responded to it, as he often did, with a simple directness. Even if it were true that the Americans wanted the highway for military purposes, he argued, then that would be all the more reason to build it. If, in the event of war, British Columbia were essential to the defence of Alaska, then it was "sheer nonsense" to talk of Canada being neutral. "What position would we be in," Pattullo asked King rhetorically, "if either Russia or Japan were to take possession of Alaska?"[38] The conservative press in British Columbia inevitably lined up against Pattullo and opposed the building of a "military highway," but the mercurial editor of the Vancouver *Sun*, R.J. Cromie, dismissed the entire argument in a sentence. "Any time Canada got tired of harbouring an American military highway, a few sticks of dynamite would allay her weariness in a most effective way."[39] Fears that a British Columbia to Alaska highway would compromise Canadian sovereignty might be easily waved aside on the west coast, but they were keenly felt by several groups, including the joint chiefs of staff, in Ottawa.[40]

Yet, as has often been the case in the history of relations between the two countries, Canadian fears were not evidence of American intentions and, certainly in this instance, the concern was somewhat ill-founded. For while Canadian opponents of the road were wary of the intentions of the American military, American proponents were annoyed because their military leaders could see little strategic value in the Alaska Highway. As late as April 1941, the United States War Department dismissed the highway as being "of no military value."[41] Given this attitude, there is little reason to doubt Pattullo's claim that during all his discussions in the United States neither the president nor any other American official ever mentioned the word "military" in connection with the highway.[42] Reporter Bruce Hutchison interviewed officials in Washington and wrote extensively, although not always accurately, on the Alaska Highway proposal. He probably was correct, however, when he observed that the Americans did not want the road for military purposes partly because they felt that Alaska was easier to defend from the sea.[43] Since both Hutchison and Pattullo were able to figure it out, it is hard to believe that Ottawa was not also aware of the low priority that military leaders in the United States placed on the road.

Knowing, perhaps, that they were on shaky ground, Ottawa officials and politicians did not consistently advance the military arguments against the highway. Even Skelton opposed the idea initially because of the cost and because he thought that east-west roads should take priority "over a north-south project in one province."[44] In August 1938, an interdepartmental committee set up by King to investigate the highway proposal reported to council. The committee advised "that the construction of the road at the present time would not be justified," but in reaching that conclusion, it did not lay great emphasis on the strategic considerations. Rather, it undercut those arguments by suggesting that the Canadian government might compromise by completing a highway to the Pacific coast at Prince Rupert: a road that the committee not only admitted would have strategic value but advocated partly for that reason.[45] Nor was the federal cabinet always unanimously opposed to the highway because of its military potential. On at least one occasion, the Canadian minister of defence, Ian Mackenzie, argued that because the defence of the Pacific coast was a common problem between the two nations, the international complications involved in American participation in building a Canadian road were without practical importance.[46] The suggestion to complete the road to Prince Rupert was a blatant piece of bribery aimed at buying off proponents of the highway. Skelton clarified this point when he indicated that a major advantage of the Prince Rupert road was that "it would traverse Mr. Pattullo's own constituency and end in his home city."[47] Ian Mackenzie may well have supported Pattullo's line on the strategic implications of the highway out of consideration for an old colleague, while knowing that there was enough opposition in the federal cabinet to defeat the project. Nevertheless, if its military potential were the paramount objection to the highway in Ottawa, then one would expect the argument to have been made more logically and consistently.

In fact neither Pattullo's "diplomacy" in the United States nor the notion that the road might pose a threat to Canadian sovereignty was the primary reason for the federal government's hostility to the scheme.[48] The international and strategic argument was largely a front: a barricade of undisputed federal jurisdiction from behind which Ottawa could shoot down a project that it objected to for other, less politically palatable reasons. Still fundamental to federal opposition to the highway was the fear of the cost. In its investigation of the highway proposal, the federal interdepartmental committee laid great emphasis on the financial considerations. It held that the Dominion was already spending more than its share on roads in British Columbia, and that, when federal money was spent in the province, other routes such as the TransCanada Highway were more important. Against this background, the committee went on to point out that, even if United States funding were accepted, the Alaska Highway would still require a considerable commitment on the part of the Canadian government. So, before it moved on to a brief examination of the strategic question, the committee had already decided that acceptance of the United States proposal was not justified even "when judged solely from the financial angle."[49]

It was undoubtedly true, as Bruce Hutchison implied, that the federal government was reluctant to spend large amounts of money in an area so far from the centre of power and where there were so few voters.[50] Pattullo also put his finger on this point, and on a traditional source of western grievance, when he observed that Ottawa was prepared to spend heavily on projects in the east like the proposed St. Lawrence Seaway that not only involved American financing but would "take scores of millions" of dollars. The British Columbia premier was getting "a little tired" of arguments in the east about western conditions and western importunities.[51]

Also underlying the federal unwillingness to finance the Alaska Highway was a basic difference between King and Pattullo on how to deal with the depression. King was conservative on fiscal policy, insisting that in tight financial times the public treasury should be defended even more firmly. Pattullo, on the other hand, had throughout his career advocated expansive government spending as the way out of economic difficulties. The two men clashed repeatedly on this issue, and neither one changed his mind.

It was clear by the summer of 1938 that the federal government intended to stall the highway project, and relations between Pattullo and King were becoming somewhat strained. The prime minister found his talks with Pattullo to be "not too helpful," and he revealed his annoyance in a rather self-righteous defence of his position. He "told the cabinet the only thing for us to do was to make up our mind for the Federal Government to do the right thing regardless of the consequences provincially, & end this business of trying to meet every demand that was made."[52] Pattullo still "radiated confidence" in public,[53] yet privately he could surely see the writing on the wall. He, too, felt frustrated after discussions with King and indicated his feeling in a letter to the prime minister. King replied at length and expressed the hope that no misunderstanding would "impair the friendship which we have enjoyed together over so many years."[54] But whatever the state of his relationship with King, Pattullo recognized that the Alaska Highway project was on hold as far as the federal government was concerned.[55] He had, after all, had plenty of experience with Ottawa intransigence.

Although his enthusiasm was waning, Pattullo did not give up. He persistently pressed the highway proposal and was "not at all prepared to admit its impossibility."[56] During June and July 1938, Pattullo was given a sharp reminder of the continuing problem of unemployment in British Columbia. When the temporary winter work camps closed down in the spring, the unemployed drifted back to Vancouver, only to be told by the provincial government that there would be no relief payments for those from other provinces. The unemployed protested this decision by occupying selected public buildings, and on 20 June, "bloody Sunday," the "sit downers" were violently evicted from the post office by the police. Pattullo met with the leaders of the unemployed but showed little sympathy for their plight. He was much more concerned about the level of public support that had developed for the "insurrectionists." In this context he wrote to King, pointing out once again that the construction of the Alaska Highway would absorb many of the single unemployed and relieve what he called the "conjestion" in larger centres. Pattullo continued to recommend "that instead of having any argument as to the propriety of accepting United States assistance, the Dominion and British Columbia join in a programme to build the road."[57] But Pattullo got no further with King on the specific proposal to build the Alaska Highway than he did on the general policy of government spending as a way out of the depression.

As was often the case, King was prepared to make an apparent concession as long as nothing of consequence was given away. In August 1938, Pattullo received a letter from Congressman Warren Magnuson pointing out that, at his instigation, the United States government had appointed an Alaska Highway commission and asking Pattullo to urge the Canadian government to appoint a similar body.[58] Pattullo immediately wrote to King suggesting that they meet to discuss the question and, a month later in Ottawa, he managed to persuade the prime minister to appoint a corresponding Canadian commission. Mackenzie King made it quite clear, however, that he was not establishing a joint commission. The Canadian commission was to be entirely separate from the American one and its appointment implied no commitment to the highway on the part of the federal government.[59]

The prime minister conceded nothing by agreeing to establish the commission, and for King this development had the added advantage of producing further delay. He waited for several months before making any appointments. In the meantime, he was advised that, since the American commissioners were all strongly in favour of the highway and any British Columbia nominees would support Pattullo's proposals, a majority of the members of the Canadian commission "should be conversant with the national implications of the problem."[60] King followed this recommendation when the commission was finally appointed on 22 December 1938. He further demonstrated his lack of enthusiasm for the project by selecting Charles Stewart, who was seriously ill, as chairman.[61] Noticing in the press that he had been appointed to the position, Stewart wrote to King from his hospital bed to inquire "what the Government has in mind in connection with this investigation."[62] It was June 1939 before Stewart was able to do much work, and by then he had been schooled by Skelton. Stewart decided that the Canadian commission should clearly formulate its own position before it met with the Americans and, when the two commissions eventually did get together, he was very anxious not to be "indiscreet" in his discussions with the United States commissioners. When the chairman of the American commission, Warren Magnuson, made enthusiastic statements to the press, Stewart was adamant that they did not reflect the views of his group which, he repeatedly stated, had "nothing to do with constructing or financing the proposed highway."[63] Hearings began in Victoria with Stewart making it clear that the Canadian Highway Commission had been appointed to investigate only the feasibility and approximate cost of the road to Alaska, and that it was not authorized to consider the question of financing.[64] The commission had, in other words, been rendered ineffective by being precluded from discussing the one matter that, as Pattullo correctly observed, was still crucial.

Before the commission had begun its work, the premier of British Columbia had hoped that its investigation would lead to a resolution of his difficulties with Ottawa, an expectation that soon proved to be naive.[65] Pattullo spent a lot of time and effort providing Stewart with detailed information and putting him in touch with the American commission. In April 1940, after a year's work, the Canadian commission presented a preliminary and inconclusive report. The commissioners emphasized the advantages of the "B" or easterly route but admitted that they did not have enough information to discuss all of the merits of the coastal or "A" route that the Americans favoured. The report included some engineering data and gave rough estimates of the cost of the "B" route, but it made no comparisons with the "A" route and forwarded no recommendations.[66] Pattullo realized that the commission certainly would not make, and probably would not even influence, any major decision. He wrote to King that, even though the commission had not made a final report, there was sufficient information to know that the project was feasible and what its approximate cost would be, so the question remained one of policy.[67]

As far as Pattullo and the public were concerned, federal policy was unchanged, but behind the scenes there was some movement. Pattullo had heard, presumably from Ian Mackenzie, that some individuals in the Department of Defence opposed the road because it would make a Japanese invasion into British Columbia easier. It seemed almost impossible to Pattullo "that men holding responsible positions could give vent to so ridiculous opinions."[68] Although he never took much comfort from being right in retrospect, Pattullo might have been gratified, had he known, that others were now advising King of the strategic value of the highway. In a memorandum dated July 1940, Skelton made a very similar case to the one that Pattullo had argued two years before. Given the Japanese threat in the Pacific, Skelton now recognized that Canada would inevitably have to look to the United States to help defend the west coast. He thought that Canada might contribute its share to the common pool by offering to construct the Alaska Highway at its own expense. He cited figures from the preliminary report of the Canadian commission indicating that the expense would be substantial but added that it would be offset by a reduction in unemployment.[69] Before long, the Canadian-American Permanent Joint Board on Defence, hastily established at Ogdensburg, was discussing the development of airfields and highways in the northwest.[70]

Unaware of this about-face, Pattullo was despondent about the prospect of progress on the road. He wrote again to Roosevelt to say that unless the highway were considered necessary as a war measure or the United States made a special request that it should proceed, he was convinced that it would be a generation before the road was constructed. He concluded that, "having put forth so much effort under considerable handicap to see this matter put through, I very much dislike to see it dropped."[71]

To the end of his premiership, Pattullo remained an advocate of the highway and of northern development. He fostered exploration for oil in the Peace river area and developed a programme to grubstake young men to prospect along the proposed route of the Alaska Highway. Concerned as always that British Columbia benefit from the opening up of the north, Pattullo wrote to King urging that the Alaska Highway should not be allowed to go through Alberta, as some were suggesting.[72] He took another flying trip to the north in the late summer of 1939, during which he learned that his country was at war. Pattullo immediately assumed the inevitability of American involvement in the war and, in this context, he talked of the need for the highway as a means of defending British Columbia. In March 1941, he went once more to Washington to discuss the highway project.

But international events and local politics were moving beyond Pattullo's control. His criticisms of the federal government were less acceptable in British Columbia in wartime, and, after a poor showing in the provincial election of October 1941, Pattullo's leadership was rejected by his own party. He resigned as premier on 9 December 1941. Two days before, at Pearl Harbor, there had occurred an event that was more important than all of Pattullo's advocacy for getting work started on the Alaska Highway. Once the threat of Japanese invasion made the road a strategic requirement, rather than a depression panacea or a tourist highway, the federal government was persuaded to act.

At the opening of the highway, Pattullo was relegated to anonymity. In the euphoria of the event, all of his arguments in favour of the highway and all of his efforts to get an unwilling Ottawa government to accept American assistance to build the road were forgotten. One wonders whether Ian Mackenzie appreciated the double meaning when he proclaimed to those attending the ceremony that they were standing on the "borderline of brotherhood."[73] Prior to the outbreak of international conflict, co-operation between Canada and the United States on the Alaska Highway proposal had been forestalled because Ottawa rejected proposals made by a demanding provincial premier. While Prime Minister King remained concerned about the implications of a large American presence in Canada's north,[74] now that the highway was opened, it could be seen as indicative of the common interests of Canada and the United States. But it had been long delayed because of differences between the federal government and one of its provinces.

In relative retirement as a private member of British Columbia's legislative assembly, Pattullo took little pleasure in the completion of a project for which he had worked so tirelessly as premier. The highway was built for reasons that were quite different from those that he had deemed important. A few days after the ceremony at Soldier's Summit, Pattullo wrote to J.L. Ralston, the Canadian minister of national defence, that he had little confidence in the men responsible for building military roads in British Columbia. Those who had once opposed his proposal because they thought the highway would facilitate a Japanese invasion had now, he bitterly observed, put through a road in great haste and in the wrong place.[75]

Notes

* Research for this paper was facilitated by a grant from the Social Science and Humanities Research Council of Canada.
1. Ian Mackenzie, speech, 20 November 1942, Ian Mackenzie Papers, PAC, MG 27, III, vol. 33, file B10.
2. *The Weekly Sentinel-Review and Dominion Diaryman,* Woodstock, Ontario, 22, 29 March and 3 May 1898.
3. Tolmie to King, 6 December 1929, W.L. Mackenzie King Papers, PAC, MG 26, J1, vol. 205.
4. Tolmie to B.W. Howard, 19 November 1929, Simon Fraser Tolmie Papers, UBCL, vol. 4, file 2; King to Tolmie, 13 January 1930, King Papers, J1, vol. 169.
5. R.L. Maitland, House Log, 16 February 1931, Maitland Family Papers, PABC, Add. MSS 781.
6. Tolmie to A.J.T. Taylor, 13 November 1931, and Taylor to Tolmie, 28 December 1931, Tolmie Papers, vol. 3, file 78.
7. Memo from minister of national defence, April 1937, King Papers, J4, vol. 171.
8. Tolmie to R. Lomen, 11 January 1930, Tolmie Papers, vol. 4, file 4.
9. Pattullo, press statement, 6 September 1929, Pattullo Papers, PABC, Add. MSS 3, vol. 33, file 9.
10. Pattullo, press statement, 9 June 1932, ibid., vol. 49, file 8.
11. E.H. Coleman, under secretary of state to Hon. J.W. Fordham Johnson, 8 April 1936, ibid., vol. 72, file 1.
12. Vancouver *Province,* 24 March 1936.
13. Ibid., Victoria *Daily Colonist,* 21 June 1935.
14. Pattullo to King, 5 February 1936, Pattullo Papers, vol. 76, file 17.
15. T.A. Crerar to Pattullo, 5 March 1937 and Pattullo to Crerar, 8 March 1937, ibid., vol. 76, file 17.
16. See Crerar to King, 27 August 1937, King Papers, J1, vol. 233; and for a discussion of the separate schools issue in particular, Richard Stuart, "Duff Pattullo and the Yukon Schools Question of 1937," *Canadian Historical Review,* 64, no. 1 (March 1983): 25-44.
17. Pattullo to Crerar, 6 October 1937 and Crerar to Pattullo, 8 October 1937, Pattullo Papers, vol. 76, file 17.

18. Pattullo to King, 4 March 1937, King Papers, J1, vol. 239.
19. Pattullo statement in Vancouver *Sun,* 9 February 1938.
20. King to Tolmie, 23 March 1937, King Papers, J1, vol. 243. Tolmie had written to King to ask if there had been any developments on the highway project.
21. King, diary, 18 October 1937, ibid., J13.
22. Norman Armour to secretary of state for external affairs, 14 September 1937, ibid., J1, vol. 231.
23. Memo to L.C. Christie, 12 November 1937, ibid., J4, vol. 171.
24. King to Armour, November 1937, ibid., J4, vol. 171.
25. Pattullo to Roosevelt and Pattullo to King, 4 March 1938, Pattullo Papers, vol. 72, file 1.
26. Roosevelt to Pattullo, 25 March 1938, ibid.
27. Pattullo to King, 23 April 1938, ibid.
28. Skelton to King, 23 April 1938, King Papers, J4, vol. 171.
29. H. Marler to secretary of state for external affairs, 24 March 1938, ibid., J1, vol. 254.
30. Vancouver *Sun,* 4 June 1938; Bennett to Pattullo, Pattullo Papers, vol. 62, file 2.
31. See, for example, Vancouver *Province,* 23 May 1938.
32. Pattullo to King, 6 June 1938, Pattullo Papers, vol. 72, file 1.
33. King to Pattullo, 27 June 1938, ibid.; King, diary, 3 May 1938, King Papers, J13.
34. King memo to E.A. Pickering, 7 April 1938, King Papers, J4, vol. 171.
35. Skelton memo to prime minister, 25 April 1938, ibid., J4, vol. 171; King, diary, 26 April 1938, ibid., J13.
36. King to Pattullo, 28 April 1938, Pattullo Papers, vol. 70, file 2.
37. Skelton memo to prime minister, 25 April 1938, King Papers, J4, vol. 171.
38. Pattullo to King, 17 October 1938, Pattullo Papers, vol. 72, file 1.
39. Vancouver *Sun,* 25 April 1938.
40. Joint staff committee memo to minister of defence, 5 April 1938, Mackenzie Papers, vol. 30, file X-29.
41. The point is made by Ernest Gruening, *The State of Alaska* (New York: Random House, 1968), p. 315; see also David A. Remley, *Crooked Road: The Story of the Alaska Highway* (New York: McGraw Hill, 1976), pp. 120-21.
42. Pattullo to King, 17 October 1938, Pattullo Papers, vol. 72, file 1.
43. Bruce Hutchison, "Highway to Alaska," *McLean's Magazine,* 15 November 1939, pp. 45-46; and in *Victoria Daily Times,* 31 January 1939.
44. Skelton to Armour, 8 February 1937, Department of National Defence Papers, PAC, RG 24, vol. 2448.
45. Interdepartmental Committee, "Report to Council on the Proposal to Construct a Highway through British Columbia and the Yukon Territory to Alaska," n.d. (August 1938), Pattullo Papers, vol. 72, file 1.
46. King, memo of discussion with Mr. Pattullo, 26 September 1938, King Papers, J4, vol. 171.
47. Skelton, memo to prime minister, 13 August 1938, ibid.
48. See Remley, *Crooked Road,* pp. 118-20.
49. Interdepartmental Committee, "Report to Council," (August 1938), Pattullo Papers, vol. 72, file 1.
50. Hutchison, "Highway to Alaska," p. 13.
51. Pattullo to King, 28 January 1939, Pattullo Papers, vol. 72, file 1.
52. King, diary, 3 May 1938, King Papers, J13.
53. Vancouver *Sun,* 7 May 1938.
54. King to Pattullo, 23 May 1938, Pattullo Papers, vol. 75, file 6.
55. See Lapointe to King, 31 May 1938, King Papers, J1, vol. 252.
56. Ibid.
57. Pattullo to King, 6 July 1938, Pattullo Papers, vol. 75, file 6.
58. Magnuson to Pattullo, 25 August 1938, ibid., vol. 72, file 1.
59. Pattullo, press statement, 28 September 1938, ibid., vol. 64, file 2; King, diary, 28 September 1938, King Papers, J13.
60. Memo from H. Keenleyside, 15 December 1938, King Papers, J4, vol. 171.

61. Minute of meeting of the committee of the privy council, 22 December 1938, ibid.
62. Stewart to King, 5 January 1939, ibid., J1, vol. 280.
63. Stewart to Pattullo, 4 April 1939, Pattullo Papers, vol. 72, file 1; Stewart to King, 5 March 1941, King Papers, J1, vól. 205.
64. British Columbia-Yukon-Alaska Highway Commission, "Preliminary Report on Proposed Highway through British Columbia and the Yukon Territory to Alaska," April 1940, p. 63, King Papers, J4, vol. 278.
65. Pattullo to E. Gruening, 12 October 1938, and Pattullo to Magnuson, 21 October 1938, Pattullo Papers, vol. 72, file 1.
66. British Columbia-Yukon-Alaska Highway Commission, "Preliminary Report," King Papers, J4, vol. 278.
67. Pattullo to King, 7 August 1940, Pattullo Papers, vol. 75, file 8.
68. Ibid.
69. Skelton to King, 1 July 1940, King Papers, J4, vol. 278.
70. J.L. Granatstein, *Canada's War: The Politics of the Mackenzie King Government, 1939-1945* (Toronto: Oxford University Press, 1975), pp. 128-29.
71. Pattullo to Roosevelt, 17 January 1941, Pattullo Papers, vol. 76, file 4.
72. Pattullo to King, 14 January 1941, ibid., vol. 70, file 5; see also William Aberhart to King, 10 October 1940, King Papers, J1, vol. 283.
73. Mackenzie, speech, 20 November 1942, Mackenzie Papers, vol. 33, file B10.
74. Granatstein, *Canada's War,* pp. 321-22.
75. Pattullo to J.L. Ralston, 23 November 1942, Pattullo Papers, vol. 73, file 9.

3

The Realities of Strategic Planning: The Decision to Build the Alaska Highway

M. V. BEZEAU

At first glance, the strategic reasons for building the Alaska Highway appear obvious. On 7 December 1941, the Japanese attacked Pearl Harbor, Hawaii and destroyed a large part of the U.S. Navy Pacific Fleet. American territorial vulnerability immediately increased, especially in the north. Although the Great Circle route, the shortest distance linking Tokyo with the west coast of the United States, passed through the Aleutian Islands, American military planners earlier had concluded that a road to Alaska had little military value. Now, facing a greatly increased threat, they declared that a land link was imperative. Both American and Canadian authorities approved the construction of a highway as a defensive measure. These facts seem to indicate that the military recommendation to build the road stemmed from a careful strategic reassessment of changing defence requirements under wartime conditions. In reality, it did not.

For many years prior to the outbreak of the Second World War, various Canadians and Americans advocated construction of a road to Alaska. They stressed economic and developmental advantages but also noted the possible value of such a road for defence.[1] In response, the United States War Department repeatedly examined these suggestions and rejected them. From a military point of view, the strategic areas of Alaska were the Panhandle, the south coast, the Alaska Peninsula, and the Aleutian Islands. These all lay near ocean transport and probable air routes. Other areas had low temperatures and poor communications which made year-round operations difficult. The sea lanes connecting all the valued areas were shorter in both time and distance than any highway route. Moreover, the proposed roads did not provide links to such areas as the Alaska Peninsula, and could not do so to Kodiak, Unalaska, and other islands where important installations were located. Thus, sea transport would be required in any case. The navy saw little likelihood of any permanent interruption to sea communications in the event of war with Japan. Shipping could be in short supply in an emergency, but this was more quickly corrected by new marine construction than by building a road. Hence, the defensive value of a highway to Alaska was "negligible," and construction on the basis of military necessity alone was unjustified and unsupportable.[2] The Canadian-American Permanent Joint Board on Defence (P.J.B.D.) reached similar conclusions on 15 November 1940.[3]

Of course, military communications to Alaska could not be, and were not, ignored. Primary reliance was placed on the sea, but air routes were developed along the coast and from the prairie interior. The prairie link, the Northwest Staging Route, was especially important since it avoided the poorer coastal weather, was removed from potential enemy interruption, and was connected to the continental heartland. The staging route originated in 1935 with a Canadian Department of Transport survey for a Great Circle air route to the Orient. The line from Edmonton to Alaska was chosen and airfield sites selected at Grande Prairie, Fort St. John, and Fort Nelson, B.C., and Watson Lake and Whitehorse, Yukon. Survey parties were in the field when the European war broke out in September 1939. With the British Commonwealth Air Training Plan and other expanded air force construction about to begin, consideration was given to ending the programme. It was decided, however, that if the U.S. were to enter the war, the strategic value of the airfields would increase, so work continued. By September 1941, the route was considered usable in daylight, and radio range stations were operational along its Canadian length by the end of the year.[4]

During this construction, but unrelated to it, a new move was launched in the U.S. House of Representatives to build a highway north. On 5 February 1941, Delegate Anthony J. Dimond of Alaska introduced Bill HR 3095 to construct a road along a route to be selected by the president.[5] The army's War Plans Division was asked to examine the issue once more, and it concluded that there still appeared to be little military justification for constructing a land route to the north. The division recommended, as it had before, that the bill not be considered favourably in the interests of national defence.[6] This staff work took time, however, and was not finished until early June. By then the strategic balance was about to undergo a dramatic change.

On 22 June 1941, Hitler launched a massive invasion of the U.S.S.R., slicing easily and deeply into Soviet territory, and the great Russian empire trembled. In the Far East, Japan was an Axis power, allied with Germany and Italy for mutual aid and assistance since the previous September. Although Japan had also signed a neutrality treaty with the Soviet Union in April 1941, the United States had no guarantee that the German attack would not ultimately lead to a Japanese presence in Siberia if the Soviet armies collapsed. Prudence seemed necessary, at least until the situation became clearer.[7]

Two days after the German invasion, the American chief of staff, Gen. Marshall, returned the War Plans Division's report. "In view of recent developments in the international situation," he advised, a highway was "desirable as a long range defense measure, providing this construction is controlled so as not to delay or interfere with other more pressing military construction requirements." Marshall directed that the report "be rewritten to interpose no objection to the passage of the authorization bill."[8] This new War Department position was subsequently passed to the House Committee on Roads. A recommendation which mentioned "certain military limitations" which justified only "a low priority" and merely interposed "no further objection" was scarcely a ringing endorsement of quick construction.[9] Nonetheless, it was a significant shift from clear opposition to gentle support and helped ensure that the issue did not die.

A few short months later, the Japanese attacked Pearl Harbor, and the United States was at war. Delegate Dimond and others now pressed William Cartwright, the chairman of the House Committee on Roads, to give active consideration to the bill. In turn, Cartwright solicited departmental views and on 6 January asked the War Department if the changing international situation now increased the military importance of the road.[10] The War Plans Division referred the request to the G-4 staff, responsible for logistics, noting in passing that the division now felt that conditions justified more active support than before.[11]

Meanwhile, other departments were also concerned with the highway proposal. On 16 January, Secretary Ickes of the Department of the Interior raised the issue at a cabinet meeting. President Roosevelt, who had previously gone on record as favouring an early route survey, was interested, and cabinet sentiment was generally favourable. Roosevelt appointed Secretaries Stimson (war), Knox (navy), and Ickes as a committee to "agree on the necessity for a road and the proper route."[12] Since the matter was then being studied by the War Department, a meeting of the committee was delayed until the army's in-house assessment was complete and its expert opinion obtained.[13]

The critical moment for a professional military contribution had arrived. Soldiers are carefully trained to make staff estimates — "appreciations of the situation" in Canadian terminology — and to weigh all factors, such as the enemy threat and considerations of time and distance, before giving their balanced conclusions. The G-4 staff's procedure was less dispassionate but perhaps more interesting.

The House Roads Committee's request, with the War Plans Division's note, went to the Transportation Branch, which would be responsible for the effective use of the highway if built. The branch disagreed with giving more active support to the bill. To do so without also giving funds, manpower, and other resources, it argued, would be ineffectual, while allocating these would only divert scarce assets. The branch strongly suggested that the immediate needs of higher priority projects meant that more support was unjustified.[14]

This advice led to some soul-searching within the G-4's staff. The War Department, it felt, was now forced to take a definite stand on the issue. The Transportation Branch's opinion, if accepted, would reverse the chief of staff's 1941 position, repeated by the secretary of war, that highway construction should no longer be opposed, and this in spite of the fact that the international situation had since deteriorated. On the other hand, it was argued, a road would eventually have to be built to Alaska anyway, and "it could be started now in the interests of the national defense," even if this meant "diverting materials and machinery from other necessary important road projects." Under the current wartime circumstances, Canada could be expected to look favourably on the project but might not do so later. Accordingly, it was recommended that the War Department "take advantage of the present war to secure the necessary agreements from Canada to start work now and finish perhaps many years to come."[15]

Col. A. R. Wilson, the author of this recommendation, drafted a carefully-worded reply, which was repeated to the War Plans Division.[16] He wrote:

> It is believed that hearings should be scheduled on this Bill as early a date as practicable ... construction of a highway to Alaska ... is a desirable undertaking to initiate. However, the amount of work to be undertaken at the present time or in the immediate future depends upon a careful evaluation of the amount of machinery, material, engineering talent, labor and funds which can be diverted from other national defense projects which may be more important.
> The Bill should provide that no unit of work should be started or no funds appropriated ... until approval has been obtained from the War and Navy Departments and the necessary priorities board.[17]

This reply seemed "generally favourable" to the division, which had a predisposition toward more active support. To the chief of staff, the division noted that increased Alaskan garrisons and the possibility of enemy interference with water routes indicated a greater need for an alternate land route for supplies and reinforcements. The road should follow the line of the Northwest Staging Route airfields in order to supply them and to support additional airfield construction.[18] The proposal now had a life of its own.

A subsequent War Plans Division draft paper clearly spelled out the army's position. It acknowledged that the cost of the highway in man hours, equipment, and supplies would be greater than the same expenditure for an equivalent amount of transport ship-building; that the estimated construction time of two years made the road "unavailable in the present emergency"; and that the road would not reach vital installations such as Kodiak, Dutch Harbor, and Sitka, all of which would still need sea transport. Nevertheless, the division concluded, somewhat unconvincingly, that the security of a supply line to the central portion of Alaska outweighed all disadvantages. It recommended that the highway be authorized.[19] The gist of this paper was passed orally to the secretary of war on 2 February.[20]

By then, both Stimson and Knox had also received the State Department's opinion. They were told that the highway would have to be negotiated with Canada, but "if the United States Government really wanted it, Canada would accede." Route selection was left to the expert opinion of the army engineers, but since a road would be needed to ease northwest airfield supply difficulties, that route seemed logical: a choice, it was noted, which would "break the hearts of the politicians in our Pacific Northwest." The State Department deliberately refused to advise on whether or not the highway was important enough to justify immediate construction.[21] The army, of course, had already recommended that it was.

Armed with this information, the American cabinet committee decided to obtain engineer surveys of the highway route and the availability of road-building equipment and to commence the survey work before the spring thaw in the north.[22] Brig.-Gen. C. L. Sturdevant, assistant chief of engineers, was immediately given this task. He was told that the decision was to build the highway via the airfield line and was ordered to submit a survey and construction plan within a few days.[23] Sturdevant's report was ready two days later, on 4 February 1942.[24]

Although Knox, the secretary of the navy, was a member of the special cabinet committee, the chief of naval operations had not yet been formally asked for his opinion, in spite of recommendations to consult him and the persistent concern over the security of sea links. On the day that Sturdevant returned his outline plan, Gen. Marshall finally signed a letter to Adm. King. He asked for "a brief statement as to the ability of the Navy, considering all its commitments and probable future requirements, to maintain, under all circumstances, uninterrupted communications" to Alaska. King replied immediately. Guarantees of uninterrupted communications were impossible, but he assured Marshall that the navy would provide adequate protection for the garrisons and civilian population. King believed it improbable that the enemy could gain any foothold in Alaska which would make the communication links dangerous. Specifically, he rejected the thesis that a road to Alaska was necessary because the navy could not afford adequate shipping defence.[25] By now, however, this opinion was irrelevant.[26] Plans were already being made. On the 11th of February, President Roosevelt approved the project and authorized the army to proceed immediately.[27]

Canadian permission to build was still necessary, but the State Department's confidence that American approval would gain Canadian concurrence was firmly based. Such support had been all but guaranteed previously when American officials visited the Canadian Department of External Affairs in mid-1941. Canada, then already at war, made it clear that the primary consideration in such matters was national defence, but the Permanent Joint Board on Defence had downplayed the highway's importance in 1940. If the board now recommended construction, however, Canada would do its share. It was strongly implied that if the United States put up the bulk of the money, it could probably choose the route. After the meeting, Norman Robertson, the Canadian under-secretary of state for external affairs, conferred further with J. Pierrepont Moffat, the U.S. representative in Ottawa. Robertson said that he was personally sympathetic to the project, but that the government would only agree to it if it were really needed for the war effort. He assured Moffat that if the United States Army "really went to the mat for it in the Permanent Joint Defense Board . . . then . . . any opposition at this end would automatically disappear."[28] The U.S. Army was now quite prepared to take such action. Shortly after the initial plans were ready, the army's senior member on the joint board, Lieut.-Gen. S. D. Embick, took steps to ensure that the American army and navy representatives would speak with one voice favouring the project. Presidential approval assured that this would be so.[29]

There was still some reason to expect opposition from Canada. After all, the Canadian members of the board had joined in the 1940 judgment that the military value of such a road was "negligible." There was no reason for them to have reversed their opinions. As late as 4 February 1942, the Canadian chiefs of staff considered the question and decided that, from their point of view, a highway to Alaska would only indirectly affect the defence of the west coast, even if it could be completed during the war. Canadian construction of the road, therefore, was unwarranted.[30] American construction for American purposes, however, was another question.

On 10 February, the secretary to the Canadian Cabinet War Committee noted that Canada was about to receive a request to allow American army engineers to survey a highway route via the Peace River to Whitehorse. The matter was discussed at a meeting two days later. The committee agreed to allow the survey. Such permission, noted C. D. Howe, the minister of munitions and supply, would in any event not commit Canada to actual construction.[31]

The American request was formally presented by Moffat the next day. It asked for permission both to make a survey and to construct a pioneer road, noting that four regiments of engineers were scheduled for employment on the project and that the United States would defray all associated costs. In reply, Norman Robertson passed on the Cabinet War Committee's approval of the survey but queried the definition of a "pioneer road." Specifically, he wished to know if, by approving it, the Canadian government would be automatically committing itself to the construction of the entire road. This, he said, would require further cabinet consideration, since only the survey had been approved so far. Moffat sought clarification from Washington and reported back the same day that a commitment for the final road would be sought later through the joint board. As for the pioneer road, he defined it as "a rough working road . . . considered part of the survey . . . [which] would be in part the site of an eventual road." Robertson was satisfied with this explanation and was pleased that Canada and the United States had come to a mutual understanding about limiting Canadian liability.[32]

The United States War Department now directed its chief of engineers to proceed with the project. Robertson may have visualized the pioneer road as a rough trail for survey parties, but the American army engineers were under no such delusions. Orders were given for a corridor thirty-two feet wide, subsequently much enlarged, with log bridges and culverts, to provide complete access for the whole distance for civilian contractors who would build the permanent road.[33] The United States Army's official historical chronology rightly regards 13 February, the day Robertson and Moffat met, as the date that Canada approved construction.[34]

In Canada, discussion continued. It was decided that the Canadian members of the board would agree to a proposal to build the highway if the Americans asked for it for defence reasons and accepted all construction and maintenance costs. Subsequently, the board formally advocated this proposal on 25-26 February 1942. The Canadian chiefs of staff still did not think the road warranted by Canadian defence standards but were willing to accept American reasons for justifying construction at their own expense.[35]

Others were more frank. H. L. Keenleyside, the Canadian assistant under secretary of state for external affairs and the secretary of the joint board's Canadian section, noted before final Cabinet approval that the board's recommendation should be accepted, but not for defence reasons. The military arguments advanced were questionable, especially since the road was not expected to be finished until 1944, and adequate ship construction and other plans would obviate its requirement by then. Nonetheless, he concluded, "the United States Government is now so insistent . . . that the

Canadian Government cannot possibly allow itself to be put into the position of barring ... land access to Alaska." Canada "should agree," he declared:

> but this agreement should be recognized, in our own minds at least, as being based on political and not on strategic grounds. The political argument, given the attitude of Washington, is inescapable; the strategic argument, in my opinion, is a most dubious egg.[36]

To this Norman Robertson could only add: "I agree that on political grounds we cannot be put into the position of blocking its construction."[37]

Whatever the value of the arguments, the board had supported the proposal, and now the Canadian government prepared to do its part. On 5 March 1942, the Cabinet War Committee approved the recommendation.[38] The last legal obstacle to construction had been passed.

We now know that the Japanese never intended to invade mainland Alaska. Planners in 1942 did not, and they had to be prepared to respond to any reasonable enemy capability. Still, it is fair to assess both the actual and perceived strategic requirements for building the highway during the war. Two issues stand out: the ability of the U.S. Navy to protect the sea lanes of communication north, and the availability of sufficient sea transport to handle all the foreseeable supply and reinforcement requirements of Alaska.

Prior to Pearl Harbor, the U.S. Navy's ability was virtually unquestioned. With the destruction of a large part of the American Pacific fleet, however, it was reasonable for the issue to be reexamined. The U.S. Army certainly voiced some doubts about the navy's capability to maintain sea communications to Alaska but carried out no detailed assessments to see if they were valid. The navy was not asked for its opinion until after all vital decisions had been made. Its rejection of the idea that it could not provide adequate protection was then no longer relevant. Beyond this general point, there are two additional significant facts. There always was a reasonably secure route along the Inside Passage as far north as Skagway — and the Americans took steps to increase the Passage's defences — with only the few hundred additional miles of open sea to Seward remaining.[39] From there, sea transport was required, highway or no highway, to the important forward installations on Kodiak Island and points west. Navy protection had to be relied upon at these advanced locations in any case.

Sea transport required ships, and these were the Allies' most critical logistical resource. Losses were then far exceeding new construction, and the highway could have been justified on the basis of freeing a depleting resource for other uses. Plans were already underway for massive new ship-building programmes, however, and from the summer of 1942, the Allies experienced a net gain, not loss, in available cargo space. Military shipping requirements to destinations other than Alaska had a much higher priority, but there was no reason to suspect such a severe shortage of ships in 1944 — the planned highway completion date — that the essential maintenance of the Alaskan garrison and population would be prevented. Indeed, the road at first contributed to existing shortages, since a great deal of construction material in the critical summer of 1942 was transported by water to Skagway and mainland Alaska.[40]

There were other opportunity costs as well. Despite assurances that sufficient men and material were available, resources sent to Canada reduced those available elsewhere.[41] In early 1942, it was already clear that the U.S. Army did not have enough engineers to handle all its tasks. To provide them for the highway required breaking an existing policy not to send black troops to extreme northern climates.[42] Demands for heavy transport trucks led to shortages and shipping difficulties as far away as the Persian Gulf, while later reallocations of road-building machinery designated for British use led to controversy and compromise in the Allied Munitions Assignments Board.[43] All this would have been justified, of course, if it had been needed to meet real or perceived strategic requirements. But it was not.

With hindsight, one can see that the highway never really contributed much to Alaskan supply even after its completion. Although the first trucks from Dawson Creek rolled into Fairbanks on 21 November 1942, in essence the territory remained an "island" for military transportation purposes throughout the war.[44] When Gen. DeWitt, the commanding general of the U.S. Western Defense Command, was informed at the end of October 1942 that the opening of the highway would lead to a curtailment of available shipping, he took immediate steps to stop such action. Completion of the highway, he pointed out, did not alleviate the need for shipping during the westward movement to the Aleutians.[45] As a strategic measure for the direct support of Alaska, therefore, the highway's impact was, as previously assessed, virtually "negligible."

But as a construction project, it was a great success. It captured the public imagination as few things did in those dark and forbidding midwar years. Work on it had a frontier spirit on a scale which seemed to typify the best in American pioneering tradition: men and machines against the wilderness in a race against time.[46] It was a magnificent achievement carried out as a military project in time of war. But it was not needed for defence. The highway was actually planned and built for other reasons.

Notes

1. Karl C. Dod, *The Corps of Engineers: The War Against Japan,* United States Army in World War II (Washington: United States Army, 1966), p. 299; C. P. Stacey, *The Military Problems of Canada* (Toronto: Ryerson, 1940), pp. 36-37.

2. Stimson to Cartwright, 2 August 1940, McNarney to Cofs, 24 April 1941, NARS, RG 165, WPD 4327.
3. Army Service Forces, "The Alaska Highway," May 1945, exhibit B (Gen. Somervell's desk file), NARS, RG 160.
4. Stanley W. Dziuban, *Military Relations Between the United States and Canada 1939-1945,* United States Army in World War II (Washington: Department of the Army, 1959), pp. 201-2; C. P. Stacey, *Arms, Men and Governments: The War Policies of Canada 1939-1945* (Ottawa: Queen's Printer, 1970) pp. 379-80.
5. Army Service Forces, "The Alaska Highway," exhibits B and E.
6. Gerow to Cofs, 9 June 1941, NARS, RG 165, WPD 4327-11.
7. See, for example, warnings to Western and Alaska Defense Commands in early July 1941, in U.S. Army, Western Defense Command, "History of the Western Defense Command," MS (1945), I: ch. 1, p. 6, ch. 2, pp. 5-6, copy in U.S. Army Military History Institute, Carlisle Barracks, Carlisle, Pa.
8. Ward to Cofs, 24 June 1941, NARS, RG 407, WPD, AG 611.
9. Gerow to Cofs, 30 June 1941, NARS, RG 165, WPD 4327; Stimson to Cartwright, 6 October 1941, in Army Service Force, "The Alaska Highway," exhibit E.
10. Cartwright to Stimson, 6 January 1942, NARS, RG 407, AG 611.
11. Gerow to Cofs, 19 January 1942, NARS, RG 165, WPD 4327-25.
12. "Notes on Cabinet Meeting of January 16, 1942," in Army Service Force, "The Alaska Highway," exhibits B and F.
13. Smith to Cofs, 19 January 1942, Stimson to Ickes, 21 January 1942, NARS, RG 165, WPD 4327-25, 26.
14. Hamblen to Construction and Real Estate Branch, 17 January 1942, NARS, RG 407, AG 611.
15. Wilson to chief, Construction and Real Estate Branch, 18 January 1942, ibid.
16. Ibid.
17. Somervell to WPD, 20 January 1942, ibid.
18. Gerow to Cofs, 23 January 1942, ibid.
19. Draft Gerow to Cofs, n.d., NARS, RG 165, WPD 4327-27.
20. Tully minute, n.d., ibid.
21. Hickerson to Berle, Berle to Knox, 31 January 1942, Knox to Berle, 3 February 1942 (Knox Office File 4-1-2), NARS, RG 80.
22. Gerow to Cofs, 6 February 1942, NARS, RG 165, WPD 4327-27.
23. Excerpt from Sturdevant's notes, in Army Services Force, "The Alaska Highway," exhibit F.
24. Gerow to Cofs, 6 February 1942, NARS, RG 165, WPD 4327-27.
25. Marshall to King, 4 February 1942, memo for record, 21 February 1942, ibid.
26. The navy did not seem to really care and in the future treated the highway with some indifference. See Knox to Cartwright, 9 March 1942 (Knox office file 4-1-2), NARS, RG 80; and lack of correspondence on CNO Confidential 1942 file on highways, ibid, NS — N2 = 8/ND3.
27. Crawford minute, 11 February 1942, on Gerow to Cofs, 6 February 1942, NARS, RG 165, WPD 4327-27.
28. "Memorandum of Conversation," 6 August 1941, enclosed with Hickerson to Embick, 11 August 1941, ibid.
29. Senior army representative to A. Cofs, 8 February 1942, memo for record, 21 February 1942, ibid.
30. Stacey, *Arms, Men and Governments,* p. 382.
31. Cabinet War Committee minutes, 12 February 1942, in Canada, External Affairs, *Documents on Canadian External Relations, 9: 1942-1943,* ed. J. F. Hilliker (Ottawa: Minister of Supply and Services, 1980), p. 1175 (hereafter cited as *DCER 9*).
32. Minister of United States memorandum on conversation with Robertson and Hickerson, 13 February 1942, ibid., pp. 1176-78.
33. Dod, *Engineers: The War Against Japan,* pp. 300, 307.
34. Mary H. Williams, *Chronology, 1941-1945,* United States Army in World War II (Washington: Department of the Army, 1960).

35. Memorandum on Alaska Highway, n.d., journal extracts, 26th P.J.B.D. Meeting, 25-26 February 1942, extracts from Cabinet War Committee minutes, 5 March 1942, *DCER 9*, pp. 1178-82, 1185-87.
36. Keenleyside memorandum: assistant under secretary of state for external affairs to under secretary of state for external affairs, 3 March 1942, ibid., pp. 1182-85.
37. Robertson note on Keenleyside memorandum, ibid., p. 1183n.
38. Extracts from Cabinet War Committee minutes, 5 March 1942, ibid., pp. 1185-87.
39. AG to CG Field Forces, 10 February 1942, Ulio to CG WDC, 4 June 1942, WDC to AG, 25 August 1942, NARS, RG 407, AG 611.
40. R. M. Leighton and R. W. Coakley, *Global Logistics and Strategy, 1940-1943*, United States Army in World War II (Washington: Department of the Army, 1955), p. 583, appendix E; R. W. Coakley and R. M. Leighton, *Global Logistics and Strategy, 1943-1945*, United States Army in World War II; (Washington: United States Army, 1968), appendix F-1.
41. Gerow to Cofs, 6 February 1942, NARS, RG 165; WPD 4327-27; extracts from minutes of 26th Meeting of P.J.B.D., 25-26 February 1942, *DCER 9*, pp. 1180-82.
42. B. D. Coll, et al., *The Corps of Engineers: Troops and Equipment*, United States Army in World War II (Washington: Department of the Army, 1958), p. 143; Ulysses Lee, *The Employment of Negro Troops*, United States Army in World War II (Washington: United States Army, 1966), p. 439. Ultimately, more than a third of the engineers working on the road were black. Ibid., p. 609.
43. Leighton and Coakley, *Global Logistics and Strategy, 1940-1943*, pp. 294, 576, 582.
44. Dod, *Engineers: The War Against Japan*, p. 315; Stetson Conn, Rose C. Engelman, Byron Fairchild, *Guarding the United States and its Outposts*, United States Army in World War II (Washington: Department of the Army, 1964), p. 225.
45. Western Defense Command, "History of the Western Defense Command," I: ch. 2, p. 17.
46. Lee, *The Employment of Negro Troops*, p. 609; Harold W. Richardson, "Alcan — America's Glory Road," Part I: "Strategy and Location," *Engineering Newsrecord* (17 December 1942): 859, copy in U.S.CMH, HRC 228.03, Geog., E., Alaska 611, "Alcan Highway."

SECTION 2:

Building the Highway

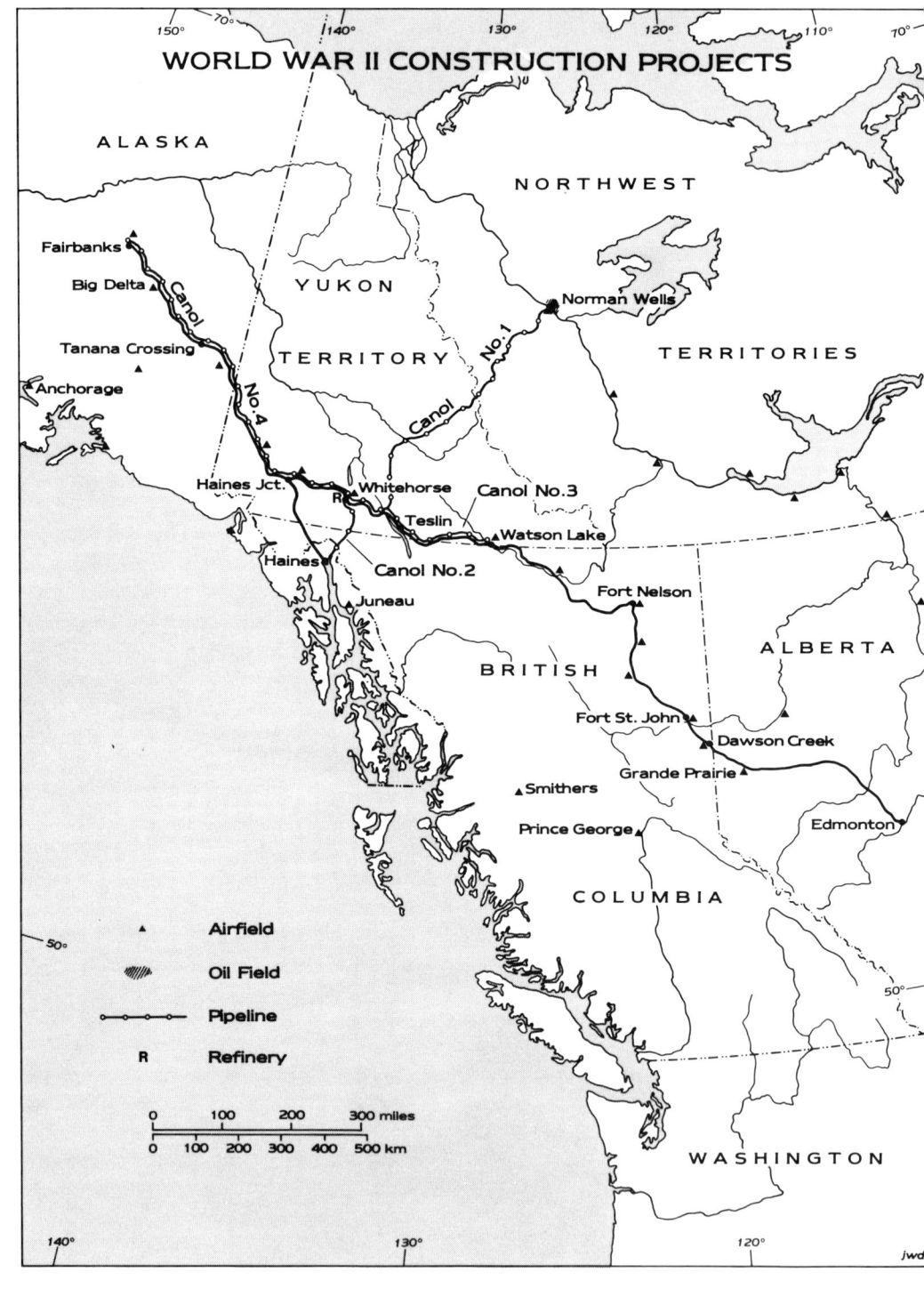

4

General Bill Hoge and the Alaska Highway

JOHN T. GREENWOOD

On 12 February 1942, Pierrepont Moffat, the American minister in Ottawa, heard the news from the State Department. The president, Franklin D. Roosevelt, had approved basic plans for the survey and construction of a military road through Canada to Alaska. Now the State Department requested that Moffat seek Canadian permission to send two engineer regiments to Whitehorse, Yukon, and two others to Fort St. John, British Columbia. This entire force and the military highway project would be under the command of Col. William Morris Hoge, who intended to visit Ottawa first for discussions with Canadian officials and engineers.[1] Although the Canadian government agreed to Hoge's visit, Brig.-Gen. Clarence L. Sturdevant, the assistant chief of engineers responsible for the project, went instead. Hoge was already on his way to Edmonton, Alberta, for his preliminary reconnaissance.

Who was Colonel, soon to be Brigadier-General, William Morris Hoge? Why was he selected to command the army engineers building the Alaska Highway? For one thing, he was stationed at Fort Belvoir, just 15 miles south of Washington, D.C., and was immediately available to begin planning with Sturdevant and the Public Roads Administration (P.R.A.) engineers who would be completing the permanent road behind him. But there was more. Hoge had previously worked for Sturdevant. While commanding the 14th Engineer Battalion (Philippine Scouts) from 1935 to 1937, Hoge had built numerous pioneer roads on the rugged Bataan Peninsula, including the Bataan Highway, when Sturdevant was the engineer for the Philippine Department. Hoge later said that Sturdevant was just searching around for somebody who had done that sort of work, pioneer work. Of course, that was all the Alaska Highway was. . . . I don't know of any other reason for it, but I was pulled out of the training camp . . . and send up to Alaska. I think that was the basis for it — the building of the Bataan Highway.[2]

Hoge had more to recommend him than just Sturdevant's personal views. His career in the Corps of Engineers since graduation from the military academy in 1916 reflected a wide variety of engineering and command assignments. His courage was unquestioned: he had won the Distinguished Service Cross for heroism in November 1918 during the Meuse-Argonne offensive. His technical engineering credentials were also first class: advanced study at Massachusetts Institute of Technology, nearly six years on engineer district and division staffs, troop commands, and tours as district engineer at Memphis and Omaha where he had directed multi-million dollar flood control and navigation projects with as many as 14,000 employees. Hoge's background suited him to such an assignment which required technical, engineering, and military leadership skills of a high order.[3]

While Canadian permission was awaited to move engineer units into Alberta, British Columbia, and the Yukon, planning moved ahead in Washington. All the early planning was done on the basis of maps and with the requirement to link the airfields at Fort St. John, Fort Nelson, Watson Lake, Whitehorse, Northway, and Big Delta. At first, Hoge admitted, there were no plans except to link these airfields.[4] "They didn't know where they were going," said Hoge. "They had this laid out purely from air photos. There were a lot of places no one had been. I later got up in there and I couldn't even find an Indian who'd been over parts of it."[5]

Hoge realized that the great distances involved, the lack of communications and reliable transportation, and the exceedingly difficult terrain determined how he organized his forces. The mountains formed a natural barrier, so he divided the project at Watson Lake and established separate northern and southern sectors. The southern sector headquarters would be at Fort St. John, and the northern sector would be located with Hoge's main headquarters at Whitehorse. He chose Whitehorse because of its good communications and transportation facilities: it had an airport; the White Pass & Yukon Route railway connected it to the port of Skagway; and it was a river port.[6] From the very first, the physical separation of the two sectors and the difficulties of travel and communication presented Hoge with a nightmarish management problem. By mid-April, it was clear that this situation was impossible and was adversely affecting Hoge's ability to control the project.[7] In May, the two sectors were completely separated, with Hoge taking the northern sector and its four engineer regiments, and Colonel James A. "Patsy" O'Connor assuming command of the three regiments in the southern sector.⁸ This division gave Hoge the much tougher and larger assignment: the 1030 miles from Watson Lake to Big Delta.

In his planning, one of the first problems Hoge faced was moving his engineer regiments into positions astride the proposed road. The short working season demanded haste. It was important to get as many units working as soon as possible. If they were to make speed, they could not work behind each other; if one ran into trouble, it would slow everything. Analyzing the problem, Hoge and Sturdevant realized that their access points were limited. They could work from either end, but in Hoge's view "that would be a hell of a long way....So we had to find some ways of breaking it into segments."⁹ Two regiments were slated for Whitehorse. From there one could work southeast to the units working from Fort St. John, and the other northwest to Alaska,¹⁰ to link up with a recently added fifth regiment that would be working from the Richardson Highway.¹¹

Of the two regiments going to Fort St. John, one would have to be moved north to Fort Nelson so it could build toward Watson Lake after the spring thaw. If it could not be moved, the gap between Fort St. John and Whitehorse would never be covered in one working season. Accordingly, Hoge pushed his efforts to move the 35th Engineer Regiment (Combat) under Lieut.-Col. Robert D. Ingalls to Fort Nelson before the winter road from Dawson Creek succumbed to the spring thaw. Hoge's greatest worry was getting the regiment, its heavy equipment, and supplies across the Peace River while the river ice still supported traffic. Hoge later recounted: "We didn't know where we were going actually at that time, but I knew we had to go to Fort Nelson." Except for the movement of the 35th, little could be gained by the early move of the other regiments. Nothing substantial could be done until after the spring thaw.¹²

With this plan of attack, Bill Hoge reconnoitered the future battlefield. He still knew pitifully little about his mission, and he had little except inadequate aerial charts and some National Geographic Society maps. In Edmonton, Hoge met Ingalls, the 35th's commander; Lieut.-Col. E.A. Mueller, the task force quartermaster; and C.F. Capes, a construction engineer from the P.R.A.'s Denver office. After discussions with the Alberta provincial government, the four men boarded the train to Dawson Creek, the end of the line and railhead for the highway's southern sector. On 20 February, Hoge, Ingalls, and Capes headed north to Fort Nelson, along with H.P. Keith from the Canadian Department of Transport's office at Fort St. John. When Hoge returned to Washington the next week, he had seen the terrain and talked to local residents but had learned few details of the route.¹³

Back in Washington, Hoge hurried preparations for moving the 35th from Fort Ord, California, to Fort Nelson. Quartermaster and engineer supply officers were already working along the route in Canada, locating petroleum products and the haulers to move them to Fort Nelson. Because Fort Nelson would be accessible only by air for some time after the thaw, the 35th had to carry 150 days of equipment, supplies, and spare parts, as well as 60 days of rations. Trainloads of equipment began arriving at Dawson Creek on 5 March. Five days later, the first elements of the 35th Engineers detrained at Dawson Creek for their 325 mile trek to Fort Nelson.[14]

The engineers laid heavy planks on the ice to reinforce the Peace River crossing and then protected it against sudden warming with sawdust insulation. The ice bridge lasted for several weeks after the 35th's last convoy cleared the river in late March. In addition to 1900 officers and men, over 900 tons of supplies and equipment, 429,000 imperial gallons of oil products, and ten 23-ton Caterpillar D-8 tractors were moved across the river. Hoge ranked the winter march of the 35th Engineers and the crossings of the Peace River among his most critical achievements. It meant that the project could now be sliced into five segments of roughly three hundred miles each which could be built separately and simultaneously. If the 35th had not made it to Fort Nelson, the road would not have been finished in 1942.[15]

Hoge received his construction directive from Sturdevant on 3 March and left for Fort St. John the next day. This order laid out Hoge's mission and granted the authority to accomplish it. Hoge was charged with surveys, construction of the pioneer road, and co-ordination with the P.R.A. for location and construction of the permanent road. The War Department wanted the general line to run along the existing Northwest Staging Route to permit the ground supply of the airfields. A provisional engineer brigade was established under Hoge's command with headquarters at Whitehorse; it included the 18th, 35th, 340th, and 341st Engineer Regiments, the 73rd and 74th Engineer Companies (Light Pontoon), and two topographic survey companies. Hoge reported directly to the chief of engineers, Maj.-Gen. Eugene Reybold, through Sturdevant, and they reported to Lieut.-Gen. Brehon Somervell, commanding general for services of supply, who had played a leading role in initiating the highway project. The Public Roads Administration was to participate in the preliminary surveys, and Hoge was to consult with P.R.A. engineers to guarantee that his pioneer road would fit the location of the permanent road. The location of the pioneer road was Hoge's decision.[16] Sturdevant's directive stressed the importance of speed:

> The pioneer road will be pushed to completion with all speed within the physical capacity of the troops. The objective is to complete the entire route at the earliest practicable date to a standard sufficient only for the supply of the troops engaged on the work. Further refinements will be undertaken only if additional time is available or if all available troops cannot be employed in pushing forward.[17]

During March and April, Hoge established the foundations for later construction. Soon, however, problems began to appear with route selection as well as with construction planning and management. For one thing, these early months revealed problems he would face in directing a construction project which involved two separate federal agencies, the Corps of Engineers and the Public Roads Administration. Each agency had a separate chain-of-command from Washington to the project. Many of the critical decisions were being made in Washington by Sturdevant and Thomas MacDonald, commissioner of the P.R.A., and then transmitted to Hoge for implementation. The local P.R.A. people received their instructions and funds from the P.R.A., not Hoge. This situation soon caused Hoge serious trouble.

On 31 March, Sturdevant authorized MacDonald and the P.R.A. to construct five sections of the highway in the northern sector.[18] These authorizations conflicted with the original route information that was the basis for Hoge's planning. Although a copy of Sturdevant's letter was forwarded to Hoge, he first learned of it from the P.R.A.'s local representative. The authorizations changed the northern end of the pioneer road from Nabesna to Slana. "These changes," Hoge wrote to Sturdevant on 11 April, "will necessitate considerable modification of my plans and the immediate initiation of further reconnaissances in order to develop the best route to Whitehorse."[19] The route already selected was considered entirely feasible but would now have to be largely abandoned. Frank Andrews, the local P.R.A. representative, had agreed with the road location, but further surveys and reports would have to be made. The final location was not determined until July.[20]

Sturdevant's actions greatly disturbed Hoge. Changes made without his knowledge or approval threw his plans into disarray and affected his command of the project. Moreover, Hoge believed that Sturdevant's letter compromised his position as field commander. Hoge argued that:

> I have made every effort to carry out this project as outlined in instructions from your office. To this end every available means have been used in making reconnaissances with the limited means at my disposal. Based on this information plans have been formulated for the carrying out of the work and the disposition of troops under my command. These reconnaissances, plans, and dispositions are rendered more or less futile when changes ... are made in the basic directive without my being informed. It is also embarrassing to receive notification of such changes through the Public Roads Administration.[21]

This episode showed the difficulties of operating without good communications between headquarters and the field. It also reflected a situation in which critical decisions were made thousands of miles from the scene, often based on inadequate information and knowledge of the local situation. Hoge had the mission but not the full authority to complete it.

During the first two months, Hoge made little headway determining the location of the highway in more inaccessible areas. The lack of adequate maps and aerial photography until late June, combined with a paucity of detailed information, especially about the sections from Fort Nelson to Whitehorse, meant Hoge could do little. The sections north of Whitehorse were already fairly well known from the surveys and report of the Alaskan International Highway Commission and Alaska Road Commission. But no action was taken, partly because so much was already known about the area, particularly by the road's vocal and persistent critics, Thomas Riggs of the Alaska International Highway Commission, and Thomas MacDonald. To the south, placement between Fort St. John and Fort Nelson progressed little during March and into April because there were no planes for aerial reconnaissances. As a result, Hoge and his locating teams had to guess about possible routes based on available information. Hoge finally hired a local Canadian bush pilot from Whitehorse, Les Cook, to fly him and his key officers around to search out locations for the road.[22]

Hoge's rides with Les Cook broke the administrative logjam. He began to issue decisions on the route between Whitehorse and Fort Nelson. From Cook, Bill Hoge learned the secrets that allowed him to extend the road through the largely uncharted region. At first, Hoge was extra baggage on Cook's contract runs. Later, Hoge remembered that:

> I had to ride on top of an old oil drum . . . to go. On the way back he would take me by different routes and he showed me a pass over the mountains — they were the Rocky mountains — down to the Yukon River from back on the Liard River. That was the bad part and he showed me where to go. Well, I got over to the pass and by following creeks — I think the top of the elevation was 3,000 feet — the place they had mapped out for me to go was up above the timber line and was in the snow country. It would have been one hell of a job to get up there and then get down and it wasn't nearly as direct as the other. They just picked it off of a map someplace, an airline map or something. They had no information . . . Les Cook was the great one. Les took me every place. He went between the mountains. We went down at elevations. We got lost, but I got to know the country pretty well, and the streams by this flying back and forth. . . . I also learned from the air that I could distinguish the type of soil from the type of timber on it. I could identify, for instance, cedar always grew on gravelly ground. . . . When you saw spruce that was usually mucky and it was soft soil. You had to have something besides some gravel and you couldn't haul gravel very far.[23]

Les Cook pointed out the best crossing of the Rockies, about 80 miles east of Teslin, with a summit of 3,208 feet. This direct route was unknown to local inhabitants, but its discovery through aerial reconnaissance proved a key to the early completion of the highway. A ground reconnaissance led by Lieut.-Col. Reinder Schilsky of the 340th Engineers followed up this lead and established the route from Teslin Lake to Watson Lake. By early June, the biggest question mark on the route was erased and this section of the road was located.[24]

Hoge also established the road's general location from Fort St. John to Fort Nelson, with P.R.A. agreement. Fort Nelson to Watson Lake was another matter because two routes could be followed: one northwest through swamp and muskeg and the other west through the mountains. After aerial reconnaissances with P.R.A. engineers, Hoge approved a route through the mountains and then along the north bank of the Liard River to Watson Lake. P.R.A. engineers favoured the south side, but Hoge opted for the north. Although Patsy O'Connor later reversed Hoge's selection after taking over the southern sector, the final road ran on the north side.[25]

Weather and ground conditions prevented detailed ground reconnaissances. In the northern sector, twelve P.R.A. locating teams worked southeast and northwest of Whitehorse with detachments from Maj. Frank Pettit's topographic survey company. Another fifty P.R.A. engineers were expected in mid-May at Gulkana on the Richardson Highway to begin site surveys of the route to the Tanana River. All the teams desperately needed aerial photographs, but photographic planes did not begin operating effectively until June. Even then, the negatives had to be developed in Seattle because no unit on the road had the proper equipment. Only in July did the locating teams have aerial photos.[26]

From May through August, ground and aerial reconnaissances continued on all sections. By this time, the marking teams barely kept ahead of the clearing crews and their D-8's. From the beginning, the sector and regimental commanders had the authority to decide the detailed location of the pioneer road. Early efforts to co-operate on placing the pioneer and permanent roads as close as possible ended because the P.R.A. locating parties could not provide detailed survey information far enough in advance of the clearing parties to prevent delay. The army engineers worked against a tight deadline dictated by the seasons and an equally tight set of specifications on the kind of road they were to build. The unexpected problem in the location issue was that the 23-ton D-8 bulldozer allowed the clearing crews to push ahead much more rapidly than anyone thought possible a few months earlier.[27]

Supplementing his 3 March instructions, Sturdevant, on 29 April, sent the final specifications for the permanent road to Hoge and O'Connor. The letter laid out the basic design and dimensions of the road, bridges, culverts, grades and curves, and the width of right-of-ways. The individual section commanders were to use these specifications to guide their location of the pioneer road. The final highway would follow that location as closely as practicable. The ultimate decision on location of the pioneer road and its specifications remained the prerogative of the sector commander because, Sturdevant said, "the mission requires Engineer troops to push through a pioneer road during the present working season, regardless of desirable specifications."[28]

During a visit to Anchorage while still in command of the entire project, Hoge was asked by a critic of the road how he was going to build it. Hoge answered, "with six machines of 1000 men each": his engineer regiments. On the Whitehorse sector after May, Hoge had two white regiments, the 18th and 340th, and the black 93rd working out of Whitehorse and Carcross. A fourth, the black 97th, landed at Valdez in mid-May and began working from Slana in mid-June. The 93rd and 340th sat in Skagway from mid-April to mid-May awaiting their heavy equipment. The 18th had arrived in early April, and despite a lack of heavy equipment, went to work north of Whitehorse with hand tools. According to Ken Rust, the regimental historian, they worked "in coolie fashion, bending pick points in frozen ground and mucking around in rivers of mud, getting nowhere." Living in tents, moving constantly, and working three 8-hour shifts, seven days a week, the soldiers cursed the endless summer nights that permitted such work schedules, the mosquitoes and flies, the monotonous army B-rations, and the lack of supplies and spare parts. Yet they steadily pushed their roads forward.[29]

With only four good months in the construction season, Hoge could not worry about the subtleties of normal road building. His mission was to push the road to completion as fast as he could. "We had to make speed," he said, "and all I was trying to do was to get this road behind me. I always had about two regiments at the most up ahead and I had to keep them supplied with food and fuel and all the repair parts and what not which was a job in itself, but that made a road. I finally punched the thing through."[30] There was not time for carefully constructed subgrades, gentle curves, and easy inclines. Hoge was continuously on the go. He personally tested the radius of the curves until he was sure that the trucks and equipment could get around them without backing up. He emphasized that the job had to be done quickly; sophistication would come with the P.R.A.'s permanent road. Hoge was once quoted as telling a subordinate: "Your road is too good, too wide, and too short."[31]

Hoge's approach to construction was simple and direct. He had "arbitrarily specified that clearings would be 50' each side of the center line. The road surface was to be 18' wide, shoulders 5' wide, maximum grades 10" and curves easy to turn."[32] As Hoge put it, "my way was to cut a swath through the woods a 100 feet wide for the right-of-way. My road was only 25 feet wide but I had that much."[33] The key to Hoge's plan was his heavy equipment, especially the D-8's, which had three basic functions: clearing, cutting and filling, and grading. Once a suitable number of the big Cats were on line, and each regiment eventually had twenty of them, ten to twelve D-8's could clear two to three miles of 100-foot right-of-way through solid forest in a day. So successful were these clearing crews that they were soon on the heels of the locating teams. Because of this, engineer and P.R.A. co-ordination on route location was discontinued, with unfortunate consequences.[34]

Despite some rainy weather in June and continuing deficiencies in equipment and supplies, the regiments completed 190 miles of pioneer road and located another 419 miles by early July. At the month's end, 368 miles were completed. Few serious obstacles slowed construction except for the major water courses, such as Slim's River, which required the 18th Engineers to build a 1040-foot pile stringer bridge. Hoge had been warned repeatedly that muskeg, pockets of decaying vegetable matter, would defeat him or seriously curtail his progress. From his experience, Hoge found otherwise. "Muskeg," he wrote, "got a lot of publicity while we were building the Alcan. Personally, I consider it to be of only limited importance. We were always able to overcome the difficulties it presented without too much trouble." Hoge carefully routed the pioneer road away from muskeg where possible. Where necessary, he used clearing techniques which allowed the muskeg to dry out.[35]

Hoge's approach was wrong for the permanently frozen subsoil, or permafrost, that lurked beneath the surface on large stretches of the located route. As Hoge later said:

> I was going just to beat hell. I was making more mileage than I'd ever made.... The first perma-frost I ran into was on my own road, building it up north of Whitehorse. I remember a spot where I had the road and everything was all right and I went back over it and it was full of water and muddy. I couldn't understand it because it had been dry before. I discovered that there was an ice lens underneath. The ice lens was quite large but it was just isolated.[36]

No sooner had the 18th Engineers mastered the area around Kluane Lake than both it and the 340th to the south ran into extensive stretches of permafrost. Their progress plummeted to less than a mile a day during August and into September. Hoge's swath-cutting policy was, as he admitted,

> the wrong thing to do, I had discovered that the hard way. The only thing to do was to cut the timber and then throw it back on top, make a mat of timber and branches and everything else to protect it and then put dirt around that.... I had to put a blanket over the perma-frost... that finally worked but it was considerable work.[37]

This procedure slowed things considerably because the clearing now had to be done by hand; the D-8's would rip the vegetation cover off the permafrost.[38]

The proper techniques for construction in permafrost areas were then relatively unknown. "Actually," Hoge said, "I doubt that any American knew anything about it until I discovered a great deal about the perma-frost end of it. Everyone talked about muskeg and everybody talked of mountains and crossing lakes and rivers, but they never heard of perma-frost which was the worst thing we had to contend with."[39]

Continuing criticism of the choice of routes prompted Sturdevant to visit both sectors during July. On 20 June, Colonel Jim Tully of the Operations Division, War Department General Staff, had forwarded a letter to Sturdevant from Thomas Riggs of the Alaskan International Highway Commission, a persistent critic of the road's location. Riggs was concerned that the P.R.A. road deviated from the line of the pioneer road so much that two parallel roads were developing. Sturdevant informed MacDonald at P.R.A. of Riggs's charges and wrote to Hoge confirming his intention of visiting the road: "I am looking forward to seeing you and the job and particularly some of the PRA activities. Some things are not working as I expected, such as building two roads somewhat parallel."[40]

Sturdevant toured the highway by air and car from 7 to 18 July, observed the work, and tried to co-ordinate the work of the P.R.A. and the engineers. The road he saw was of a much higher standard than envisioned in the original plan. The pioneer road was really a well-graded and drained two-way road for most of the distance, whereas the troops had been expected to build a one-way access road suitable only for their own supply. The P.R.A. contractors, who were to build the permanent road, had progressed little beyond establishing their camps, gathering equipment, and initiating work. Sturdevant reported to Somervell that the road would be ready to Fort Nelson by 15 September and to Watson Lake and Northway by 1 December. Winter traffic to Alaska could use the road from 1 December through the spring thaw of 1943 if there were rest camps, telephone and radio communications, fuel supply and storage facilities, refuge stops every fifty miles, warehouses and barracks.[41]

While welcome, Sturdevant's news of this unexpectedly rapid progress altered plans for the road's completion and future use. On 3 August, Sturdevant informed MacDonald that the situation required review and that a curtailment of P.R.A. work was a real possibility. Five days later, Sturdevant sent Hoge and O'Connor revised construction orders intended to improve co-ordination between the engineers and P.R.A. For sections not yet under construction, the pioneer road was to be located in close co-operation with P.R.A. teams so that it could be more easily incorporated in the later final road.[42]

By early August, another factor in Washington affected Sturdevant's more militant approach. On 3 August, Sturdevant reminded O'Connor that his job was to build a pioneer road and to reach agreement with the P.R.A. if possible. If that could not be done, the matter was to be referred to him in Washington. Then he revealed the real force at work: "General Somervell has received a letter stating that there has been an appalling lack of co-ordination between the Army and Public Roads Administration. I believe the writer's information came from the Whitehorse area, but a similar incident might happen anywhere that we build two parallel roads." Somervell was sensitive to any criticism, but this was especially bothersome one month after House and Senate investigations of the entire Alaska Highway project and the route selection. Unless Sturdevant discussed this during his visit in July, there is no indication that Hoge was told officially of this "appalling lack of co-ordination."[43]

As a result of the conferences with Sturdevant, the P.R.A., and his own project engineers during July, Hoge had already decided to change his method of operation. He discarded his previous approach which had the engineers and P.R.A. performing different and sequential jobs and concentrated their combined forces on building the pioneer road during 1942. Permanent standards were abandoned. In mid-August, Hoge advised his regimental commanders to follow P.R.A. locations as closely as possible for pioneer road construction. Under these new instructions, substantial progress was made despite the permafrost. By late August, 528 miles had been completed, but Bill Hoge received little credit for it. He had been fired the last week of the month.[44]

The early completion of the highway, the continuing criticism of route selection, and Somervell's own plans prompted his visit to Canada and Alaska from 17 to 22 August. He was probably more concerned about his pet Canadian Oil (Canol) Project than the highway, but the two were becoming increasingly intertwined now that the highway neared completion. Petroleum products from Canol were essential for the economical and efficient operation of army trucking operations on the long haul from Edmonton to Alaska. When Somervell arrived in Hoge's sector after a brief stop with O'Connor, he found plenty to dislike about Hoge's operation. After looking over the congested and uncomfortable city of Whitehorse, Somervell, whose reputation for pomp, show, and grand designs was unrivaled in the U.S. Army, decided things were a mess. The White Pass & Yukon Route railway to Skagway was inadequate, the housing was inadequate, the supplies were inadequate. Hoge's whole concept and operation were unacceptable. Hoge later recalled Somervell's visit:

> He came up there and we were living in tents. I had an old Mounted Police barracks in Whitehorse that I used as my headquarters . . . otherwise everything went on the road. Well, that didn't suit Somervell; he wanted a big show, . . . it had to be the biggest, most expensive that

anybody could have ... if I had built all the buildings he was thinking about, they wouldn't have done any good to start with except as a base camp, which would have been left several hundred miles behind in each case. But they wouldn't have been lived in. We had to move.[45]

Somervell decided to relieve Hoge. He told his chief of staff, Maj.-Gen. W. D. Styer, that O'Connor's section was "a first class construction job," but Hoge's had many problems.[46] But Somervell's dissatisfaction was personal as well as professional. Hoge had known Somervell since their cadet days at West Point and had worked for him in the Memphis district in 1932-33. Somervell was known to be vindictive, and Hoge believed that Somervell never forgot that when he left after trouble with the division engineer Harley Ferguson, Hoge became the district engineer. While Hoge and Ferguson remained close friends for many years, Somervell and Ferguson were bitter enemies.[47]

Hoge quickly found a job with Maj.-Gen. Jacob Devers, then commanding the armored force at Fort Knox. Bill Hoge never forgave Somervell for his actions, but he also never looked back and never tried to vindicate himself. He felt he had nothing to prove; he had been given a job and had seen it largely completed before his departure. In fact, Hoge later came to see that his departure "was very fortunate as it turned out for me because I would have been stuck there maybe a year or two." Bill Hoge left Whitehorse for the last time on 10 September and officially relinquished command two days later.

Before Hoge left Whitehorse, seven of the enlisted personnel from his headquarters wrote a farewell note expressing regret at his leaving. "It has been," the non-commissioned officers said, "an honor and a pleasure to serve under the direct supervision of such a capable and fair dealing commander. We wish you the best of health, success and happiness in your new assignment."[49] In a history of the Whitehorse sector written in June 1943, Capt. W.C. Palfreyman, who had been Hoge's adjutant, added an operational assessment far different from Somervell's:

> Highest individual credit, of course, should be given to the leader who planned and was responsible for the successful accomplishment of the mission. General Hoge's careful planning, forceful carrying out of plans, the understanding way in which he dealt with his subordinates, and his drive and initiative, were in large measure the principal factors in seeing the road through.[50]

On 4 September, Somervell established the Northwest Service Command to preside over his new empire in the northwest, including Canol and the services supporting the soon-to-be-opened highway from Dawson Creek to

Fairbanks. The men, material, supplies, equipment, and support for which Hoge had fought so hard were lavished upon O'Connor's new command. The road from Fort St. John to Whitehorse was completed in late September, and that section through to Alaska was ready in late October. The Alaska Highway was complete and open to truck traffic in November 1942.

Bill Hoge survived his firing to become one of the great tank commanders of the war in Europe. After commanding the Provisional Engineer Special Brigade Group that established and operated the American beachheads at Omaha and Utah beaches during the Normandy invasion, Hoge assumed command of Combat Command B of the 9th Armored Division in October 1944. He led this unit through the tough defensive fighting around St. Vith during the Battle of the Bulge in December. On 7 March 1945, his tank and infantry forces captured the Ludendorff railroad bridge over the Rhine River at Remagen and gave the Allies their first foothold east of the river. He ended the war commanding the 4th Armored Division. His postwar career included a succession of important army commands and promotion to the rank of four-star general in October 1953. Bill Hoge's last assignment prior to retirement in January 1955 was as commander-in-chief of U.S. Army Europe, the American ground element of NATO. Of all Bill Hoge's many contributions to the U.S. Army and his country in peace and war, none better demonstrated his abilities as a leader, organizer, commander, and engineer than his seven months on the Alaska Highway.

Notes

1. Message from Hull, SecState, to AMLEG, Ottawa, 12 February 1942, and Message, Moffat to Hickerson, 13 February 1942, NARS, RG 77 Acc. 3173.
2. Interview, Lieut.-Col. George Robertson, Corps of Engineers, with Gen. William M. Hoge, April 1974, 2-1, in Historical Division, Office of the Chief of Engineers (OCE).
3. Biographical file on Gen. W. M. Hoge, U.S. Army Center of Military History.
4. Memo for the Adjutant General Maj.-Gen. Brehon B. Somervell, assistant chief of staff G-4, "International Highway," 13 February 1942 in NARS, RG 77, Acc. 3173, box 15, docs. January-March 1942.
5. Interview, Robertson with Hoge, 2-17.
6. Interview, Robertson with Hoge, 2-35, 36.
7. Memo for Gen. Somervell, Maj.-Gen. E. Reybold, COE, approx. 12 April 1942, NARS, RG 77, Acc. 3173, file 52-2.
8. AG 320.2 (5-12-42) MR-M-SP, "Constitution and Activation of Sector Headquarters Detachments," 14 May 1942, in 320.2 Constitution & Activation of New Detachments 1942, Northwest Service Command, NARS, RG 338, box 4.
9. Interview, Robertson with Hoge, 3-9.
10. Memo for assistant chief of staff, war plans division, (ACS/WPD), Sturdevant, 4 February 1942, in Report, Headquarters Army Service Forces, "The Alaska Highway," May 1945, Historical Division Files, Alaska Highway.
11. Memo for chief of staff of the army, Gerow, ACS/WPD, and Crawford, "International Highway," 6 February 1942, NARS, RG 77, Acc. 3173, file 50-10.

12. Interview, Robertson with Hoge, 2-16; Sturdevant, "The Military Road to Alaska: Organization and Administrative Problems," *Military Engineer* (April 1943): 177.
13. Northwest Engineer Division, *The Alaska Highway and CANOL Projects* (Edmonton: 1944), p. 12; Theodore A. Huntley, *The Alaska Highway: First Year* (Edmonton, 31 March 1943) pp. 5, 36; Interview, Robertson with Hoge, 2-15, 2-30, 3-8/9; *Peace River Block News*, 26 February 1942, in William M. Hoge Papers, Library U.S. Army Command and General Staff College, Fort Leavenworth, KS.
14. Interview, Robertson with Hoge, 3-10; Sturdevant, "The Military Road," 174; Memo for Col. R.F. Fowler, Chief, Supply Div., OCE, from Maj. R.W. Reuter, "Report on Travel in Connection with Engineer Activities," 10 March 1942, in "Misc Notes Alcan — Transportation," NARS, RG 77, Acc. 3173; Letter, Lieut.-Col. J.S. Gullet, military attaché, Ottawa, to Sturdevant, 5 March 1942, ibid.
15. Telephone Interview, Dr. John T. Greenwood with Col. William M. Hoge, Jr., USA (Ret), 14 June 1982; Huntley, *The Alaska Highway*, pp. 11, 12; Report, Maj. A.C. Welling, Exec Ofr, Force 6968, southern sector, to chief of engineers, "Monthly Report of Operations for March 1942," 1 April 1942, in NARS, RG 77, Acc. 3173, file 50-32; Message, Welling to Hoge, 26 March 1942, in ibid., file 50-12; Memorandum for Col. Hoge, Maj. A.C. Welling, 27 March 1942, in Hoge Papers.
16. Sturdevant to Hoge, "Construction of the Canadian-Alaskan Military Highway," 3 March 1942, in NARS, RG 77, Acc. 3173, file 50-10.
17. Letter, Sturdevant to Hoge, 3 March 1942.
18. Sturdevant to MacDonald, 20 March 1942, exhibit M, in Alaska Highway Report, Historical Division, OCE; Sturdevant to MacDonald, 31 March 1942, and Message, Hoge to COE 15 April 1942, in NARS, RG 77, Acc. 3173, file 50-29.
19. Hoge to Sturdevant, "Location of Canada-Alaska Highway," 11 April 1942, in File Alaska Highway General, NARS, RG 77, Acc. 3173, Box 14.
20. Letter, Sturdevant to Hoge, "Selection of Route," 6 May 1942; Letter, Hoge to COE, "Selection of Route," 3 June 1942; and Letter, Hoge to COE, "Selection of Route," 1 July 1942, in NARS, RG 77, Acc. 3173, file 50-33.
21. Letter, Hoge to Sturdevant, 11 April 1942.
22. Hoge to Sturdevant, "Photographic Plan," 2 May 1942, in NARS, RG 160, Subject File: Alcan, Box 2, Planning Division, Army Service Forces (ASF); Hoge to Sturdevant, 3 May 1942, NARS, RG 77, Acc. 3173, Box 14, file: Alaska Highway General; Maj. A.C. Welling, "Monthly Report of Operations for March, 1942," 1 April 1942, and Report, Capt. W.C. Palfreyman, Adj., 18th ER, to COE, "Progress Report for May 1942," 26 May 1942, NARS, RG 77, Acc. 3173, file 50-32; Capt. W.C. Palfreyman, "History of the Whitehorse Sector of the Alaska Highway," 10 June 1943, Historical Division, OCE, Alaska Highway General.
23. Interview, Robertson with Hoge, 2-30, 31.
24. Sturdevant, "The Military Road," 175; Huntley, *The Alaska Highway*, p. 15.
25. *Alaska Highway and CANOL Project*, 22; Sturdevant, "The Military Road," 174; Huntley, *The Alaska Highway*, pp. 38, 39.
26. Huntley, *The Alaska Highway*, p. 44; Sturdevant, "The Military Road," 175; Memo for CG/SOS, Sturdevant, "Monthly Report of Operations, Alcan Highway, April 1942," 8 May 1942, in Documents May-June 1942, NARS, RG 77, Acc. 3173, box 15; Report, Maj. C.F. Waite, Operations Officer, Northern Sector, to COE, 24 June 1942, in NARS, RG 77, Acc. 3173, file 50-32; Col. J.A. O'Connor, Commanding Officer, Southern Sector, to COE, "Progress Report for June 1942," 22 June 1942, in NARS, RG 77, Acc. 0434, box 29, file 600.914.
27. Sturdevant to Hoge, 3 March 1942 and 29 April 1942. Alaska Highway General, Historical Division, OCE; Sturdevant, "The Military Road," 177.
28. Sturdevant to Hoge, 29 April 1942.
29. T/5 Ken Rust, "History of the 18th Engineers (Combat) in the Yukon Territory," pp. 7, 14, 18, in Historical Division, OCE; Telephone Interview, Dr. John T. Greenwood, Chief, Historical Division OCE, with Col. William M. Hoge, Jr., USA (Ret.), 11 June 1982; Interview, Robertson with Hoge, 2-20.

30. Interview, Robertson with Hoge, 2-20, 35.
31. Edmonton *Bulletin,* 5 June 1943, in NARS, RG 77, Acc. 3173, file 50-23.
32. Rust, "18th Engineers," pp. 37, 38.
33. Interview, Robertson with Hoge, 2-33, 34.
34. Letter, Hoge to Norell, Chief of Military History, 3 June 1960, in Historical Division Files.
35. Hoge, "Construction in the Arctic," p. 2, in Hoge Papers; Interview, Robertson with Hoge, 2-32; Hoge to COE, 10/1035z July 1942, and Report, Hoge to COE, "Progress Report for July, 1942," 24 July 1942, in WNRC, RG 77, Acc. 3173, file 50-32.
36. Interview, Robertson with Hoge, 2-32. 33, 34; 3-1.
37. Ibid.
38. Rust, "18th Engineers," pp. 51, 52, 64; Palfreyman, "Whitehorse Sector," p. 11.
39. Interview, Robertson with Hoge, 3-1.
40. Sturdevant to Hoge, 23 June 1942, in WNRC, RG 77, Acc. 3173, file 50-33; Memo for Gen. Sturdevant, Col. J.K. Tully, WDGS, "International Highway," 20 June 1942, in WNRC, RG 77, Acc. 3173, file 50-28.
41. Memorandum for CG/SOS, Sturdevant, "Monthly Report of Operations, Alcan Highway, July 1942," 1 August 1942, in Monthly Progress Reports, WNRC, RG 77, Acc. 3173.
42. Sturdevant to MacDonald, 3 August 1942, in WNRC, RG 77, Acc. 3173, file 50-28; Sturdevant to Hoge and O'Connor, "Instructions for Construction of Alcan Highway," 8 August 1942, in WNRC, RG 77, Acc. 3173, file 50-10; MacDonald to J.S. Bright, District Engineer PRA, "Coordination of Operations of Alaska-Canada Highway," 8 August 1942, WNRC, RG 77, Acc. 3173, in Misc. Correspondence Folder Alaska Highway.
43. Sturdevant to O'Connor, 3 August 1942, in WNRC, RG 77, Acc. 3173, file 50-29; US, Senate, Committee on Foreign Relations, 77th Congress, 2d Session, *Hearings, Alaska Highway June 1, 12, and 16, 1942* (Washington: GPO, 1942).
44. Huntley, *The Alaska Highway,* pp. 46-48; Rust, "18th Engineers," p. 56.
45. Interview, Robertson with Hoge, 3-2, 3, 4, 5, 6, 7.
46. Memo, W.D. Styer, "Resume of Remarks Made by General Somervell As a Result of His Inspection Trip to Alaska," 24 August 1942, in Styer's desk file, NARS, RG 160, box 73, NWSC-1942.
47. Interview, Robertson with Hoge, 1-57, 1-59, 2-29.
48. Interview, Robertson with Hoge, 2-38; Telephone interview, Dr. John T. Greenwood with Lt.-Col. George F. Hoge, 11 June 1942; Memo for CSA, Col. M.G. White for BG Donald Wilson, ACS, "General Officer," 31 August 1942, in File 201 Hoge, W.M., NARS, RG 165, box 46; GO 4, Hoge, Northern Sector, Alcan Highway, 12 September 1942, in file, Alaska Highway, Northwest Service Command, NARS, RG 338, box 47.
49. Note to General Hoge, n.d., Hoge Papers.
50. Palfreyman, "Whitehorse Sector," p. 16.

5

Cut, Fill and Straighten: The Role of the Public Roads Administration in the Building of the Alaska Highway

HEATH TWICHELL

Anyone who thinks about the building of the Alaska Highway during the Second World War probably visualizes U.S. Army Engineer troops cutting a narrow supply route through 1,500 miles of forest, muskeg and mountains to link western Canada with Alaska. Such a picture is accurate; this is exactly what the U.S. Army did. But it is also misleading. The Alaska Highway that was essentially complete in late 1943 was at least as much the work of the American Public Roads Administration and its consortium of American and Canadian management and construction firms as it was of the engineer regiments who began to lay out the original "pioneer" road in the spring of 1942.

For all of its continuing problems with rough spots and washouts, the highway that was gradually opened to the public after the Second World War was a far better and safer road than it otherwise would have been had it been constructed solely by the U.S. Army Engineers. This may sound like another slap at an organization that has long been a favorite target of watchdog groups of many kinds, from conservationists of land and money to civic and regional boosters playing porkbarrel politics, but there is no need to belittle the magnificent military engineering accomplishments of Generals Hoge and O'Connor and their men. There is more than enough credit to go around.

The point is simply this: few people realize that the army's bulldozed trail was never intended to be more than a sort of "rough draft" of the finished, all-weather highway that the Public Roads Administration (P.R.A.) and its civilian contractors eventually built. In addition, even though the Corps of Engineers supervised and controlled all aspects of the project, including the activities of the P.R.A., the latter organization's inherent tendency to reject temporary expedients and think in terms of permanent construction led to frequent and often bitter disputes with the engineers over construction methods and standards. Standards were repeatedly revised downward as the enemy threat to the Pacific Northwest receded and road building resources were more urgently needed elsewhere. But the P.R.A. won enough of these arguments to ensure that what would be left to the American and Canadian public at the end of the war was not just a hastily constructed and already deteriorating emergency military supply route.

Most people have some idea of both the peacetime and wartime missions of the U.S. Army Corps of Engineers; the Public Roads Administration is not as well known. The P.R.A. has been better known as the Bureau of Public Roads (B.P.R.) for most of its more than sixty years of existence as an agency in the American government. The original bureau was an outgrowth of the "Better Roads Movement" of the 1920's, whose purpose was the improvement of America's rural roads for the benefit of farmers and consumers. This remained a fundamental purpose of the B.P.R. between the world wars, but other important functions were added as the United States became an increasingly motorized nation. Among these were the setting of road- and bridge-building construction standards, research on improved materials and equipment, traffic density studies aimed at rationalizing the national highway system, and co-ordination with state highway departments (most of which had come into existence to respond to the directives and queries of the B.P.R.). In addition, the bureau was responsible for the construction and maintenance of all roads within the national park system, using civilian contractors hired for each specific project. Until 1939, the bureau was an agency of the Department of Commerce; that July it was renamed the Public Roads Administration and put under the jurisdiction of the newly created Federal Works Administration.

As this brief history suggests, the B.P.R./P.R.A. was an agency with considerable power and political influence. That it also enjoyed the respect of the transportation and construction professionals with whom it dealt was a credit to its boss, Thomas H. MacDonald, commissioner of public roads since 1919. An experienced highway engineer and a careful and farsighted administrator, MacDonald had come to the bureau after making a name for himself as head of Iowa's highway department. His longevity in Washington is the best testimony to his effectiveness as both an engineer and a bureaucrat: he retired in 1953 after thirty-four years in the same position.

Just prior to the Japanese attack on Pearl Harbor, with the war in Europe already two years old, the U.S. Congress passed the Defense Highway Act, which directed the P.R.A. to concern itself solely with highway projects that would bolster national defence. Congress had in mind upgrading the roads serving military training areas, mines, and factories, and making improvements to the existing strategic highway network. But in late January 1942, when the War Department began to study the problem of building a highway to Alaska as quickly as possible, the P.R.A. was a natural choice to supplement the already overburdened equipment and manpower resources of the Corps of Engineers. It was to be a "co-operative" undertaking between two professionally competent and powerful federal organizations, with the engineers retaining authority to make final decisions and being held responsible for the project by the War Department.[1]

The original agreement between the Corps of Engineers and the P.R.A. concerning the highway was contained in a series of letters of March 1942 between Commissioner MacDonald and Brig.-Gen. Clarence L. Sturdevant, assistant to the chief of engineers. It confirmed that overall responsibility rested with the Corps of Engineers and gave the P.R.A. a series of clearly defined tasks. Subject to the army's final approval, the P.R.A. was to: survey, locate, and lay out the route of the finished highway; prepare plans, specifications and estimates for building it; and place under contract and supervise the civilian contractors necessary to get the job done. Because the northern climate dictated a construction season of six months or less, completion of the finished, two-lane, all-weather highway (including several large permanent bridges and more than one hundred smaller spans) was not anticipated until the fall of 1943, a date some skeptics regarded as overly optimistic.

For the army's part, its troops would hastily construct a rough pioneer or "tote" road closely paralleling the route of the finished highway, to provide access to it for the P.R.A.'s contractors and their equipment. But this rough trail was intended to serve a strategic purpose as well as a practical one. In view of the perceived Japanese threat, the army's plan was to begin construction of the pioneer road at several points simultaneously with the hope of having at least a primitive overland supply route open all the way to Alaska by late 1942. Of equal, and ultimately of greater, importance, such a route would also service a chain of recently constructed airfields linking the industrial midwest with Fairbanks. Finally, completion of the pioneer road on schedule would greatly increase the P.R.A.'s chances of finishing the highway as planned in 1943.

Even as Gen. Sturdevant and Commissioner MacDonald worked out the terms of this basic agreement in Washington, the first detachments of engineer troops and equipment began arriving in Canada at the Dawson Creek railhead. Company B of the 35th Engineers, with 4 officers and 160 enlisted men, passed through Fort St. John on their way over the winter trail to Fort Nelson on 12 March 1942. Ahead and above them, working both by air and by dog sled, several joint P.R.A./engineer surveying parties were searching for the best route through more than 1,500 miles of thinly populated, poorly mapped, and very forbidding terrain.[2]

By late June 1942, most of the 10,000 troops assigned to Gen. Hoge's command had arrived and were at work on the pioneer road. The P.R.A.'s work force took a bit longer to organize, equip and transport than the seven engineer regiments. The army had assembled an impressive array of men and equipment in a remote region of North America in the space of about three months. Given what it started with, the P.R.A.'s performance was equally impressive.

The Alaska Highway was the largest single project ever undertaken by the P.R.A. Many of its best engineers and management personnel from districts throughout the central and western states were quickly diverted from less essential wartime tasks and given new assignments: survey the proposed route; find the best sites for bridge crossings, gravel pits, sawmills and work camps; requisition usable office and storage facilities in the vicinity of the proposed route; scour the United States for unused prefabricated buildings, furnishings of all kinds, tools, construction equipment and winter clothing, and make arrangements to ship it all. Last but not least, they were to select and place under contract the more than fifty construction firms needed to do the actual work.

With wartime priorities and procedures still being worked out, the scramble for resources to support the massive national mobilization then underway can well be imagined. Fortunately for the P.R.A., many of the items on its "shopping list" were still the property of two New Deal agencies made superfluous by the wartime revival of the economy: the Civilian Construction Corps (C.C.C.) and Works Projects Administration (W.P.A.). From C.C.C. camps in Minnesota, Montana, Washington and Oregon came completely furnished prefabricated buildings of all types, from dormitory barracks and mess halls to kitchens and machine shops. In padlocked C.C.C. and W.P.A. warehouses, there were thousands of other used but still supposedly serviceable items, from bulldozers and road scrapers to typewriters and adding machines. North it all went, by road, rail or ship. There wasn't much time to weed out the junk; the prevailing motto seemed to be: 'We'll sort it out at the other end and what doesn't work can be cannibalized.'

"Sorting it out at the other end" proved to be a logistician's nightmare. During one five-week period that spring, six hundred boxcar loads of P.R.A. supplies and equipment arrived at the Dawson Creek railhead, which was already jammed and chaotic from the army influx, while two hundred more carloads backed up at Prince Rupert awaiting barges for Skagway or Valdez. Covered warehouse space was nonexistent; with every gymnasium, movie theater and curling rink as far away as Edmonton and Fairbanks already bulging with supplies for the highway, there was no place left to put things but in vast piles outside in the mud until they could be brought to the various work sites.

By late May, the first contractors began to arrive. Back in March, Commissioner MacDonald had made two key decisions that enormously simplified his organization's dealings with these firms. First, the P.R.A. would not negotiate directly with every contractor and businessman interested in working on the highway. Instead, it selected five large firms to act as management contractors, (four to handle different segments of the highway and one to manage the transportation and housekeeping needs of the entire project), and gave each of these organizations the authority to hire the necessary smaller contractors and specialists. Second, since the situation made detailed cost estimates and bids a matter of pure guesswork, a special type of contract was devised under which the government agreed to pay rent on each contractor's equipment plus the cost of all his labour and supplies. On top of this came a fixed fee (subject to renegotiation) in proportion to the size and difficulty of the project. This constituted the contractor's profit. In addition, using the scrounged-up C.C.C. and W.P.A. supplies, the P.R.A. furnished each company with whatever prefabricated buildings and additional construction equipment it needed.

The four highway management contractors were R. Melville Smith Co., Ltd. (a Canadian firm that exclusively employed Canadian contractors), the Dowell Construction Co. from Seattle, the Okes Construction Co. from St. Paul, and Lytle and Green Construction Co. from Sioux City, Iowa. The E. W. Elliott Co., also from Seattle, was responsible for all transportation and camp construction. Together, these five firms managed the activities of 47 smaller companies during the 1942 construction season and 81 during 1943. The total contractors' payroll for the summer months of 1942 and 1943 grew to 7,500 and 14,100 men.

Overseeing all this, of course, was the P.R.A.'s own organization in Canada and Alaska, with a staff of more than 1,800 employees. Commissioner MacDonald's man in charge was J.S. Bright, formerly district engineer in San Francisco, who initially tried to work out of an office in Seattle but soon gave up and moved his headquarters to Edmonton. Even then he often had difficulty communicating by road or telephone with his two division officers in Fort St. John and Whitehorse, not to mention the numerous branch offices strung out along the highway and at places like Prince Rupert and Skagway. Sometimes the only way to get a message or a high priority item through was by air. Both the army and the P.R.A. made good use of local bush pilots, some of whom, like Les Cook, became legends.[3]

Except for the magnitude of the Alaska Highway project and the speed with which it got underway, there was nothing particularly unusual about the organizational structure or management methods adopted by the P.R.A. But that these worked so well in such a difficult environment was quite a tribute to the professionalism and the perseverance of Commissioner MacDonald and his subordinates. They shared a common task with the army engineers, but the partnership was not always an easy one. Patience was another virtue much in demand — on both sides.

As previously noted, the original agreement between the army and the P.R.A. envisioned the construction of two essentially separate roads, built to different standards for different purposes. The army's overriding criterion was military necessity. Gen. Hoge had been told, in effect, to connect up the airfields and push through to Fairbanks with the best road possible, but do it in one season. The P.R.A. was there to support the army, but Bright and his fellow civil engineers also had a responsibility toward future users of the highway. Safety and permanence were their guiding considerations. This divergence was understood and accepted by both sides, and it was embodied in the construction standards set forth in their original agreement. The finished highway was to have had a 36-foot-wide roadway (30 feet in mountainous terrain), surfaced to a width of 24 feet with two feet of crushed rock or gravel with an oil or asphalt topping. This was the typical, two-lane, country road the P.R.A. had been building all over rural America for the past twenty years. On the other hand, the army's pioneer road would have a maximum width of 24 feet and could dwindle to 16 feet in rugged terrain. Wherever possible, local materials would be used to provide the road surface; if gravel or rock were available, fine, but it would not be hauled in if the existing soil made a useable dirt road. A corduroy surface of logs over muskeg and marshy spots was also acceptable. Similar differences existed in the specifications for curves, grades and sight distances. For example, slopes on the P.R.A.'s road were supposed to be less than 3 per cent whenever practicable and never more than 7 per cent. The army road went over the hills, not around them; 20 per cent slopes were not uncommon. Suicide Hill is still a legend among old timers in the north.

Differences like these meant that the pioneer road tended to follow a path of least resistance in terms of ease and speed of construction, but this in turn meant a longer, meandering road compared with the route being surveyed by the P.R.A. Only in level, dry terrain would the two routes be likely to coincide. In rougher or wetter areas every attempt was made to prevent major divergences between the two, but on occasion they ended up as much as five or ten miles apart. This was a problem most often faced during the 1943 construction season, however. During the late summer and fall of 1942, the biggest question was whether the pioneer road could be pushed to completion before winter halted all earth moving operations. Much to their surprise and dismay, the P.R.A. and its contractors found themselves being diverted from their work on the permanent highway to help finish the army's road in time.

The blunt words of a directive from the army's chief of engineers in

Washington on 8 August 1942 almost managed to conceal what amounted to a major change in policy:

> 1. A recent inspection of the ... project discloses that Sector Commanders and ... [P.R.A.] engineers are not working in the close co-operation intended. ... It appears that two separate roads are in large measure being located ... the resulting duplication of effort is considered a waste of Government funds and is disapproved.
> 2. It is desired that the pioneer road be incorporated in the permanent road to be constructed by the P.R.A. insofar as practicable.

Commissioner MacDonald's letter that same day to Mr. Bright conveyed his acceptance of the army's new policy, but perhaps betrayed his real feelings:

> In view of the magnitude of our proposed operations in the limited time available, ... our entire efforts must be concentrated upon the completion of our assigned task this season regardless of Public Roads procedure and policies as followed in our regular work.

Summarizing the results of this change, the P.R.A.'s year-end report for 1942 again managed a nice blend of tact and honesty:

> Under this revised program, with Engineer troops and contractors pulling together, the pioneer road was cut through in a single short season ....
>
> The Army [also] required assistance in building warehouses, barracks, mess halls, water and sewer systems at Dawson Creek [and elsewhere], necessitating withdrawal of ... construction crews from other work on the project.
>
> By forbearance, patience and persistence all difficulties and obstacles were surmounted .... Contractors were rushed to uncompleted sections of the pioneer road ... [but much is left] to be done to make the pioneer road a useable highway for movement of freight.

Some simple statistics give a clearer idea of the amount of P.R.A. assistance on the army's pioneer road. At the time of the official opening of the "highway" on 20 November 1942, truck odometer readings gave its length as 1,619 miles. Of this, 246 miles of the route had been constructed by the P.R.A.'s contractors without army assistance, and another 979 miles were army-built pioneer road that had been widened and improved by the P.R.A. Put even more simply, 76 per cent of the original army pioneer road was built either partially or completely by the P.R.A. And, as its report so tactfully noted, much work indeed remained to be done.

No real attempt was made to keep the highway open for long distance hauling during the winter of 1942-43. The army changed its mind several times as to who would be responsible for winter maintenance but finally, on 31 December, gave the P.R.A. a sizeable share of the job. Some five thousand civilians remained on the contractor's payrolls over the winter to supplement the army's efforts to keep local traffic moving and minimize weather damage. Temperatures as low as -72°F were recorded that January, and all outside work ceased for several weeks on the upper end of the road. At such temperatures, metal becomes brittle; broken equipment began to accumulate in the repair shops and sometimes, quickly trapped by the flow of freezing ground water, along the highway as well. In places, such a flow produced six feet or more of ice on the roadbed. In the streams and rivers, ice also wore away at bridge pilings and piers. Breaking up into huge chunks during the spring thaw, it quickly battered down many of the temporary structures it had been grinding against all winter.

By May, with a new construction season beginning, all that was left of the original pioneer road in many places was an endless soggy swath through the forest punctuated by swollen streams and the wreckage of washed-out log bridges. But such a situation had been anticipated by the P.R.A. Its planners had spent the winter combining their recently completed survey data with the experienced gained the previous season. The best parts of the pioneer road would be saved and incorporated into the final highway; the worst parts had lasted long enough to serve their purpose and would be replaced that summer with an all-new roadbed. However, it did not quite work out that way.

Through June and early July, the mood along the highway was optimistic. The ground was finally dry, every contractor reported good progress, and work had begun on all the new bridges. The biggest bottleneck of all, the Peace River suspension bridge, was almost completed. Supplies were moving up the highway in quantity. Anticipating no more major problems, the army was getting ready to transfer overseas the few remaining elements of the construction regiments originally assigned to the project. Then it began to rain.

On 9 and 10 July 1943, more rain fell than most natives in the region had seen in fifty years. Hardest hit was the area within two hundred miles either side of Fort Nelson, where 24 of 25 bridges were washed away along with countless culverts and many thousands of cubic yards of fill. Hardly had all this damage been repaired and additional bridging materials been stockpiled at the most critical sites, when, in early August, the rains returned. This time only four bridges went out, but massive mud slides blocked several other sections of the road. By now well prepared for this sort of thing, the P.R.A.

simply diverted men and equipment from less critical assignments. Within five days, traffic was moving again. But the project as a whole was now several weeks behind schedule and the Army had set 31 October, now less than three months away, as the date for all construction to be complete. To meet this deadline, shortcuts and compromises would be necessary.

During late August and September, the army ordered work stopped on a whole series of jobs. Most of these involved the relocation of sections of the route away from the original pioneer road in order to provide greater protection against floods or mud slides or to improve grades and curves. Instead, to save time and money, the P.R.A.'s contractors were ordered to do the best they could to upgrade the existing trail. In addition, the army now encouraged the P.R.A. to use less permanent and time-consuming construction methods. For example, bridge decking could now be made of wooden planks instead of poured concrete. Wooden culverts, rather than steel or concrete, would also suffice. Most of these orders, particularly those halting major relocations, produced angry confrontations between the army and the P.R.A. Bright and his subordinates usually took the position that not finishing such improvements was not only wasteful of resources already expended, but shortsighted as well. But the army's argument made equally good sense: why build a better road than you need, particularly when other wartime construction projects now had a higher priority? More often than not, the army's arguments prevailed, but occasionally the P.R.A. got its way. Sometimes a relocation project was so near completion that the army could be convinced that it was cheaper to complete it than abandon it and go back to the pioneer road.

Under these revised "ground rules," the P.R.A. essentially met the army's target date for completion of the highway. By the end of October 1943, all of the contractors working on the road itself had ceased operations and released their men to return home. A few bridges remained unfinished; most of these were turned over to the army. In November, the P.R.A.'s Edmonton office packed up and moved to Chicago, while the field offices along the highway only retained skeleton staffs to supervise the evacuation of equipment and remnants of the contractors' forces. Maintenance of the completed highway was to be an army responsibility for the duration of the war, using mostly Canadian civilians recruited from the ranks of the departing construction workers. Here again, the army turned to the P.R.A. for assistance. The man who organized that maintenance force and helped it develop the skills and experience necessary to keep the highway open on a year-round basis was a P.R.A. highway engineer named Frank C. Turner. He remained behind as a maintenance consultant until Canada assumed control of its segment of the highway in April 1946. A P.R.A. engineer was thus the last American to come home from the Alaska Highway when the war was over.[4]

The finished highway can be credited in surprisingly large measure to the work of the P.R.A. and its civilian contractors. Of the 1,420 miles of completed highway between Dawson Creek, British Columbia and Big Delta, Alaska, more than two-thirds, a total of 970 miles, was composed of the original army pioneer road, all of which had been substantially improved and upgraded by the P.R.A. The other 450 miles of road was strictly P.R.A.-built. Here, the army's pioneer road had served its original purpose as an access route but was abandoned thereafter.

In addition to its major role in completing the Alaska Highway, the P.R.A. can claim credit for a large number of the highway's bridges. Using its own architects and draftsmen, the P.R.A. designed 133 permanent bridges of various types for the highway. Of these, contractors had completed 99 by the end of October 1943. Their average length was 340 feet, but placed end to end the bridges would have had a total length of about 8½ miles. More than half were fairly short wooden trestle spans built with native timbers, similar in appearance to the army's temporary bridges but far sturdier. (Most of the original temporary spans on the pioneer road did not survive the spring thaw of 1943, and the summer floods swept away many of their replacements.) Among the remaining structures, a few were constructed of reinforced concrete, but most were of steel. The most spectacular bridge on the entire highway was the Peace River suspension bridge, opened in the summer of 1943, but the largest was the high span across the Teslin River. It was one of the few bridges not completed until the 1944 construction season. Wartime steel shortages were the main cause of such delays. In several cases, the P.R.A. solved this problem by dismantling unused bridges in the U.S. and shipping them north to be reassembled on new foundations. Some of these 133 bridges have since been replaced (including the Peace River bridge), but many are still in use and in good shape.[5]

The U.S. Army Corps of Engineers gets the overall credit for the Alaska Highway. This is as it should be. Nothing but wartime military considerations and the hardnosed professionalism of those pioneering engineer regiments could have brought the highway into existence. But the credit for the fact that the Alaska Highway is still here goes mostly to the Public Roads Administration.

Notes

1. Frank C. Turner, interview with the author, Arlington, Va., 26 May 1982. Mr. Turner became a highway engineer for the Bureau of Public Roads in 1929. He was assigned to the Alaska Highway project from 1942-46 and later (1957-58) became acting head of the bureau; "Preliminary Inventory for Records of the Bureau of Public Roads", NARS, RG

    30, (1962), pp. 4-7. This finding aid contains an excellent short history of the BPR; U.S., Interior Department, Office of Territories, NARS, RG 126, box 372; 9-1-55 (Alaska, Roads and Trails), U.S., Interior Department, Office of the Secretary, NARS, RG 48, box 3674, File 9-1-10 (British Columbia - Alaska Highway). The last two references contain data on proposals for the highway and the decision to build it.

2. Theodore A. Huntley and R.E. Royall, *Construction of the Alaska Highway* (Washington: Public Roads Administration (?), 1945), pp. 5-7, 102-10; U.S., War Department, World War II Operations Reports, NARS, RG 407, boxes 19523, 19534, 19549, 19553, 19555, 19579, 19580, 19581. These are the operations reports of the seven engineer regiments that built the pioneer road.

3. Huntley and Royall, *Construction of the Alaska Highway*, pp. 3-16, 77; F.C. Turner, interview, May 1982; U.S., Bureau of Public Roads, NARS, RG 30, boxes 242-286, file 003.12 (Alaska Highway, 1942-44). These contain copies of all the contracts executed between the P.R.A. and private firms and individuals for goods and services needed during the construction of the highway.

4. U.S. Army Military History Research Collection, Senior Officer's Debriefing Program. Transcript of Interview of Gen. W.M. Hoge by Lieut.-Col. G.R. Robertson, Section 2, pp. 16-20; Section 3, pp. 1-2; Huntley and Royall, *Construction of the Alaska Highway*, pp. 7-14, 26-29, 39-52. The passages quoted may be found on pp. 14, 127 and 130; Turner, interview with author.

5. Huntley and Royall, *Construction of the Alaska Highway*, pp. 52-53, 58-68; Turner interview with author; the author drove the length of the highway in the summer of 1980.

6

The Army Medical Department and the Construction of the Alaska Highway

DWIGHT D. OLAND

"The town is one vast cess pool." This was Maj. Mendel Silverman's description of Whitehorse in February 1943. In October 1942, Lieut.-Col. W.F. von Zelinski described the sanitary conditions at Dawson Creek as "just above a primitive level" and stated that those at Fort St. John, "while much better than at Dawson Creek, left considerable to be desired." The comments of these U.S. Army medical officers pointed to a basic health problem in the north when the Alaska Highway was under construction. Although the Canadian government had a very good public health organization, the small, remote towns of the north suffered from endemic disease, which the influx of workers threatened to make worse. Prior to the Second World War, Whitehorse had a population of less than 600, half of whom left the area during the winter, while Dawson Creek and Fort St. John had populations of 500 and 250. With the coming of the highway, all three towns were quickly surrounded by military and contractor camps and facilities.[1]

In general, water supply, garbage disposal, and sewerage handling were barely adequate for the small populations; they were grossly inadequate given the sudden increase in demand. Whitehorse had the worst conditions, made even more serious when the Alaska Highway and the Northwest Service Command located their headquarters there. The sole municipal public health official received little or no assistance in improving sanitary conditions. Only two of the eleven restaurants in the town had acceptable standards: chlorinated water, sterilized dishes, and refrigerated food. Water was supplied from shallow wells and the Yukon River. Garbage and other wastes were dumped on the ice of the river to be carried away during the spring thaw. No proper sewerage system existed. Instead, privies, cesspools, septic tanks and tile fields were used, and they were not always properly maintained. If the major towns along the Alaska Highway offered these sanitary conditions, what could the camps and villages along the route be like?

Conditions along the route were certainly not much better. The Indian villages had similar or worse problems with water, garbage, and sewage. The camps established by the army during the construction of the pioneer road were primitive and moved with the crews. Pit latrines and straddle trenches were used for sewerage, water came from the closest streams, creeks, or lakes, and garbage was either buried or burned. The men were housed in tents, which were difficult to heat during the coldest parts of the year and in summer were barely adequate to keep out the mosquitos, flies, midges, and dust. They had few facilities for personal hygiene and had to tolerate inclement weather and a monotonous diet. In addition, outbreaks of cerebrospinal meningitis, diphtheria, and measles occurred in the civilian population, and tuberculosis was a major killer, especially of Indians. Bacillary dysentery was endemic in settled areas, particularly during spring and fall. Under such conditions, the paradox was that disease rates were quite low.

This result represented a triumph of preventive medicine. The medical department had both experience with and up-to-date research on most of the current diseases which affected troops. Troops and their commanders were made aware of the preventive medicine regulations and were expected to follow them. All echelons of medical service were well trained to report outbreaks of disease, establish sanitary and personal hygiene measures, and maintain proper conditions through frequent inspections. However, these measures were effective only within the military community, thereby creating a potentially volatile relationship with Canadian public health agencies in the area along the Alaska Highway route.

Fortunately, both the army medical personnel and the Canadian public health officers were working toward a common goal: the protection of the health of everyone living and working in the area. Relations between the two groups were harmonious. Because of a shortage of personnel and a desire to expedite the defence projects, the Canadians relinquished their responsibility for preventing contagious diseases from entering the country. The army handled the examination and quarantine of Americans. In Whitehorse, medical and sanitary officers of the medical department also inspected the restaurants and enforced most other preventive measures. A rapid improvement in sanitation was soon noted. In many instances, the army provided better quality medical facilities than had previously existed in local communities. In the more remote native villages, they attempted to separate residents from construction forces to prevent the exchange and spread of disease.

In Alaska, the territorial Department of Health and the army Medical Department co-operated to ensure that the intrusion of construction, operation, and maintenance personnel would be as limited as possible.[2] A rather delicate aspect of this co-operative spirit was the control of venereal disease. Alaska sanctioned prostitution (it was illegal in Canada but the law was not rigidly enforced) and public health authorities preferred to treat prostitutes in known locations. However, much local venereal disease was attributed to amateurs. All reports of contacts were followed up by the civil agencies, including the Royal Canadian Mounted Police. The close liaison between the military and civil health organizations along the highway routes used by men on furlough was a major reason for the low incidence of locally contracted venereal disease.

This network had developed from simple beginnings. No elaborate medical organization had been planned for the Alaska Highway because the army intended to pull out during the winters. Medical aid men and battalion and regimental aid stations accompanied the engineer regiments. The Clearing Company, 58th Medical Battalion, consisting of two clearing platoons, was also sent. They established clearing stations at Whitehorse and Fort St. John to offer the construction forces treatment and evacuation to the U.S. Natives and Canadian citizens were also taken as patients.

The medical troops who accompanied the engineer regiments during construction of the pioneer road shared the same harsh, unpleasant conditions as those they served. The aid men were constantly in the field, and aid stations and dispensaries operated out of tents. Pitching their tents in the spring of 1942, the Whitehorse platoon discovered that "in April, the Yukon Territory is not a very inviting place." Snowfall and freezing temperatures alternated with thaws, all of which were alien to many of the soldiers who had just arrived from training camps in the southern United States. Local sanitary conditions were "execrable" and water supply was practically nonexistent because of the freezing of the streams, the storage containers, and the transportation trailers. In addition, the arctic ration baffled the platoons' cooks.[3]

As word leaked out that an American medical organization was available, patients were evacuated there from nearby construction forces. Soon the platoon was operating as a station hospital. Heated showers and latrines were erected and a laundry machine purchased. The operating tent was equipped for major surgery and the enlisted personnel were trained for advanced duties.

The change in function to a station hospital, along with a rapid increase in patients, necessitated a further expansion of facilities. In June, the army rented an old gymnasium in Whitehorse and partially renovated it for medical use. Plumbing and kitchen facilities were placed in nearby tents. According to Maj. Silverman, "It was far from an ideal of an adequate hospital but it constituted a definite improvement over our tent installations." As winter approached, better facilities had to be found to protect patients and staff from the rigorous cold. The army appropriated a fifty-bed expansion unit, designated for the Public Health Service, and the hospital occupied the building before plumbing and water supply could be introduced and sanitary deficiencies corrected. The hospital remained in this building until 1945.[4]

After leaving a small detachment at Dawson Creek to handle casualties at the railhead, the other clearing platoon moved to Fort St. John. As with the platoon at Whitehorse, this one operated as a station hospital from the onset because "no higher echelon of medical service" existed nearby, and transportation was inadequate for prompt evacuation of the injured. Therefore, all patients were kept at the hospital for treatment except for extremely critical cases and those whose recovery would be prolonged. The original organization used tents, but by May, two prefabricated frame buildings had been erected to form the nucleus of a fixed hospital. In September 1943, it was moved into better facilities at Dawson Creek where it operated until October 1944.[5]

Station hospitals also provided definitive treatment for nearby forces and served as collecting points for evacuation of patients to the U.S. at Ladd Field and Skagway, Alaska, and at Edmonton, Alberta. Another hospital was activated at Fort Nelson in December 1943, but it was reduced to a dispensary three months later.

The clearing platoons were not the only field medical units to become fixed organizations. Although the company aid men and the various aid stations continued to follow the road crews as construction of the pioneer roads progressed, more permanent dispensaries were flown in. A dispensary had been included in the medical plan of 25 February 1942, and several were called for in the northern sector medical plan of 13 June 1942. Their number increased rapidly in the ensuing months. Dispensaries were ten- to fifteen-bed units with steel beds, sheets, pillowcases, and other equipment normally found at established camps and posts. The dispensaries did not change location as the aid stations did, and when a new regiment assumed responsibility for a section of the road, it also operated the dispensary. Upon completion of the pioneer road, dispensaries were added to the rest camps and way stations. By now, company men helped staff the dispensaries; the aid stations had departed.[6]

Patient treatment followed a well-thought-out chain of evacuation. It started with the aid men and moved back through aid stations, dispensaries, and station hospitals to major hospitals in the U.S. Each location sent the most seriously ill or injured patients further along the chain and kept less serious cases for return to duty. Patients were evacuated by truck or ambulance along the highway route, with the exception of those who were gravely ill or hurt. These were moved by airplane to the nearest hospital, or medical officers were flown in to perform operations in the field. Those who needed treatment in the larger U.S. Army hospitals were sent back by train, boat, or plane. Throughout the chain, the life-saving benefits of aeromedical evacuation were clearly evident.

Even more fundamental than treatment was prevention. Great care was taken over preventive measures designed to keep disease incidence low. Such measures involved the proper selection of personnel and included providing the best possible clothing, housing, nutrition, personal hygiene, water supply, waste disposal, immunizations, insect and rodent control, and the previously mentioned quarantine.

Although all military personnel originally assigned to duty on the pioneer road met the physical qualifications for overseas duty, those units which replaced them in 1943 were composed mainly of over age and limited service men, many of whom had pre-induction physical defects. However, after 1943, the soldiers sent to the Northwest Service Command were younger, better trained, and more carefully selected. The civilians employed in the area were as a rule less physically qualified because of lower selection standards. These men contracted more illnesses and diseases than their military counterparts, by ratios of up to four to one, even though all were required to pass two physical examinations to screen out the unfit.

During the winter, proper clothing was essential for survival. All men quickly learned how to cope with the cold. Soldiers were supplied with several light garments to form insulating airspaces rather than stiff, heavy apparel. Constricting clothing hindered blood circulation, which increased the chance of being frostbitten. The sleeping bag, though not classified as clothing, was an indispensable item of cold weather equipment which was carried at all times along the highway. It was used not only for sleeping but as a warm "cocoon" for stranded drivers and passengers.

A wide range of housing units was used on the Alaska Highway. During 1942, the majority of housing was in tents because the troops were moving frequently. Gradually, prefabricated and frame units were built as the construction phase ended. All were winterized and heated. The change from tentage to buildings also meant that the net square footage available per man could be increased, thereby improving ventilation and reducing the spread of respiratory disease. By 1944, pit latrines and makeshift showers had been completely replaced with flush toilets and shower units. Recognizing the importance of proper housing to soldier health, army and civilian contractors rapidly built sturdy housing which offered vastly improved protection from the elements. The cost of replacing sick men was far greater than the cost of providing decent housing.

The old saying that an army travels on its stomach was certainly true, because proper nutrition was essential to maintain the soldiers' strength and health. Working in cold weather required an additional 1500 to 2000 calories per day solely for heat production. The first troops dined on field rations in the open or in mess tents. Gradually, as the troops were assigned permanent stations, frame or metal mess halls were constructed which vastly improved eating conditions. Although plentiful and quite nutritious, the field rations became monotonous after several weeks and many men threw away their meals. Loss of appetite, general malaise, and weight loss were noticed. These complaints disappeared as fresh food, including local produce and wild game, became available. As transportation and storage facilities improved, more fresh meat, vegetables, and fruits were imported to supplement the field rations. By the end of 1943, all units along the highway were supplementing their rations in one way or another.

Because most men considered powdered milk to be unpalatable, they turned to local sources of raw milk. But cows and milk handlers had not been tested for disease and the sanitary conditions involved in milk production were poor. In May 1943, the army finally ordered all milk to be obtained from army inspected and approved sources in the Edmonton area. Unfortunately, milk could not be safely shipped to all camps along the highway. These camps received fresh frozen milk or milk from "mechanical cows"; machines which reconstituted powdered milk.

Personal hygiene included foot care, dental and oral hygiene, maintenance of general health, control of venereal diseases, and immunizations. Foot diseases were minimal in the Northwest Service Command because the men changed into dry socks whenever their feet got wet, bathed and dried them daily, and wore properly fitting footwear. Dental hygiene was rather haphazard in 1942 until the number of dental surgeons and amount of dental equipment and supplies was sufficient for large scale work. In November 1943, a yearly dental survey of all military personnel was initiated primarily to determine if a soldier had enough good teeth to chew the army ration. The construction forces attended lectures on dental hygiene, their eating habits were studied, and they were encouraged to consume a balanced diet high in calcium.

Cleanliness was encouraged to prevent the spread of diseases and other health disorders. All men were repeatedly advised to bathe daily, to wash their hands before each meal and after visiting the latrine, to brush their teeth at least once a day, to keep their nails cut short and clean, their hair cut short, their clothing and bedding clean, and all soiled clothes in barracks bags. Frequent inspections by medical officers ensured cleanliness, and commanding officers were reprimanded for slackness. All food handlers were examined monthly for communicable diseases.

Prior to the summer of 1943, daily bathing was extremely difficult because no showers existed in the field, and stream and lake water was too cold. The only method available was sponge bathing, and even this usually depleted the camps' limited supply of water. By 1944, however, hot showers were available in almost all quarters. Laundry facilities were constructed as camps became more permanent.

Venereal disease was a serious threat to the efficiency of the army, and various preventive measures were used. Except for illness contracted prior to arrival, cases of venereal disease were practically non-existent during 1942 because the men were in remote areas away from women. However, beginning in December 1942 when furloughs were given, the rate of venereal disease increased as the men visited local settlements and the United States. Venereal disease control officers were appointed to supervise a programme which included monthly and special troop inspections, education, diagnosis and treatment, prophylaxis, and liaison with army, air force, and civilian agencies. Areas where contacts were made were placed off limits and women involved were sought out and treated. Men were prohibited from visiting villages where venereal diseases were epidemic or endemic.

The use of immunizations had been a tradition of the U.S. Army practically since its formation. Anyone arriving to work on the Alaska Highway had to have up-to-date smallpox and triple typhoid vaccinations and tetanus toxoid immunization. Civilians who refused immunization were dismissed. Ironically, the only serious epidemic among the construction crews was an outbreak of jaundice in 1942, which was traced to contaminated yellow fever vaccine.[7]

The water supply along the highway was from army-constructed and controlled sources which were supposed to be chlorinated. Not understanding that clear running water could be contaminated, some workers refused to take the trouble to treat it. A reprimand to the commanding officer was sufficient to rectify the situation. All camps used either hypochlorinators or hand chlorination. In Whitehorse and Dawson Creek, the army constructed water systems to which the towns eventually connected after correcting their more serious sanitary conditions. All water was checked frequently for potability and sufficient chlorination so that all deficiencies could be corrected immediately.

Waste and sewerage disposal was more complex in the settled areas than in the field camps. Camps initially used pit latrines but gradually installed septic tanks and leach fields to handle flush toilets. The civilian settlements used a variety of methods of waste disposal, all of which were barely adequate for their usual population and totally unsatisfactory for the influx of troops and civilians. Until the Army constructed sewerage systems in the towns of Whitehorse and Dawson Creek, the citizens used privies, cesspools, septic tanks, and tile fields. In Whitehorse a sewerage line had been laid in the same trench as the water line. Whenever the level of ground water reached above the woodstove pipes which formed the two lines, sewerage would seep into the water supply, causing an outbreak of dysentery. The utilization of the Army's water and sewer systems eliminated periodic dysentery epidemics among the citizens. All refuse and garbage were either incinerated, buried outside of town, or disposed of in garbage dumps located at least one mile from camps and villages.

Insects were more a nuisance than a health hazard. Mosquitos, flies, and midges were generally uncontrollable in the field, though head nets, bed nets, and screening were used. The muskeg formed innumerable pools during the mosquito season, making it impossible to kill all the mosquito larvae. However, the streams around Dawson Creek were oiled successfully. All camps were supplied with insecticide and fly paper to use in the mess halls. The areas around pit latrines were oiled regularly and all garbage dumps were located outside the camps. Barracks were fumigated with hydrocyanic gas and DDT to exterminate bedbugs, while various insecticides were sprayed to eliminate roaches. No arthroped-borne diseases were transmitted in the Northwest Service Command. A few cases of malaria were traced to prior duty in a malarious region. Rodents offered no medical problems except as flea reservoirs. Flea-borne diseases were nonexistent and rodent control measures were employed only for the protection of foodstuffs.

As a result of such measures, disease incidence along the highway was low compared to other military theatres. Among the most frequently occurring intestinal diseases were bacterial food poisoning, common diarrheas, bacillary dysentery, and dysentery unclassified. Proper sanitation, protection of water supplies, and fly control kept diseases from becoming epidemic; and, although dysentery was endemic within the civilian population, at times becoming epidemic, it was never a severe problem. Food poisoning, attributable to unsanitary handling of food, was more prevalent among civilian employees than soldiers. Common diarrheas, the most prevalent intestinal diseases, were directly related to food management and fly control. Again, army camps had better success than contractor camps because of better personnel control. However, the number of cases of common diarrhea among military personnel was probably greater than reported, because many commanders would rather ignore small, easily controlled outbreaks than face the stigma of being seen as unable to maintain healthy troops.

Respiratory infections were also lower among the military than among civilian workers. Upper respiratory disease was expected during the fall and early winter. Tuberculosis, influenza, mumps, measles, pneumonia, and scarlet fever were common in the civilian settlements, but hardly any effect was felt among the construction forces. The cold, dry air and a strict observance of housing regulations were the major factors in keeping the incidence low. The widespread dispersal of personnel, the quarantining of contagious patients, and the improvement of mess management also contributed to the low incidence of respiratory infection. Placing villages off limits to highway personnel to prevent the spread of infectious disease was always more beneficial to the native residents, who suffered greatly from epidemics caused by contact with outsiders. In 1942, for example, a native village at Teslin Lake suffered from epidemics of measles, mumps, whooping cough, tonsillitis, and meningitis.[8]

Dental health fell within normal ranges for the army worldwide. Most problems could be traced to improper dental hygiene, overindulgence in sweets, lack of fresh milk and vegetables, and unsanitary mess conditions. Besides the usual dental caries, the most prevalent disease was Vincent's anginia which affected 2 per cent of the military personnel and 4 per cent of the civilians. In some settled areas, the incidence rate approached epidemic proportions among civilians. Ascorbic acid and thiamine complex compounds were used in treatment, but instruction in the proper care of teeth and improvement of mess operation usually reduced the number of cases. Surprisingly, the overwhelming preponderance of oral problems occurred in settled areas where a complete and balanced diet was readily available.

Frostbite and exposure were two problems which could have been rampant among men inexperienced in cold weather operations, but in fact the incidence was very low. Approximately 120 cases of frostbite were reported during the construction stage, resulting in fewer than six amputations of fingers and toes for a force of 22,000 men. One death from exposure occurred on the Slana Cutoff when a driver decided to walk ten miles to camp instead of waiting for help with his disabled truck. Enforcement of clothing, diet, and housing regulations were the principal control measures which accounted for this success.

A much more exciting story could be told if the construction forces had suffered great losses attributable to the climate or the sanitary conditions of the area. The frigid weather, execrable sanitation in towns, endemic diseases, and poor working conditions were all conducive to a widespread attrition rate. Considerable planning, based upon previous experience, helped solve the major problems affecting the Northwest Service Command's health. A dovetailing of civil agencies' expertise and army Medical Department experience was vitally important not only to the health of the construction forces but also to that of the local communities. Preventive medicine, a U.S. Army Medical Department tradition, was the main reason for low disease rates. Without the strict supervision of preventive measures by Medical Department officers, the enormous task of building a highway rapidly through a vast and alien wilderness would have been much more difficult and costly.

Notes

1. Maj. Mendel Silverman was commanding officer of the Clearing Co., 58th Medical Battalion, and Lt.-Col. W.F. von Zelinski was surgeon for the Northwest Service Command. Annual Report, Station Hospital, Whitehorse, 1942; Annual Report NWSC, 1942-43.
2. NARS, RG 112, box 1, declassification no. 795145, ALASKA, folder HD:040.
3. Annual Report, Station Hospital, Whitehorse, 1942.
4. Annual Report, Station Hospital, Whitehorse, 1942.
5. Medical History, Fort St. John Sector, 1942.
6. NARS, RG112, box 3, declassification no. 795145, ALASKA, both medical plans.
7. U.S. Army Medical Dept., *Communicable Disease Transmitted Through Contact or by Unknown Means,* Preventive Medicine in World War II (Washington, D.C.: Government Printing Office, 1960), 5: 419-31.
8. John F. Marchand. "Tribal Epidemics in the Yukon," *Journal of the American Medical Association,* 123 (1943): 1019-20.

Each paragraph would be supported by numerous and repetitive footnotes. The following list provides an outline of sources consulted.

NARS, RG112, box 1, declassification no. 795145, ALASKA HD:032.2 House Committee Report — The Alaska Highway, March 1946

NARS, RG112, box 3, declassification no. 795145, ALASKA Annual Report, Whitehorse Sector Alcan Highway 1942; Medical History, Whitehorse Sector Alcan Highway 1942

NARS, RG112, box 4, declassification no. 795145, ALASKA Memo, Tatum to All Unit Commanders, Whitehorse Sector, 7 Nov. 42, subject: Winter Hygiene and Sanitary Measures.

NARS, RG112, box 230, declassification no. 795145, entry 54A Medical History, Fort St. John Sector, Canadian-Alaskan Military History, 1942

NARS, RG112, box 234, declassification no. 795145, entry 54A Annual Report, 340th Engineers Regt General Service 1942; Annual Report, 477th QM Regt. (Truck) 1942-43

NARS, RG112, box 235, declassification no. 795145, entry 54A Annual Report, NWSC, 1942-43, 1944

NARS, RG112, box 236, declassification no. 795145, ent. 54A Annual Report, Station Hospital, Edmonton, 1944; Annual Report, NWSC Med. Lab., Edmonton, 1943; Annual Report, Station Hospital, Fort St. John, 1942; Annual Report, Station Hospital, Whitehorse, 1942, 1943, 1944; Annual Report, Station Hospital, Dawson Creek, 1943, 1944; Annual Report, Station Hospital, Fort Nelson, 1944

NARS, RG338, box 3, declassification no. 735044 W.C. Palfreyman, "History of the Whitehorse Sector of the Alcan Highway", June 1943; Regt. Hist., 340th Engineers Regt (GS), 1942; Regt. Hist., 341st Engineers Regt (GS), 1942

NARS, RG338, boxes 4, 5, 8, 9, 10, 11, 12, 47, 49, declassification no. 735-044 Official Directives, NWSC

NARS, RG338, box 6, declassification no. 735044, Essential Tech. Med. Data, Aug. 1943 - Feb. 1944

NARS, RG407, box 6, declassification no. 735017, entry 427 G-2 reports 16 July 42 - 2 Jan. 43

Frank G. Manning, "Preventive Medicine in the Northwest Service Command Northwest Division, United States Engineer Department and Northwest District, Sixth Service Command," 1946, unpublished manuscript on file in Medical Records Collection, United States Army Center of Military History.

The assistance of Mr. George C. Chalou, Asst. Chief, MMFB, Military Archives Division, Mr. Frederick W. Pernell, Archivist, and Mrs. Victoria S. Washington, Archives Technician, NARS, is gratefully acknowledged.

7

Surveying the Line: The Canadian Participation

DON W. THOMSON

The Alaska Highway, begun in 1942, ranks among the world's superlative feats of engineering enterprise. The pioneer roadway, 1,523 miles (2,437 kilometres) in total length, was built in record-breaking time. Some critics of this highway-building concept regarded the proposal as a mind-boggling monstrosity impossible to implement. But the impossible became a reality in a great hurry. Nine months and six days after the issue of the United States War Department's directive in Washington, D.C., the pioneer road was completed between Dawson Creek, B.C., and Fairbanks, Alaska. The highway was formally dedicated on 20 November 1942. Most of the highway, about 1200 miles of it, is located within Canada.

Credit for the actual construction of this Alaska Highway belongs to the U.S. Army engineers, to the U.S. Public Roads Administration, to thousands of enlisted men as well as to American and Canadian private contracting firms and thousands of their civilian employees. However, without detracting from the impressive American accomplishment, it is important to clarify two misconceptions concerning this unique international highway, misconceptions widely held on this continent when the road was under construction and still rather widely accepted. The first is the persistent belief that this highway was conceived in wartime for entirely wartime purposes; the second is that the project was an American achievement from start to finish, with a minimum of Canadian participation, apart from providing the overland right-of-way.

The facts are that the Alaska Highway was a peacetime concept and that Canadian surveyors, on the ground and in the air, were involved in its planning and other preliminary stages to a highly important extent. In addition, following the end of the Second World War, Canadian military and civilian organizations became responsible for road maintenance and improvements. This development involved legal surveys and resurveys by Canadians, including the widening of the right-of-way, at least throughout the Yukon Territory, from 200 feet to 300 feet.[1]

For years before the attack on Pearl Harbor, several alternative routes for this international overland roadway had been considered, officially and unofficially. As early as 1928, a location engineer in Fairbanks, Donald MacDonald, campaigned for such a road. In 1930, recognition of the desirability of this project was expressed in actions of both the government of Canada and the government of the United States. In that year, nine years before the outbreak of war, the president was authorized by the U.S. House of Representatives to designate three commissioners to co-operate with Canadian representatives on a feasibility study of the plan.[2] Three Canadians were named, but the severe economic depression of the 1930's in both countries postponed any action. The idea was revived in 1938, and a five-man Alaskan international highway commission was appointed by President Franklin D. Roosevelt. A counterpart commission was set up in Canada, and the two bodies carried out investigations of various proposed routes for the road. Canadian commissioners flew over much of northern British Columbia and, as a result, recommended certain alternative routes. The government of B.C. favoured the route of the Rocky Mountain trench, as it had the lightest annual snowfall, the longest open season, the best grades and road alignment, and the shortest total distance of any route. The government and the commissioners also had an eye on the possible benefits of such a highway for the promotion of tourist trade and the development of mineral resources. But the end result of these investigations was a rejection of all the recommended routes when the road was finally built.

Some time before the official inquiries were launched, an unpublicized but highly significant air probe had taken place in northwestern Canada. In a sense, it was a search for a northwest passage to the Orient by air. In the summer of 1935, Dan McLean, acting superintendent of airways and airports for the federal Department of Transport, along with bush pilot Punch Dickens, had flown on an aerial reconnaissance survey across northern Alberta, northern British Columbia, the Northwest Territories and the Yukon. Apparently, Ottawa's air transport officials were planning for the long future in the realm of international airlines. They had decided to seek out the shortest and best route for an airway across northwestern Canada via the Great Circle route to Siberia and thence to China. In effect, McLean's findings transformed the Edmonton-Dawson Creek-Fort St. John route from a dream road to a road of destiny.

In the spring of 1939, Ottawa authorized a survey of the proposed airway. Location of intermediate airfields took place, and landing strips and radio range stations were installed. Without any doubt, the fact that these landing fields had been located and surveyed and were, in varying degrees, ready for use, weighed heavily in favour of what had come to be known as the Northwest Staging Route. This was a decisive factor in choosing the course which the road was to follow when the Alaska Highway project was finally undertaken.

In 1939, Canadian authorities initiated a detailed survey of the airway project, including the location of airfields at Grande Prairie, Fort St. John, Fort Nelson, Watson Lake, and Whitehorse. Later, intermediate fields were added. In February 1941, Canadian surveyors were engaged at Fort Nelson, laying out runways and setting in grade stakes. Just one year later, American military forces were to travel over this same territory during the initial stages of planning for the Alaska Highway. In any event, before the highly destructive attack by the Japanese on Pearl Harbor, and thus before the declaration of war by the United States, there was a Canadian-built airway across northwestern North America, equipped with navigation aids and with at least some rudimentary airfield lighting equipment.

Combined with disaster at Pearl Harbor, the loss of Britain's two major battleships, in Far Eastern waters, the *Prince of Wales* and the *Repulse,* drastically altered the balance of naval power in the Pacific. The whole of the western coast of the United States and Canada was exposed to Japanese attack and invasion. Japanese forces were advancing throughout Southeast Asia. Hong Kong had fallen to them, as had Singapore. Alaska had become particularly vulnerable. Panic set in.

Suddenly there was a desperate need for a protected overland link between the continental United States and Alaska as a defence measure and as a base for ferrying warplanes to Russia. All of these pressing factors spurred the Canadian government into agreeing with the United States to build a highway connecting the airfields of the Northwest Staging Route with Fairbanks.

A trail investigation group from the United States came to the Sikanni Chief River early in 1942 and consulted with Dominion Land Surveyor Knox F. McCusker and others who had first-hand knowledge of the region. McCusker assured the group that if advance units of road-builders could be in position at Fort St. John by mid-March 1942, he could guide them in location work for a pilot road across some 500 miles of wilderness before the spring break-up brought everything to a halt.[3]

Soon McCusker was fully occupied with organizing outfits to guide U.S. engineers. This reconnaissance was accomplished within one month. In the main, the scouted line followed very closely a proposed trail tentatively sketched by McCusker seven years before. By mid-March 1942, soldiers as well as machinery and supplies were pouring into the small town of Dawson Creek.

For the record, McCusker wrote:

> The area I am most familiar with is what is known as the Muskeg Area. The highway skirts the west side of the big muskeg, stretching east to Hay River and north from Blueberry River. Until the roadbuilders appeared on the scene in 1942 this region was served by a sleigh trail cut by the Topographical Survey of Canada in 1922. This trail ran from Fort St. John to a tiny water post on the Sikanni Chief River, known as Horsetrack. Over this rough trail went trade goods from the north to be taken on scows down that river each year in the spring. After the spring break-up in 1941 the Canadian Department of Transport widened this road using bulldozers and extended it to the site of the airport at Fort Nelson. . . .We had gas tanks, gas pumps and eating houses stationed along that trail. Tractors kept the road smooth and snow-plowed for trucks . . . . When the trail investigation group came from Washington, D.C. to look over the possibilities the fact that the trail was ready may have had something to do with the decision to go ahead with the Alaska Highway Project . . . . The highway survey from Dawson Creek to Fort St. John was completed.[4]

McCusker commented on the changes the Alaska Highway project brought to the north. "At Fort St. John," he wrote:

> everything had changed from a one-restaurant town where the proprietor was his own best customer to a place supporting seven eating places and unable to handle the traffic. Sleeping places were almost impossible to get. Parking space in the feed barn hayloft sold at one dollar per night. My neighbour's field was an army camp. His hogs wore a bilious look presumably from imbibing too freely of army swill.[5]

McCusker, in his unpublished memoirs, described early procedures followed on highway construction work. Two men, guided by him, blazed the initial rough trail. After them came the stadia party. Its members ran the preliminary line and cut a pack trail of sorts for the use of advance transport. The surveyors were quickly followed by a single bulldozer cutting a swath through tree growth along the centre line so that the next bulldozers, in squads of six, could concentrate on cleaning up the resulting debris. This clearing operation made way for rough as well as finished grading work all along the line of construction. After the Cats had levelled the roadway for grading, subsequent parties located the final route, building corduroy roads wherever required. The general scene was one of intense activity. Pack trains threaded their way through tangles of tractors, graders and men. Radio equipment enabled workers to keep in close, constant touch with each other's work all along the line. At this stage of the project, men worked extremely long shifts. Motors were seldom turned off. Trucks moved night and day.

Before the entry of the United States into the war, Ontario had developed a system of employing air photographs to locate lines for proposed highways. Alaska Highway officials, aware of Ontario's progress in this field, asked for the services of Ontario government employees directly involved with this special survey activity. As a result, R. W. Johnston and K. H. Siddall arrived at Fort St. John in June 1942 and were at once attached to the American Southern Sector Task Force. As it turned out, all road construction records for speed of progress were surpassed as the road between Dawson Creek and Fairbanks reached completion. On 20 November 1942, in weather well below freezing, the official highway dedication ceremonies took place at Soldier's Summit overlooking Kluane Lake, Yukon.

The surveying, guiding and mapping activities of Canadians made possible the rapid launching and speedy building of this major engineering achievement, constructed at a critical stage in the defence of North America. The efforts of all involved represent triumphs of the human spirit over heavy physical odds. What was accomplished reflects high credit upon the engineering and surveying professions.[6]

Surveys by Canadians multiplied after the Canadian takeover of the highway in April 1946. In the early 1950's, B.C. surveyors completed work on most of the Alaska Highway lying within that province. In the mid-1950's, the highway, at least all of it within the Yukon Territory, was widened, involving a considerable amount of resurveying as well as the replacement of survey markers or monuments lost in washouts or displaced during construction activities.[7]

With the completion of the Alaska Highway, the long isolation of northwestern Canada from the remainder of the world was brought to an abrupt end. Although the immediate and pressing purpose of the road link was to serve perceived military needs, its potential for promoting peacetime development in the regions it crossed was impressive. To most observers it appeared that, at long last, a northwest passage to the doorstep of Asia had become a reality both by air and by highway.

Notes

1. Deputy Minister Jackson (I.A. and N.R. Dept.) to Deputy Minister Hume (M. and T.S. Dept.) Ottawa, 26 July 1956, Legal Surveys Division, Ottawa file 5486-1 vol. 3.
2. House of Representatives, Washington, D.C., bill no. 8368 (1930).
3. McCusker, K. F. *The Canadian Surveyor*, vol. 8 (July 1943): 8.
4. McCusker's unpublished memoirs (c/o Mrs. McCusker at 7720-108th St., #324, Edmonton, Alberta).

5. McCusker, *The Canadian Surveyor,* vol. 8 (July 1943): 8.
6. The effort continued after the original pioneer road had been pushed through. In the summer of 1943, J. Earl Ross, Dominion Topographical Surveyor of Ottawa, reporting to Surveyor-General Peters of Dominion Lands, proceeded to the 60th parallel in order to establish accurately the latitude of highway crossings there. It is interesting to note that Ross had to obtain permission from U.S. Traffic Control officers at Edmonton to travel over the new highway and to obtain supplies of gas, oil and food. J. E. Ross diary, Legal Surveys Division, SMB (EMR), Ottawa.
7. Deputy minister (I.A. and N.R. Dept.) to assistant deputy minister (M. and T.S. Dept.) Ottawa, 26 July 1956, Legal Surveys Division, file 5486-1 vol. 3.

SECTION 3:

Canadian Sovereignty and the Alaska Highway

8

The Army of Occupation: Malcolm MacDonald and U.S. Military Involvement in the Canadian Northwest*

CURTIS R. NORDMAN

Whether or not the story is true that the switchboard at Northwest Command Headquarters was occasionally answered, "Army of Occupation," the fact remains that, as late as March 1943, the Canadian government was not terribly bothered by the massive and virtually unsupervised activities of the U.S. Army in the Canadian north. Indeed, were it not for the daring of a rather unusual British diplomat, the Honourable Malcolm MacDonald, it might have been even longer before this Canadian complacency was shaken.[1] One could say daring because it was presumptuous in the extreme for a diplomat to report to Canadian Prime Minister William Lyon Mackenzie King, in almost Paul Revere fashion, that a virtual American invasion was underway. How was it that the Canadian government could cast a blind eye to what was obviously a major political problem, and who was this man who was able to motivate the Prime Minister?

To be charitable, there were real reasons for the Canadian War Cabinet not to be overly concerned with what Stan Cohen has referred to as the "Forgotten War."[2] By the spring of 1943, the allies were just emerging from the darkest period of the Second World War. The Fall of France had been followed by the Battle of Britain, and prospects remained bleak for the next two years. December 1941, for example, saw not only the decimation of the American fleet at Pearl Harbor, but the loss of the British warships *Prince of Wales* and *Repulse* to Japanese aircraft, and the capitulation of Hong Kong. This latter event was particularly bitter for Canada, which was informed on

Christmas day that an entire Canadian army brigade had surrendered. Shortly after, Manila and Singapore met a similar fate, while in the desert of North Africa, Rommel was making his mark. In May 1942, as the construction of the Alaska Highway began, Tobruk fell to the Axis powers, and soon the Afrika Korps was within seventy miles of Alexandria. At the same time, on the Russian Front, the Soviet army was being humiliated. Then, in August 1942, Canada suffered a major reversal on the beaches of Dieppe. As the opinion polls of the day indicate, fiascos like Dieppe were traumatic and fostered divisions on such emotive issues as conscription.[3] While it is true that by early 1943 the Germans had met their match at Stalingrad, Leningrad, and El Alamein, and the Japanese had been dealt a serious blow in the Battle of the Coral Sea, the war was still far from won. There were, therefore, good reasons why the King government was more concerned with Europe and the Pacific than the Canadian northwest, where the major battle appeared to be with the blackfly.

In fact, with the tide of war turning, the time was ripe for the Canadian War Cabinet to come to grips with the situation in the northwest. King's diary indicates that the government was not totally oblivious to the problem. For example, in March 1942, the prime minister recorded a conversation with Malcolm MacDonald concerning the Alaska Highway in which King stated that the road "was less intended for protection against the Japanese than as one of the fingers of the hand which America is placing more or less over the whole of the Western Hemisphere."[4] By the end of 1942, he was confessing to a fear of postwar American domination. He referred to

> the efforts that would be made by the Americans to control developments in our country after the war, and to bring Canada out of the orbit of the British Commonwealth of Nations into their own orbit. I am strongly opposed to anything of the kind. I want to see Canada continue to develop as a nation to be, in time, as our country certainly will, the greatest of nations of the British Commonwealth.[5]

From this it can be seen that Malcolm MacDonald's role was not so much to make the Canadian prime minister aware of the situation in the northwest as to galvanize him into action.

Malcolm MacDonald's appointment as high commissioner to Canada is intriguing because, superficially, it represented a demotion. At the time of his selection, in April 1941, he held the post of minister of health, a position that was certainly senior to that of high commissioner. MacDonald, however, was not being slighted. What one must appreciate is that, during the early years of the war, Canada played an important role in Anglo-American relations. Such programmes as Lend-Lease, which were absolutely crucial to the British war effort, were the product of significant Canadian effort.

Consequently, the office of British high commissioner in Canada assumed an importance it had not held before, and MacDonald's acceptance of this post must be viewed in this light.

What made MacDonald a prime candidate for this position was his close relationship with the Canadian prime minister. The son of Ramsay MacDonald, England's first Labour prime minister, Malcolm had made King's acquaintance when the latter visited Britain on official business. Over the years, MacDonald and King became close friends. Indeed, as the wartime secretary to the Canadian cabinet has written, King was "predisposed" towards MacDonald long before his appointment.[6] MacDonald built upon this foundation to create a position of considerable influence. As King's most intimate advisor has recorded, "throughout his period of office, Malcolm MacDonald had the closest relationship with Mackenzie King."[7]

But just how did MacDonald become influential on a topic as unlikely as the Canadian north? And why would the British high commissioner make not one, but two trips to the region at a time when there must have been many more serious problems demanding his attention? The answer to these questions is to be found in a brief examination of a small informal Ottawa clique referred to by one scholar as the "Northern Nationalists."[8]

One must be extremely careful when employing a term like the Northern Nationalists because, as the then director of northern research for the Bank of Canada has pointed out, there was no formal organization.[9] What did exist was a number of people who were vitally committed to the north; a group that was alarmed by the almost cavalier attitude of the Canadian government towards the region they considered a key to Canada's destiny. In the postwar period, they would form the core of Canadian representation for the Arctic Institute of North America.[10]

What really dismayed the Northern Nationalists was the fact that, although many of them were prominent civil servants, they had been unsuccessful in forcing the government to come to grips with the situation in the northwest. Because official channels of communication had proven inadequate, they adopted novel means to further their cause. As Trevor Lloyd has revealed, the situation in the northwest was often discussed at social gatherings such as cocktail parties. It was in such an atmosphere that Malcolm MacDonald, a man who had the prime minister's confidence, was briefed on and enlisted in the Northern Nationalists' cause.[11]

But what were the concerns that were relayed to MacDonald? The concerns grew out of the massive development projects that the Americans had begun in northern Canada. This involvement centred upon three major, interrelated undertakings. First, there was the Canadian-inspired Northwest Staging Route: the series of airports from Edmonton to Alaska that passed through Grande Prairie, Fort St. John, Fort Nelson, Watson Lake, and Whitehorse. Although this was a Canadian project, the need to accelerate construction in order to allow for the ferrying of lend-lease aircraft to the Soviet Union led to significant American participation. The second project was the Alaska Highway, which was designed in large measure to provide land connections for the staging route. And finally, there was the Canol project, which was to ship oil by pipe from Norman Wells in the Northwest Territories to Whitehorse in the Yukon, where it would be refined and distributed along the Alaska Highway and the staging route. To these projects there could also be added the development of radio-telegraph networks and weather stations. The magnitude of these projects can be seen in the numbers they involved. Canadian estimates in April 1943 indicated that there were 9,337 U.S. Army engineering troops, and 14,570 American civilians engaged on the Alaska Highway alone. The total number of Americans working in the Canadian northwest was expected to swell to 46,000 by the summer of 1943.[12]

What worried the Northern Nationalists was not the projects themselves, but the licence that the Americans took when placing airfields and aligning roads. They were concerned that much of this work was being conducted with definite postwar considerations in mind, and they feared that if the Canadian government did not assert itself, it would soon find its interests compromised. It was this message that prompted MacDonald to make his first trip north in August 1942.

Unfortunately, MacDonald's August expedition was not to have the impact hoped for by the Northern Nationalists. It was more or less an official visit, and he was accompanied by T.A. Crerar, the minister of mines and resources, and his deputy, Dr. Charles Camsell, who doubled as commissioner of the Northwest Territories. Both MacDonald and Crerar kept diaries of the trip, but these diaries bear more resemblance to travelogues and provide little insight into the military situation in the north.[13] Perhaps, however, these documents reflect the fact that, by August 1942, with the defence projects still in their infancy, a major problem was not yet obvious. What does emerge from the MacDonald diary is a clearly sympathetic view of northern Canada. His vivid descriptions of the land, its people, and its wildlife, and his infrequent references to the frantic efforts to complete military installations, leaves the reader with a sense of forboding if not impending tragedy.

Through the winter of 1942-43, a sense of crisis began to grow among the Northern Nationalists, and, if Trevor Lloyd is correct, this led directly to MacDonald's second journey north in March 1943.[14] Again, his diary proves of minimal value. His notes amount to a few pages and are written in his characteristic travelogue style. But the situation was not the same.

Immediately upon his return, MacDonald went to visit the prime minister at home. That evening, King recorded in his diary:

A long talk with Malcolm MacDonald who had just returned from Edmonton. Says Americans sending 46,000 workers to construct another highway along MacKenzie River. I said to him that we were going to have a hard time after the war to prevent the U.S. attempting control of some Canadian situations. He said already they speak jokingly of their men as an Army of Occupation.[15]

The process that would lead to a definition of northern policy had begun.

Two days later, MacDonald appeared before the Canadian War Cabinet to present his findings,[16] and, six days later, he submitted a major report to Canadian officials.[17] MacDonald also despatched a copy of the document to London, and, in his covering letter to Clement Attlee, minister responsible for the Dominions Office, he confided:

> it is, as it says, a "personal, informal and frank note on the subject." I fear that it may be impertinent, not to say unconstitutional, for a High Commissioner to send such a Note to the Canadian Government, but the situation in the North-West is so disturbing that I felt something had to be done. And as a matter of fact the Prime Minister and his colleagues seem to have welcomed my move.
>
> The situation is pretty alarming. I have set it down as tactfully as I could in the Note, and have probably understated rather than overstated the case. I felt so concerned when I got back from Edmonton that I discussed my impressions immediately with Mackenzie King.... The result is that the Government is now fully aware of what is happening, and I hope that they will take vigorous action. They were already beginning to feel very uneasy before my recent trip. Mackenzie King encouraged me to write the enclosed note for their further consideration.[18]

The enclosed note to which MacDonald referred is a seminal document and merits detailed attention. Its explosive quality was reflected in the comments of the under-secretary of state for external affairs in his covering letter to the prime minister which accompanied MacDonald's note. "It is," he wrote, "a frank and very personal memorandum, and his interest in the whole question might easily be misconstrued if, for instance, it got in any way to the ears of the United States Government that the United Kingdom High Commissioner had been taking the initiative in this question."[19]

Indeed, the Americans would have been more than a little angry at MacDonald's remarks. The high commissioner began by noting the "serious deterioration" of the situation compared with the previous August. He continued, spelling out the difficulties as he saw them:

it is perhaps easy to overstate the danger of so much initiative and decision belonging to our American allies. Admittedly it is highly important from the point of view of the vigorous prosecution of the war that these roads and routes should be built forthwith, and they will in any case be of immense value to Canada after the war. But it is surely unfortunate that the Canadian authorities have little real say as to, for example, the exact placing of these airfields, and the exact route of these roads on Canadian soil. The Americans decide these according to what they consider American interests. Responsible American officers will tell you frankly in confidence that in addition to building works to be of value in this war, they are designing those works also to be of particular value for (a) commercial aviation and transport after the war and (b) waging war against the Russians in the next world crisis. . . .

The American Army calls itself "the Army of Occupation." Much of this annoys the Canadian citizens of the territory, yet they cannot help realizing that it is largely the Americans who *are* now opening up their country. The Canadian counterparts of the Americans who swarm through the country are conspicuous by their absence. The inhabitants of those regions are beginning to say that it seems that the Americans are more awake to the importance of the Canadian North-West than are the Canadian authorities. This state of affairs tends to play into the hands of those Western Canadians who are inclined to assert that the West receives little sympathy and help from Eastern Canada and that its destiny lies in incorporation with the United States of America.

Having said all this, MacDonald concluded his memorandum with the recommendation that a commissioner be appointed to supervise American activities in the north, and that this commissioner be given powers and staff sufficient to do the job.[20] (See Appendix for the complete text.)

It should be noted that MacDonald's motives were not entirely altruistic. While the files extant in London are far from complete, they do indicate certain preoccupations on the part of the British.[21] For example, there are constant references to Canada's strategic position in commercial aviation. Reading between the lines, one gets the impression that the British feared that America would capture the field for itself by the end of the war. It is fair to say, therefore, that Malcolm MacDonald was not simply attempting to safeguard Canadian interests; he was actively promoting those of his own country as well.

In any event, back in Ottawa, the senior civil servants who had desired that the situation in the northwest be made clear to the prime minister now had a problem: they had to prove that while prospects of American domination were serious, they were not the result of a dereliction of duty on their part! Hugh Keenleyside of external affairs was quick to moderate

MacDonald's findings. As he put it, "Although the situation is not by any means as deplorable as 'MM' and some others have suggested, there is no doubt that concern over developments is fully justified." However, his enumeration of junior ranking officials in the region who were supposedly monitoring U.S. activity, and his admission that these officials did not have the authority to deal with the American army, weakened his defence.[22]

In the Privy Council Office, J.R. Baldwin attempted to keep the debate on the critical issue identified by MacDonald:

> [T]here still remains one problem, much greater in extent. The United States had undertaken the economic development of one of Canada's largest and strategically most important areas, without any measure of Canadian participation or control in the development. U.S. interests are gaining a permanent foot-hold in Canada in the development of certain Canadian resources. In addition, the U.S. Government is establishing its influence in an area of great strategic importance to it in the event of any future conflict with an Asiatic power.

Like the British, Baldwin was deeply suspicious of America's commercial interests in the northwest. He could not conceive of a company, like Standard Oil, making significant investments in the region "unless it felt that it would achieve lasting benefits and gain a permanent foot-hold."[23]

This MacDonald interpretation, if it can be styled so, was reinforced by another, less celebrated document submitted to the Department of External Affairs. It was written by Bob Beattie, the director of northern research for the Bank of Canada. Beattie was in Edmonton at approximately the same time MacDonald was making his second trip. He submitted his report "because very few in Ottawa seemed to be having much direct or even indirect contact with developments in the Northwest."[24] As a banker, Beattie began by placing developments in their financial perspective:

> Based on what information I could get, however, I would guess that there might be 50,000—75,000 Americans in Edmonton and the Northwest this summer, and that the total cost of the projects mentioned above might run well over $500 million .... However, even in physical terms this capital development is equivalent to perhaps ¼ of the whole of Canada's wartime capital expansion. Moreover, the men and resources have been poured into a region with a population of only a few thousand before the war and with probably not more than 10,000 Canadians now. Canadian government expenditures in this region, other than for the benefit of Indians, is in the order of $5 million a year .... So far as Canada is concerned the Northwest is today in many respects a foreign country.

The political consequences of this, he argued, would soon become apparent: "As knowledge of what is going on in the Northwest becomes more widespread throughout Canada the feeling that 'the Americans are developing our country while we are fighting the war' might become or might be made into an important political issue." Beattie concluded his report with harsh words for both America and Canada alike:

> From such personal contact as I had with them on the spot, it is certain that the Americans in the Northwest are no supermen. In carrying out projects I should think they are definitely inferior to Canadian engineers and workmen. Privately they will admit mistakes of a kind and magnitude which are almost unbelievable. But they are not afraid to set bold objectives and if one method bogs down they keep trying others until they find one that works. This is the spirit in which Canada has tackled most aspects of her war effort. My own feeling is that unless we can approach the development of the North in the same spirit she will never regain effective control of the region, nor will she deserve to.[25]

In stark contrast to his comments on Malcolm MacDonald's report, Keenleyside minuted, "In general, I think that this is a very sound appraisal — though I would change details and modify phrasing."[26] This despite the fact that, in substance, Beattie and MacDonald were in agreement. Keenleyside, however, could afford to be more candid because this document was not as widely circulated as MacDonald's.

MacDonald's report did lead to action. As the secretary to the cabinet wrote:

> The serious situation revealed by Mr. Macdonald's report, and in recent discussions of specific problems resulting from already large and continually expanding U.S. developments in Northwestern Canada, fully justify the War Committee's conclusion last week that special steps should be taken, at once, to safeguard the Canadian position and to provide for a larger measure of Canadian participation in these activities on Canadian soil. It was agreed that adequate government representation in the area was of first importance.[27]

At the Cabinet War Committee meeting of 16 April, direction was given for the appointment of a commissioner to oversee U.S. activities.[28] Draft instructions were developed by the 20th,[29] and refined the next day.[30] The requisite order-in-council was prepared on 6 May.[31] Finally, on 20 May, Mackenzie King wrote the commissioner, Gen. W. W. Foster, to give him his orders. In this briefing, certain familiar themes emerge. As the prime minister wrote:

> The northwest possesses valuable natural resources and is an area of strategic importance in the event of conflict between the United States and any Asiatic nation. The Canadian government desires to ensure that the natural resources of the area shall be utilized to provide the maximum benefit for the Canadian people and to ensure that no commitments are made and no situation allowed to develop as a result of which the full Canadian control of the area would be in any way prejudiced or endangered.[32]

Thus armed, Gen. Foster was entrusted with the task of reasserting Canadian sovereignty in the north.

However, it would not be an easy task, as British high commission reports to London on the situation in the northwest indicate. One of the last despatches sent by Malcolm MacDonald was issued in November 1944, after a British official had visited the northwest and talked with Gen. Foster. According to Sir Patrick Suff, "the policy of asserting Canadian rights in respect of their territories and of the development created there by the United States but since purchased by Canada is, within limits, progressing steadily. Certainly there is a most substantial change since the High Commissioner drew the Canadian Government's attention to the general situation in April, 1943." But, having conceded this, Sir Patrick was forced to comment:

> the Canadians on the North West Staging Route are only caretakers in their own house. They are the guests of the United States in the latter's palatial messes, where they see money poured out like water.
>
> And, worst of all, the Canadians see perpetually the United States rolling up the Highway or streaming through the air to war along the Aleutians, while neither they themselves nor a single Canadian vehicle nor a single Canadian aircraft are on a similar errand. The men along the route feel themselves just hewers of wood and drawers of water; and trammels at headquarters frequently prevent them from carrying out even these services with adequate despatch and efficiency.
>
> [The] ignoring of Canadian interests combined with the spectacle of the overwhelming amount of United States material constantly flowing up the route, the possible peace time uses of so many of the installations, and their permanent appearance, causes a number of officers . . . . to apprehend the intention on the part of the United States to make the North West Staging Route a Polish Corridor.[33]

While this appraisal was hardly reassuring, it did indicate that Canada was taking steps to gain control over its northern hinterland.

In the end, the price of Canadian sovereignty came high: about $123,500,000. Of this amount, some $88.8 million was paid to the U.S. for permanent installations along the staging routes and the Alaska Highway.[34] Mackenzie King justified these expenditures to the House of Commons on the grounds that it was "undesirable that any other country should have financial investment in improvements of permanent value such as civil aviation facilities for peacetime use in this country."[35]

While extinguishing American claims to the Canadian north, the government had finally begun to formulate a northern policy, and the British high commissioner played a significant role in alerting Canada to its northern responsibilities. However, in the last analysis, it was the construction of the Alaska Highway and other related military projects by the United States that forced the Canadian government to seriously consider the future of its northern districts.

Notes

At the outset, I would like to acknowledge the assistance of an old Oxonian colleague of mine, Dr. William Beaver, and Anne Thurston who kindly checked the Dominions Office files in the Public Record Office, London, England for Mac-Donald's despatches to his superiors.

1. While the role played by MacDonald has not gone unrecognized by historians, it is fair to say that it has not received the attention it warrants. Brief references to the episode are to be found in Donald Creighton, *The Forked Road: Canada 1939-1957* (Toronto: McClelland and Stewart, 1976), pp. 73-74; C.P. Stacey, *Canada and the Age of Conflict: The Mackenzie King Era* (Toronto: University of Toronto Press, 1981), p. 362; and J.L. Granatstein, *Canada's War: The Politics of the Mackenzie King Government, 1939-1945* (Toronto: Oxford University Press, 1975), pp. 321-22, and more recently J.L. Granatstein, *A Man of Influence: Norman A. Robertson and Canadian Statecraft, 1929-68* (Toronto: Deneau, 1981), p. 121. The most complete reference to MacDonald's influence is to be found in Richard J. Diubaldo, "The Canol Project in Canadian-American Relations," Canadian Historical Association, *Historical Papers, 1977*, pp. 179-95.
2. Stan Cohen, *The Forgotten War: A Pictorial History of W.W. II in Alaska and Northwestern Canada* (Missoula, Montana: Pictorial Histories Publishing Co., 1981).
3. Granatstein, *Canada's War*, p. 360.
4. W. L. Mackenzie King diary, 21 March 1942, as quoted in Granatstein, *Canada's War*, p. 321.
5. J.W. Pickersgill, ed., *The Mackenzie King Record: Volume I: 1939-1944* (Toronto: University of Toronto Press, 1960), p. 436.
6. Arnold Heeney, *The things that are Caesar's: the memoirs of a Canadian public servant* (Toronto: University of Toronto Press, 1972), p. 91.
7. Pickersgill, *The Mackenzie King Record: Volume I*, p. 179.
8. Shelagh D. Grant, "The Northern Nationalists: Crusaders and Supporters of a 'New

North', 1940-1950," a paper presented to the Canadian Historical Association Annual Meeting, Ottawa, 1982.
9. Bob Beattie, correspondence with author, 19 December 1981.
10. For details, see Shelagh Grant, "The Northern Nationalists," pp. 3-6. According to Grant, the groups are composed, among others, of such distinguished people as the renowned anthropologist Diamond Jenness; Bob Beattie, the director of northern research for the Bank of Canada; Hugh Keenleyside, assistant under secretary of state for external affairs; A.D.P. Heeney, secretary to the War Cabinet; and Trevor Lloyd, a geographer then in the employ of the wartime information board. One of the driving forces behind this group was Raleigh Parkin who, through business (Sun Life), politics (a major influence in the Liberal Party who had organized the First Liberal Summer Conference in 1933), and marriage (son-in-law of Vincent Massey), was able to provide those concerned with much needed contacts and support. In particular, he was a direct line to Malcolm MacDonald. The foregoing was also confirmed in a personal interview with Trevor Lloyd, 13 August 1980.
11. Trevor Lloyd, interview with author, 13 August 1980.
12. Department of External Affairs (DEA), file 52-Bs: memorandum from deputy minister of mines and resources to Cabinet War Committee, 13 April 1943.
13. A few months before his death, Malcolm MacDonald kindly provided the author with a photostatic copy of his diary. The original is to be found with his papers in the Public Record Office, London, England. This diary provided the basis for the book, *Down North* (Toronto: Oxford University Press, 1943). The Crerar diary is to be found in the archives of Queen's University, Kingston, Ontario, box 155, series 4.
14. Trevor Lloyd, interview with author, 13 August 1980.
15. W.L. Mackenzie King Papers, diary, 29 March 1943.
16. Minutes, Cabinet War Committee meeting, 31 March 1943.
17. This memorandum, entitled "Note on Developments in North-Western Canada" and dated 6 April 1943, may be located in three archival sources: Department of External Affairs, file 52-Bs; the Mackenzie King Papers, vol. 309, file 3282; and the Public Record Office (PRO), London, England, file D035/1645/WG533/7. This important document has also been reprinted in its entirety in John F. Hilliker, ed., *Documents on Canadian External Relations: 1942-1943* (Ottawa: Canadian Government Publishing Centre, 1980), pp. 1567-73.
18. Malcolm MacDonald to Clement Attlee, 7 April 1943, PRO, D035/1645/WG533/7.
19. Norman Robertson to prime minister, 8 April 1943, DEA, file 52-Bs.
20. Malcolm MacDonald, "Notes on Developments in North-Western Canada," 6 April 1943, ibid.
21. See PRO, D035/1208WG533/8; D035/1208/WG533/10; D035/1646/WG533/11; and D035/1648/WG533/18 for miscellaneous correspondence.
22. Hugh Keenleyside, "United States Activities in North Western Canada," 9 April 1943, DEA, file 52-Bs.
23. J.R. Baldwin, "Situation in Canadian Northwest," 12 April 1943, ibid.
24. Bob Beattie, correspondence with author, 19 December 1981.
25. Bob Beattie, "Memorandum on Trip to Northwest," 12 April 1943, DEA, file 52-Bs.
26. Hugh Keenleyside, minute on above document, undated, ibid.
27. A.D.P. Heeney, "Canadian Northwest: Improved Government Representation," memorandum to prime minister, 13 April 1943, ibid.
28. Minutes of Cabinet War Committee meeting, 16 April 1943, ibid.
29. A.D.P. Heeney, "Memorandum for the Prime Minister," 20 April 1943, ibid.
30. Minutes of Cabinet War Committee meeting, 21 April 1943, ibid.
31. Order-in-council, P.C. 3758, DEA, file 5221-40.
32. Prime minister to Gen. Foster, 20 May 1943, King Papers.
33. Sir Patrick Duff, "Notes on trip up the North West Staging Route in October, 1944," 7 November 1944, PRO, D035/1648/WG533/18.
34. Shelagh Grant, "Canada Rediscovers Her North, 1943-1953" (Trent University: unpublished paper, 1979), appendix H. This figure represents total Canadian expenditures for

U.S. defence projects in the north and can be broken down as follows: $76,800,000 paid in 1944 for permanent installations along the northeast and northwest staging routes and the Alaska Highway; an additional $12,000,000 paid in 1946 for facilities along the staging routes and the Alaska Highway; and $34,700,000 in Canadian expenditures that were to have been reimbursed but which were written off by Canada.
35. Canada, House of Commons Debates, Volume 6, 1 August 1944, p. 5708, as quoted in Shelagh Grant, "Canada Rediscovers Her North."

Appendix

NOTE ON DEVELOPMENTS IN NORTH-WESTERN CANADA

*A memorandum prepared by Malcolm MacDonald
for Prime Minister W. L. King, 1943*

I have recently returned from a second visit to the Canadian North-West to see the development works being accomplished there. They leave two major impressions on a casual visitor. First, they are colossal, and their significance may be very far-reaching indeed. Second, the Americans are doing the greater part of the planning and execution of these works, and at present at any rate the Canadian authorities have too little influence on the shaping of these important affairs in Canadian territory. The situation even seems so disturbing that I venture to write this personal, informal and frank note on the subject.

There can be no question of the Canadian Government's wisdom in giving every encouragement to these enterprises. The development works are to be wholeheartedly welcomed. They will open up the North-West a generation sooner than would otherwise have been the case, and will add immensely and immediately to Canada's importance in world affairs. Moreover, the Canadian Government has been right in agreeing to the Americans doing much of the work. When so much of Canada's energy was being thrown into other parts of the war effort it was beyond her power to achieve some of these additional works quickly, and from the point of view of the military defence of North America they had to be accomplished without delay. Again, the Canadian Government has been right in announcing that the work as a whole should be an act of co-operation between the American Government and the Canadian Government working as partners together. They have been right also in insisting that after the war the Americans should withdraw from the work except insofar as the Canadian authorities might be willing for them to continue, and that every part of the development works which remained on Canadian soil then should belong in undisputed ownership to Canada.

So the Canadian authorities have nothing to reproach themselves with on the general policy. On the contrary they have acted with foresight, broad-mindedness and courage. Where things seem to have "slipped" is in the practical carrying out of the third principle of policy outlined in the above paragraph. In theory the Canadian and American Governments are co-operating as equal partners in the work. But in practice the American authorities have gained increasing control of what is done, how it is done and where it is done, whilst the Canadian authorities' influence on events is comparatively small. There are explanations for this. Circumstances have been extremely difficult for the Canadian authorities. For one thing, they have thrown so much of their best personnel into organizing Canada's tremendous war effort at many other even more urgent points that they have so far not been able to spare enough good men to make their influence sufficiently felt in these perhaps rather remote North-Western developments. For another thing, on the Americans' side difficulties have been greatly increased for the Canadians by the fact that the State Department through whom the Canadian Government quite properly deal with the American Government has been largely ignored by the American Army and other authorities carrying out the works on the spot in the North-West.

But whatever may be the reason for what is happening, the facts of the situation are clear and disturbing.

I need not give a list of the works being accomplished or projected. When Mr. Crerar, Dr. Camsell and I visited the North-West last August there were four principal undertakings, and the Canadian and American authorities truly divided responsibility for them. There were the building of the Alaska Highway, the creation of a chain of airfields from Edmonton to Fairbanks, the production of oil at Norman Wells and the laying of a pipeline to convey the oil from Norman Wells to Whitehorse. American authorities were responsible for the carrying out of the first and fourth of these works whilst Canadian authorities were responsible for achieving the second and third. The first three were proceeding with remarkable speed and efficiency. The fourth was making disappointing progress owing to American miscalculations about the ease of transport in the Mackenzie country.

Generally speaking — though there were signs that matters might develop unfortunately — the situation from the point of view of the preservation of Canadian interests was reasonably satisfactory in August. It is since then that there has been a serious deterioration. The following are some of the developments which alter the general picture:

1. Last August it was assumed that the chain of airfields then being built by the Canadians from Edmonton to Fairbanks along the general route of the Alaska Highway would provide, in war and peace, the principal air way from America to Asia. Since then the opinion of the American and Canadian experts in those parts seem to have changed. Of course, that opinion may swing back again. But at present it holds that, although the route through the mountains may always be important as an alternative flying route, for reasons which I need not go into a new chain of airfields from Edmonton down the Athabaska, the Slave and Mackenzie valleys and thence across northern Yukon Territory to Fairbanks will be the more important. This air route is now being built solely by the Americans. They settle exactly where the airfields shall be; they decide where the auxiliary works shall be placed; they are building the airfields; and they are providing the equipment and administrative staffs. These new

airfields are magnificent, all of them with 5,000 feet runways and some of them with runways already stretching 7,000 feet.

2. Just as the Americans have built the Alaska Highway partly as a feeder to the earlier chain of airfields, so they have now begun to build roads partly to serve this air route down the river valleys of Alberta and the North-West Territories. The world was astonished when the Americans built the Alaska Highway 1600 miles long. But now already they are at work, and far advanced, on the construction of nearly 2,000 miles of other roads further east, from Grimshaw to Norman Wells, Fort Smith to Alexandra Falls, Fort Nelson to Willow Lake and Fort Norman to Whitehorse. The Americans are solely responsible for this road-building, and the decision as to when, where and how the roads shall be brought into existence rests mainly with them. No doubt they have yet other plans for the not too distant future.

3. It is perhaps easy to overstate the danger of so much initiative and decision belonging to our American allies. Admittedly it is highly important from the point of view of the vigorous prosecution of the war that these roads and air routes should be built forthwith, and they will in any case be of immense value to Canada after the war. But it is surely unfortunate that the Canadian authorities have little real say as to, for example, the exact placing of these airfields and the exact route of these roads on Canadian soil. The Americans decide these things according to what they consider American interests. They pay no particular heed to this or that Canadian national or local interest. This aspect of the matter assumes even greater importance when one realises fully the considerations which the American Army, and the other American interests working with them, have in mind in all their efforts in the North-West. Responsible American officers will tell you frankly in confidence that in addition to building works to be of value in this war, they are designing those works also to be of particular value for (a) commercial aviation and transport after the war and (b) waging war against the Russians in the next world crisis.

4. With the same considerations in view, the Americans are pushing ahead with many other development works, such as the building of oil pipelines (there are already three such projects besides the Norman Wells-Whitehorse one), the improvement of navigation on the Athabaska, Slave and Mackenzie Rivers, the extension of railroad facilities, etc. In some of these matters they engage in only a minimum of consultation with Canadian authorities.

5. There has been a very encouraging expansion of oil production at Norman Wells during recent months. The Americans are very alive to this and to the possibility that further prospecting may reveal an oil field of considerable importance in the Mackenzie valley. American oil

interests are watching the situation closely, and if developments look good they will seek to gain control there. Canadian oil interests do not seem so alert to the possibilities. I was told at Norman Wells that no senior representative of the Imperial Oil Company has visited the place for a long time past.

6. The American Army is sedulously collecting all the information that they can about the Canadian North-West. For example, their aeroplanes are flying widely over the territory photographing it. I doubt whether they recognise any limits to what they can do if they want to do it. All the information that they collect goes to the War Department in Washington. Does it come likewise to Ottawa? I doubt whether all of it does. In fact the American authorities probably now know much more about this part of Canada than the Canadian authorities do, which is a most undesirable state of affairs.

7. Do the Americans intend to surrender all control over the works which they have established after the war? There can be no question at all of the good faith of the American Administration in supporting the agreements which they have made with the Canadian government. But certainly many influential American individuals who have had a hand in these developments in the North-West have no serious thought that the interests which they represent shall withdraw. American money, energy and labour have been spent on an immense scale whilst the Canadians have had comparatively little to do with some of the most important undertakings. One can imagine some of these people stirring up quite an unpleasant agitation in Congress circles to force the hands of the Administration, if they feel so disposed.

These are some of the worrying elements in the present situation. From them may flow other unfortunate consequences. For example, the political effect in Western Canada of these developments may be significant. Wherever you travel north of Edmonton there are large numbers of American military officers, troops and airmen and civilian workmen and representatives of American business and finance. Everywhere these Americans are talking eagerly about the development of the North-West, and their words are being translated into deeds. The American Army calls itself "the Army of Occupation." Much of this annoys the Canadian citizens of the territory, yet they cannot help realising that it is largely the Americans who *are* now opening up their country. The Canadian counterparts of the Americans who swarm through the country are conspicuous by their comparative absence. The inhabitants of those regions are beginning to say that it seems that the Americans are more awake to the importance of the Canadian North-West than are the Canadian authorities. This state of affairs tends to play into the hands of those western Canadians who are inclined to assert that the West receives little sympathy and help from Eastern Canada, and that its destiny lies in incorporation with the United States of America.

The centre from which these various activities are generally directed is Edmonton. Some other places have also assumed a new importance, such as Whitehorse, which is the headquarters of the American builders of the Alaska Highway. But the growth of Edmonton under American stimulus in connection with these North-Western developments has been most remarkable. The Americans fill a large part of the MacDonald Hotel, they have taken over completely many other pre-existing buildings, and I am told that their Army and civilian organisations have caused the erection of eighty or ninety new buildings in the city during the last four months alone.

They have recognised the importance of their work by stationing a whole Army division in the region. Their local organization runs to one General, eight Colonels, other high ranking officers and an assortment of civilian business executives presiding over military and civil departments established to examine, check and approve of field investigations, construction works, aerial reconnaissance, aerial photography, camouflage, public relations, postal service, legal matters, contracts, labour relations and various other branches of activity staffed by about 13,000 military and civil employees.

The regular Canadian organisation in Edmonton on the other hand consists of one man. He is Mr. Leonard E. Drummond, who is a consulting mining engineer and the secretary of the Alberta Chamber of Mines. He acts as representative of the Department of Mines and Resources, but is not strictly speaking a Government servant. Even his correspondence on behalf of the Canadian Government with the American authorities about all those works is conducted on either his Chamber of Mines or his private notepaper. I must say at once that I doubt whether any better choice could have been made as the semi-official representative of the Canadian Government. Mr. Drummond has an excellent knowledge of North-Western Canada and he is keen, industrious and tactful. His defence of Canadian interests is stout, and at the same time his relations with the Americans are excellent. American military and civilian officers alike speak in high terms of his wise and helpful advice. The extent to which he has been able to keep in touch with their multifarious activities is remarkable. But as often as not, as is inevitable in the circumstances, he only learns about these activities after they have happened, instead of being brought into consultation, as should invariably be the case, before decisions and actions are taken. He works from one small room in the Chamber of Mines office, and I believe his staff consists of one stenographer.

In addition the Department of Mines and Resources has other representatives in smaller centres in the North-West. The Commissioner for the Yukon in Dawson City and such men as Dr. Urquhart at Fort Smith and Dr. Livingstone at Aklavik in the North-West Territories are admirable representatives of the Federal Government. They are doing excellent work as local Canadian advisers and liaison officers to the Americans in their respective districts. But they have other duties also to perform for the Department, and I expect (though I do not know) that they have insufficient staffs under them to achieve satisfactorily the many new tasks which fall to them as a result of the new developments.

Besides these permanent representatives of the Canadian Government, individual departments in Ottawa send officers to Edmonton or elsewhere in the area for 'ad hoc' discussions with the American authorities on particular questions.

These arrangements clearly do not any longer measure up to the situation. One should not exaggerate the extent to which the Canadian authorities have lost their influence over events. The Departments concerned in Ottawa have sought to keep a keen eye on every development, and the Americans may have had to secure their authority in general terms for every project. This control from Ottawa might have worked reasonably satisfactorily if the control on the American side had remained in Washington. But, as has already been said, the dynamic American authorities in Edmonton and elsewhere in the North-West have tended to ignore Washington. At any rate, the War Department has ignored the State Department. And in any case Washington and Ottawa could only deal satisfactorily with the general principles of development policy. Speed required that much of the important detailed work should be settled in Edmonton. The Americans feel handicapped by the inadequacy of the Canadian organisation on the spot there. I understood from one of them that some time ago they offered to finance a considerable increase in Mr. Drummond's staff and office accommodation! Quite apart from other considerations, the effect of this state of affairs on the Americans' opinion of Canadian government is not good.

I am not qualified to propose the remedies. My visits to the North-West have been too superficial for me to claim any real grasp of the problems. Nor am I sufficiently acquainted with the difficulties of Canadian administration in war-time, and anyway it is no business of mine. But perhaps it would help those who read this Note if I risk censure by making some positive suggestions, however impractical or inappropriate they may turn out to be, so that they have something to "get their teeth into." In that spirit I throw out the following tentative suggestions:

1. Someone in the nature of a special Commissioner should be appointed to represent the Canadian Government and be at the head of its organisation in Edmonton dealing, under the general supervision of the Government in Ottawa, with all questions of war-time development in North-Western Canada.
2. He should be assisted by a "general staff" living and working in Edmonton. On it should sit appropriate senior officers of all the Government Departments concerned (Department of External Affairs,

Department of Mines and Resources, Department of Transport, Defence Department, Air Ministry, etc.). They should have an adequate complement of juniors, clerks, stenographers, etc.
3. This staff should be sufficiently large to allow some of its members to travel from time to time through the North-West, maintaining contact with the work in the field.
4. They should be housed in office quarters in Edmonton sufficiently imposing to impress everyone with the presence and authority of the Canadian Government.
5. They should be given appropriate powers. Their two main duties would be:
a) to guard Canadian interests as such in all matters connected with the developments. They would naturally co-ordinate the efforts of all the Canadian Departments concerned.
b) to act as a co-operative partner organisation with the American organisation. Real consultation and co-operation between the Canadians and the Americans before decisions and action are taken should be organised in every department of the work.
6. The staffs of the Government's representatives in the Yukon and the North-West Territories should, if necessary, be increased. It might also be found desirable to appoint local representatives in some places where they do not at present exist.

These suggestions deal only with organisation. Other suggestions concerning other aspects of the situation naturally leap into one's mind. But I am very conscious that my observation of these affairs has been too cursory to make me in any way a reliable judge, and I repeat that I mention even the above suggestions diffidently on that account. This leads me to the one proposal which I do make with confidence. It is that two or three really good men should be appointed at once to proceed to Edmonton and the North-West forthwith as an official Commission to enquire into the situation and make recommendations to the Government. For obvious reasons their appointment should be rather informal and should be attended by no publicity.

I would only add that I expect some of the authorities concerned will find mistakes of fact or of emphasis in this Note. I have not consulted them on those matters because this is in no sense a formal or official document. When I started out for the North-West I did not expect to find myself writing this Note, and so did not collect information with a view to its production. However, I submit it with all its imperfections, for I believe that the general picture which it presents is true.

M.M.

9

The Alaska Highway in Canada-United States Relations

RICHARD J. DIUBALDO

Before the Second World War, the north existed more as a state of mind than anything else. Little had been done to integrate this huge area with the rest of Canada, primarily, one suspects, because there was no reason to, given more pressing southerly concerns. It was nice to have, to reinforce the idea of "The True North Strong and Free" — with obvious emphasis on the latter, as cheapness was the operative policy. Those individuals who had any "northern vision" were politely tolerated. Not being a developmental priority, the north received few financial resources; if Canada had any preoccupation with its higher latitudes, they revolved around the question of sovereignty. To be sure, the Canadian Geological Survey became quite active in this incredibly vast frontier in the 1880's, but the main thrust from the Klondike gold rush to the 1920's was to maintain and enhance an official Canadian presence. Government sponsored expeditions under the likes of Joseph E. Bernier and Vilhjalmur Stefansson were one way in which this was achieved. A more lasting presence was provided by the Northwest Mounted Police (after 1920 called the Royal Canadian Mounted Police) whose prime functions, aside from law, order, and being jacks-of-all-trades, was to show the flag and give lip-service to the care and well-being of Indians and Inuit. There was no long-range policy, merely knee-jerk reactions to real or perceived threats. Most activities and responsibilities were left to agents in the private sector, initially whalers and later fur traders and missionaries. One can hardly say that before 1939 Canada had "asserted" itself in the north. An earnest assertion — certainly not reassertion — of control came with the trauma of the Second World War, somewhat of a blessing in disguise for Canada's north and its inhabitants.

The Alaska Highway played a prominent role in Canada's decision to take a more active stance in the north, but the actual conversion revolved around larger issues. In the case of the Alaska Highway, political considerations more than anything else prompted Canada to take over a road which was viewed as a liability and embarrassment. Yet Canada's position as it evolved in the war years was designed to thwart American aspirations for postwar rights in the Canadian northwest. The highway was an integral part of the Northwest Defense Projects, huge undertakings calling for hundreds of millions of American dollars to defend its Alaska possessions but using Canadian territory. The highway would follow a string of airfields, the Northwest Staging Route, linking Edmonton to Whitehorse and Alaska. The project which caused the greatest amount of anxiety for Ottawa, however, and the one which forced the Canadian government to dig in its heels and establish a policy regarding the future disposition of these American undertakings, was the Canadian Oil Project (Canol). Through the Canadian position on Canol, one can appreciate the problem confronting Canada and gain insights into its dealings with the United States. It is in this broader context that one must place the Alaska Highway and its eventual Canadian take-over.

Shortly after the route for the Alaska Highway had been chosen, along with the appropriate exchange of notes between the two countries, orders were given by Washington on 30 April 1942 to construct a pipeline from Norman Wells to Whitehorse. The line, running some 577 miles, was to be 4 inches in diameter (with some sections 6 inches) and would connect with a 3000 barrel-a-day refinery to be constructed in Whitehorse. The Canadian government was notified once the American decision was made and formally acquiesced in late June 1942, even though Ottawa questioned the soundness of the idea.[1]

In reality, the Canadian government had had little say in the planning and execution of these wide-ranging projects and appeared oblivious to the long-range problems such activities could create.[2] The war abroad required more attention than the goings on in the northwest, and the government's preoccupation was not to exercise control in the area but merely to be informed in advance of American intentions. After all, it was American money and it certainly helped the Canadian balance of payments. This attitude continued well into 1943, and Canada seemed satisfied as long as proper channels were followed and ruffled feathers avoided. It would take the intervention of a non-Canadian to rouse Ottawa to action, and this in itself was a bit of an embarrassment.[3]

The jolt came from the British high commissioner to Canada, Malcolm MacDonald. On 31 March 1943, the high commissioner, who had just returned from a tour of the northwest, informed the Cabinet War Committee of his analysis of American activity. It had become "quite evident," he reported, "that these vast undertakings were being planned and carried out with a view to the post-war situation."[4] MacDonald elaborated on these remarks in a secret and personal memo to Prime Minister Mackenzie King on 6 April 1943, pointing out that Canada was in a precarious position.

MacDonald's recommendation that the government create the office of special commissioner was undertaken almost immediately. On 19 May 1943, the government appointed Maj.-Gen. W.W. Foster to strengthen the Canadian presence in the northwest and to watch over American activities, making sure that no situation be "allowed to develop as a result of which full Canadian control of the area be in any way prejudiced or endangered."[5] As watchdog, it was Foster's responsibility to ensure that no American projects were initiated without prior approval.

Foster began to appreciate his position and Canada's predicament. When Charles Camsell, deputy minister of mines and resources, asked Imperial Oil for data on geological formations and on the Norman fields drilling data, for instance, the Canadian company advised him that they could do so only with U.S. approval. Foster sought out the appropriate U.S. officials to clear the matter, but was told that to accede to his request was impossible as it would be a breach of secrecy.[6] The special commissioner was informed that there was no intention to withhold information to which Canada was "properly entitled," but "it seems inadvisable at the present time to disclose information secured by the Imperial Oil Company under a contract with the United States Government until we have accomplished our directive."[7] Ultimately, the block was removed by officials in Ottawa and Washington, but the Canadians were clearly upset.

In reality, the presence of Foster, and Canada's stepped-up publicity campaign to tell the Canadian and American public of its input into the Northwest defense projects were merely holding actions. As Ottawa saw it, "[t]here were three outstanding characteristics [of] United States activity in the North Pacific area — its *scale,* its *intensity,* its *permanence.*"[8] The major question of resolving the American presence remained. True, the various formal exchanges of notes and the recommendations of the Permanent Joint Board on Defence (P.J.B.D.) theoretically protected Canada's postwar position, and "if existing agreements are maintained and executed all Canadian interests will be adequately protected."[9] Yet there were strong feelings that American pressure would increase to change these arrangements.[10] There seemed little opportunity to deflect American sentiments.

The chance came from an unexpected quarter — the Americans themselves. Through October and November 1943, the Canol project and its creators were subjected to unrelenting questioning by Senator Harry S. Truman's special committee investigating the National Defense Program. Exposed were the messy details of how the project had been started, how the army had turned a blind eye to its critics, and how American money had been squandered. The war department was left standing naked before its inquisitors.[11] Congressman Leon H. Gavin of Pennsylvania reflected the committee's frustration:

> Why didn't we have some good horse trader handling the contract for us who would try to make a deal that would be beneficial to our own people who have to foot the bill? I feel we are all fighting the war together, and I am of the opinion that we all ought to assume our proportionate share, particularly as this is a Canadian oil development and at the termination of the war Canada will take it over, and we have just carried on a gigantic W.P.A. project for the benefit of the Canadian people, opening up the Canadian wilderness, and Uncle Sam isn't getting anything out of it.[12]

Gavin's remarks were not lost upon the Truman Committee. The issue was Canol, but such sentiments could undoubtedly be applied to the Alaska Highway as well. The wheels for such renegotiation had been set in motion in late November 1943.

In Canada, this development caused some alarm. Assistant Under Secretary of State for External Affairs Hugh Keenleyside pointed out to a special meeting of departmental and political representatives on 30 November 1943 that "this case is probably the first of a number of United States efforts to re-negotiate wartime agreements with Canada, using as an excuse the development of public opinion in the United States."[13] Nevertheless, the Truman Committee's revelations of the War Department's empty logic in defence of Canol now provided Canadian authorities with the lever for which they had been searching. Three days later, on 3 December, the Canadian government decided literally to "buy" the Americans out of the potentially valuable Northwest Staging Route and the related facilities constructed at U.S. expense[14] — a strategy they had been toying with since the spring of 1943.[15] Any changes to the Canol agreements would open the floodgates for the establishment of postwar rights along the Alaska Highway and along the chain of airfields established in eastern Canada, and if this happened, "Canada will ... be committed to the consequences of future United States' Policy."[16] The American presence had to be extinguished in one fashion or another. Negotiations between the two countries stretched from December 1943 to the spring of the following year. From the outset, the Canadian position remained firm, giving the United States little latitude for further concessions.[17] By the end of January 1944, through skillful negotiation and determined argument, the Canadians were able to lead their American counterparts to the idea of a strategic reserve.[18] The initial

Canadian position had remained firm and the Americans encountered a toughness that they had not anticipated, a signal that they would receive little sympathy should they try to press on the staging routes and the Alaska Highway.[19]

After 1944, Canol was allowed to wither, subsequent to some fancy diplomatic footwork which upset the Americans,[20] and remained a junkyard monument to military stupidity.[21] A key fact of Canada's policy regarding the north had been established. It was largely a reaction to the American presence and the fact that the United States was developing a taste for the mineral potential and strategic value of Canada's northern hinterland.[22] But much was owed to the work of a number of farsighted, enthusiastic, and influential members of Canada's governing elite — a band of northern enthusiasts, or "arcticians," scattered throughout government departments who were, at bottom, most instrumental in formulating northern policy.

In external affairs, for example, individuals such as Hugh Keenleyside, Norman Robertson, Escott Reid, Hume Wrong and Lester Pearson had a broad, perhaps romantic, vision of Canadian nationhood and the place of the north in Canada's future. Most were members of the Canadian Institute for International Affairs, founded in 1928 and dedicated to providing a forum for informed opinion amongst academics, businessmen and government leaders.[23] They knew that Canada must take the lead in developing its backyard; otherwise control of the north might be lost by default should the United States do more than Canada. A northern focus, wrote the dynamic and articular Escott Reid in 1943, could prove therapeutic to Canadians:

> After the emotional debauch of the war there is going to be a bad hangover in all the former belligerent countries. In order that people's lives will not feel too empty, some peacetime equivalents to the exciting national objectives to the war must be found. The opening of a new frontier in the Canadian North can, I think, become a national objective of some importance to the Canadian People. Even if, from the point of view of securing the highest possible national income, the Canadian North is not worth a large expenditure of national energy and capital, a very large expenditure might nevertheless be justified in an effort to realize an inspiring and somewhat romantic national objective.[24]

To achieve this, Canadian policy called for the careful removal of the American "occupation." Diplomatic manoeuvering would take care of Canol; cash reimbursement would take care of the staging routes. Taking over the Alaska Highway, however, was another matter.

The Canadian government knew it must some day take over the highway, but it was extremely reluctant to do so. From the moment U.S. military authorities began their irresistible pressure for its construction, Canada had doubts about the highway and its route but based its assent on political, not military, factors. Ottawa had entertained, but rejected, building and paying for the road itself; it would have been "a monument to our friendship for the United States but would otherwise be pretty much of a 'white elephant'."[25] What concerned Canadian planners in the spring of 1942 was the prospect of the United States and its military acquiring a moral, if not a legal, right to use the road after the war.[25] The formal exchange of notes in 1942, however, were quite specific. The highway would be turned over six months after the end of the war, unless Canada preferred to assume responsibility at an earlier date, and at no time thereafter would Canada impose any discriminating conditions on American *civilian* traffic.[27] A year later the United States pressed for an extension of the agreement between the two countries to include postwar military use of the highway, but the chiefs of staff, along with the Canadian section of the Permanent Joint Board on Defence, wisely resisted such an arrangement on the grounds that "it was impossible to foresee the circumstances which might exist on the cessation of the present hostilities, and from time to time thereafter."[28]

Despite Ottawa's severe reservations, it appeared that Canada just might be getting a bargain as the initial U.S. plans and construction unfolded. On 29 May 1942, C.K. LeCapelain of the Lands, Parks and Forest Branch of the Department of Mines and Resources had been appointed Canadian liaison officer with U.S. Army officers in charge of construction. LeCapelain became Ottawa's "eyes," and his detailed and penetrating reports became the basis for much of Canadian policy regarding the Alaska Highway. LeCapelain, after establishing warm contacts with the American army engineers, waxed enthusiastic about the progress of the highway during the summer of 1942. "The U.S. Engineer Corps, for whom I have nothing but the highest praise, had what seemed to me the right idea. They were building a military road fit to carry a fair truck traffic and capable of continual improvement afterwards.... They went about it efficiently and economically and with no frills."[29] He was not too pleased, however, with the extravagance and duplication exhibited by the Public Roads Administration in paralleling the army's efforts.[30] Nevertheless, Canada would in the long run benefit from the P.R.A.'s efforts: "No one in Canada need worry about the standard of permanent highway which the Public Roads Administration is building. It is being built for heavy traffic and to a standard and with a better foundation to support heavy truck traffic than any road I have personally seen or know of in any Dominion National Park or in the Province of Alberta."[31] When LeCapelain hinted that the duplication and jurisdictional friction might lead to the curtailment of the P.R.A.'s work — as was eventually done — officials in Ottawa became unsettled.[32] To Charles Camsell, deputy minister of mines and resources, such a development meant "a distinct departure from the terms of the exchange of notes, for a modern highway has been promised by the U.S. Government."[33] His remark would anticipate the quandary Ottawa would face when it came time to consider the highway takeover. Meanwhile, the army got its way and pushed through a pioneer and tote road from Dawson Creek to Fairbanks. The road, officially opened on 20 November 1942, was testimony to American determination to get *a* job, but not *the* job, done. But the highway was never completed to original plans or Canadian satisfaction.

A year after his initial enthusiasm, LeCapelain was reporting a gloomy scenario in the northwest to his superiors in Ottawa. He pointed out that many stretches of road, especially west of Whitehorse near the Yukon-Alaska border, had been poorly located, subject to glacial runoffs "and permanently frozen ground which becomes a bottomless quagmire when exposed to sun and air ... [A]s an experienced engineer who has spent many years locating, building and maintaining highways, roads and trails in the Rocky Mountains ... I would have used the greatest endeavour to have avoided the present route of the Alaska Highway from Kluane Lake to the Yukon-Alaska border." A permanent road would be built over this stretch but it would require an extended effort, piling thousands of yards of rock and coarse gravel until a stabilized condition was reached, requiring probably twenty years of attention by Canadian authorities. Reflecting on the entire highway, LeCapelain concluded that,

> when the Alaska Highway is finally turned over to our government to maintain, it is likely to get considerable of a liability. This condition is not confined to the Kluane Lake section discussed in this report. There are other sections extending over most of the length of the Alaska Highway where the road was located as a tote road and in a great hurry by inexperienced men ... Due to poor location and that many of the bridges are being built of untreated native timber, the highway over these stretches is likely to prove a decided liability.[34]

LeCapelain was not the only one to make such observations for, within two weeks, Ottawa received a similar report dealing with the whole highway which corroborated LeCapelain's:

> Taking into consideration the entire Alaskan project, it does not impress me as an engineering feat but as a great demonstration of determination on the part of those who assumed responsibility for putting through the road, the efficiency of high-powered mechanical road-building equipment. A first-class road at less expense could have been built had there been time to properly survey the route ....
> When the Canadian Government takes over the Alaska Highway of approximately 1500 miles, provision will be necessary for a maintenance

cost of about $750 per mile for just ordinary maintenance .... In addition, a large sum would be required to undertake the necessary revisions, replacement of bridges, culverts, cribbing against slides, etc., etc., spread over a number of years.... Another expenditure which will have to be considered when this road is being taken over is in regard to disposal of material which has been bulldozed to the sides of the right-of-way and not disposed of for almost the entire length of the highway in Canada from about Mileage 25J north of Fort St. John to the Alaska-Yukon Boundary. This material certainly is a potential fire-hazard to surrounding country and an eyesore. It is a matter of great concern to the British Columbia authorities from a forest fire protection standpoint, as well as to our Yukon administration.[35]

When Canadian members of the P.J.B.D. paid a summer visit to Pacific defence areas, they likened the road to that "of a poor country road in Ontario."[36] Originally, the standard for the permanent road was to have been a graded road section 36 feet wide with 20 feet surfaced with crushed rock or gravel. In early 1943, the standard was reduced to a width of 26 feet, and by the fall of that year, the road sections were being built or finished to a width varying from 20 feet to 26 feet. These latter changes were partly a reflection of the improved situation facing the Americans in the Pacific theatre of war which diminished the urgency and energy of their efforts in the north.[37]

Canada's position was complicated by glowing but highly misleading newspaper reports throughout 1943 emanating from the northwest which suggested that the road was fully operational and had opened up areas of tremendous economic potential and incredible scenic beauty for tourists. The U.S. public was certainly under that impression, as were Canadians. Charles Camsell went to the heart of the matter in this respect for he feared that "Canada is going to have some explaining to do when it is found out that the Alaska Highway is not to be a tourist highway but merely a serviceable road connecting airports."[38] The consequences of such misrepresentation would, of course, force Canada to submit to the pressure of public opinion compelling it to take on, maintain and possibly rebuild an unwanted road.[39] Takeover was one thing; permanently maintaining and improving a less than desirable project was another. It could not be made to die like Canol. But if Canada refused to continue maintenance of the road, it would not only alienate the U.S. government but would solicit unfavourable public opinion in both countries giving the impression that the Dominion was not interested in the future of the northwest.[40]

Canada would have to make a decision on the highway soon. By the winter of 1943, the Interdepartmental Panel on Joint Defence Construction Projects directed various departments to prepare argued briefs regarding the future of the road.[41] While these studies went ahead, the Canadian position became clearer and stronger. The Canol revelations and a public exposé by

Congressman Warren Magnuson in May of 1944 undercut the U.S. Army's credibility in these projects and affected even more the pace and scale of construction along the highway.[42] By the summer of 1944, the U.S. would abandon the so-called Haines Cutoff running from Haines, Alaska to Haines Junction on the Alaska Highway proper.[43] Although U.S. military authorities hotly denied this shutdown, the evidence suggested otherwise and led Canadian officials to view the action as a possible signal regarding American intentions for the overall highway system.[44] Technically, this was a violation of the official international agreement between the two countries,[45] because the cutoff was legally part of the highway package.[46] "In abandoning the Haines Cutoff the United States would seem to have broken their understanding to maintain the Alaska Highway until six months after the war. This abandonment has raised fears that the main highway will similarly fall into disuse."[47]

Early in September 1944, the United States moved. Through its senior army representative on the P.J.B.D., Maj.-Gen. Guy V. Henry, it suggested that Canada might wish to take over responsibility for the administration and maintenance of the highway at an earlier date.[48] The Cabinet War Committee's consideration of Henry's proposal, in September 1944, coincided with the submission of the Joint Defence Construction Projects Panel's report on the highway. The prime minister and his committee were told by the panel that to take over the highway at that juncture would cost Canada $4.5 million for the first year of maintenance and $1.5 million thereafter per annum, and that this estimate was based upon maintenance of the road to "minimum standards". To improve the highway substantially would incur additional millions, a prospect which the government did not wish to face at that time. Parsimony may have been one factor, but undoubtedly the Canadians, who by now were resigned to taking over the road, wanted more time and wanted the United States to fulfill its obligations to the letter and spirit of the agreements. This Canadian reticence helps to explain the Dominion's resentment over the Haines Cutoff episode, for instance. As well, the Cabinet War Committee was counselled that, though the road would technically be in Canadian hands, there were reasons other than cost not to move too quickly. Admittedly, it had become Canadian policy "to give maximum cooperation to the United States defence forces in Canada, and at the same time facilitate their withdrawal whenever they have found it expedient to do so." But the Alaska Highway was different. United States interests and "present" obligations required their keeping control of the road transport operations, and "the authority operating the road should dictate its maintenance, otherwise both harmony and efficiency might suffer; also those responsible for construction should be in charge during the period of stabilization."[49] Nevertheless, at some point, Canada should take over the route:

> The highway provides an easy form of transport into the immense

country between Fort St. John and Whitehorse, which were previously accessible only with difficulty. In these areas, before the highway was built, no industry could be carried on that involved the transportation of heavy or bulky materials; the necessities of life were taken in, and any exports were of small bulk and high value, such as furs and gold, which could be transported by pack horses, back packing or along the traditional inland waterways in canoes. To what extent the building of the highway will give rise to changes in the economic life of the country and resultant traffic cannot be forecast until the resources along the route have been more thoroughly investigated. Failure to maintain it for at least a trial period might seriously impair the prospects for development of these areas....

Apart from the consideration of beneficial use of the highway, there are other factors that will influence the decision as to whether or not it should be maintained in whole or in part after the war. Publicity of a favourable and often extravagant nature given to this highway has led to the impression that it traverses a country of unlimited natural resources and commercial possibilities and also of considerable scenic interest, and that it has been completed by the United States to a very high standard and will shortly be paved or at least given a surface treatment of some kind.

Failure of Canada to continue maintenance after the responsibility of the United States ends, would result in most unfavourable reactions by sections of the public in both countries; and some bitterness that an investment of over $100 million had been abandoned. The obvious permanency of the larger bridges tend to reinforce public belief in the permanency of the whole.

Finally it will be recalled that the decision to build the highway was based solely on military considerations. These related not merely to the exigencies of the moment but to the long-term defence of the continent. Hence the United States view that while the general situation had improved, the necessity remained for both a highway and an air route suitable for large operations as a part of the *permanent* Alaska defence.[50]

Though the future value of the road remained unclear, it was difficult for Canada to pursue any other course but takeover and maintenance.

For the moment though, the Cabinet War Committee decided to turn down the American proposal. The Canadian government drew American attention to the abandonment of the Haines-Cutoff, done without the consent of the Canadian government, and also informed their partners-in-arms that Canada was not at present prepared to assume responsibility for the road.[51] It appears, also, that the government was angered and would not welcome any future requests from the United States suggesting that Canada relieve the Americans of the highway before war's end. In a personal and confidential letter to J.D. Hickerson of the State Department, Hugh Keenleyside told of the War Cabinet's decision and that the Canadian members of the P.J.B.D. were all aware of Canada's position; he went on to say that the proposal should not be brought up again. "It seems to me that there is something to be said for avoiding a discussion which must have either a negative result or an affirmative result which would be based on a divided vote."[52]

The issue of takeover was put to rest when the Americans were informed through the P.J.B.D. that Canada would not take over the road before the date originally agreed upon; six months after the termination of the war.[53] There would be no more talk of Canada assuming authority over the road any earlier, but government officials would soon be pressured to sustain the road for reasons of continental defence. As the war wound down, and new international confrontations were perceived, it became obvious that the United States did not want the highway to fall into disuse. At a meeting of the P.J.B.D. on 8 June 1945, Maj.-Gen. Henry, the leading spokesman for the U.S. military, requested that the Canadian members consider the continental defence value of the various projects in northwestern Canada, arguing that the defence of Alaska should not be merely a concern of his country but of Canada's too: "The defence of Alaska in case of war with an Asiatic power is of major importance to the defence of the North American continent."[54]

Initially, Canada did not see eye-to-eye with the United States about the imminent threat of the Soviet Union, Henry's unnamed "Asiatic power," but had concluded by 1945 that the defences of Canada should be "closely co-ordinated" with the United States in the postwar period.[55] Interestingly, by the summer of 1945, the Post Hostilities Problems Committee, considering the defence of northwest Canada and the true value of the Alaska Highway, wished to avoid putting all of Canada's efforts into protecting and developing or improving northern defence facilities solely to protect Alaska. "Steps should be taken to ensure that any such pressure does not lead her to neglect the defence of strategic sectors which lie wholly in Canadian territory, such as the Mackenzie River Valley, and the Arctic Barrens to the East. These areas may prove to be more vulnerable as a line of [enemy] approach than the highland area of Alaska and the Canadian corridor."[56]

Looking back, one can see that Canada had reviewed her options and, largely in accordance with the policy first generated by anxieties over Canol, concluded that the highway, though a liability, had to be retained, more for political than economic, military or strategic reasons. That was the price to be paid if Canada was to assert herself in the north. The transfer of the Alaska Highway took place on 1 April 1946, and Canada promised to maintain the highway in the postwar world.[57] The road would be maintained by the Canadian army as a military road, but the United States received no permanent military rights along the right-of-way. Much would have to be done because the road was "in very indifferent condition due to an economical policy instituted by the Americans" and required "a great deal of corrective work."[58] For this reason, and because regular highway facilities and amenities were virtually nonexistent, the road was closed to most civilian traffic, and U.S. pressure to the contrary was resisted.[59] To open the road at that time to civilian traffic, especially unlimited tourist traffic, could have proven embarrassing given false impressions generated during the war years. Canadian military and, later, civilian authorities would shoulder the obligation of integrating the road into the Canadian system of highways. Ultimately, as one Canadian member of the Permanent Joint Board on Defence acidly commented, Canada in the postwar years would "build and maintain the kind of road that the United States promised but did not construct."[60]

Notes

1. Records of the Department of State, file 842.6363 (hereafter Department of State Papers). Memorandum by J. Hickerson, 16 May 1942. For terms of the Canol arrangements see, Canada, *Treaty Series,* 1942, Supplement No. 15, "Exchange of Notes (June 27 and 29, 1942) between Canada and the United States of American Constituting and Agreement for the Construction of a pipeline and a refinery in the Yukon Territory."
2. See Department of External Affairs Records, External Affairs Archives, file 4349-40C, Hugh Keenleyside to Norman Robertson, 6 October 1942; ibid., Pearson to Robertson, 26 February 1943.
3. William Lyon Mackenzie King Papers, PAC, MG 26, J4, Robertson to King, 8 April 1943, fol. 213758.
4. PAC, Records of the Privy Council Office, cabinet war committee, 1939-45, PAC, minutes RG 2/7c, vol. 12, 31 March 1943; Malcolm MacDonald to King, 6 April 1943, King papers, PAC, fol. 213758.
5. Minutes of the cabinet war committee, document No. 519, draft instructions to the special commissioner, 19 May 1943.
6. P.A.C., Records of the Special Commissioner for Defense Projects in Northwest Canada, PAC, RG 36/7, A.D.P. Heeney, 8 October 1943. vol. 2, Brig. Gen. L.D. Worsham, U.S. Army Engineers, to Foster, 14 September 1943.
7. Ibid., Worsham to Foster, 28 September 1943.
8. Keenleyside to King, 29 July 1943, External Affairs Records, file 4228-40.
9. Memorandum by Keenleyside, 11 December 1943, entitled, "Evidence Relating to United States Efforts to Obtain Postwar Advantages from Wartime Expenditures in Canada," External Affairs Records, file 3634-40C.
10. Ibid.; see also, Foster to Heeney, 30 August 1943, file 463-BQ-40; Address of Ray Atherton, 30 September 1943, King Papers, vol. 240.
11. United States Congress, Senate, 78th Congress, *Special Committee Investigating the National Defense Program* (hereafter, Truman Committee).
12. Testimony of Representative Leon H. Gavin, Truman Committee, p. 9549.
13. Minutes of Meeting held on 30 November 1943 to discuss the Canol Development, External Affairs Records, file 463-N-7-40C.
14. A.D.P. Heeney to Norman Robertson, 14 December 1943, ibid., file 3634-40C.
15. Cabinet war committee, minutes, vol. 12, 17 March 1943 and 7 April 1943.
16. Memorandum: "Defence Aspects of the Canol Project," n.d. and unsigned, probably 1 December 1943 by Group Captain W.F. Hanna, Director of Plans, Department of

National Defence for Air, and Wing Commander P.A. Cumyn, Secretary of the Interdepartmental Panel on Joint Defence Projects, External Affairs Records, file 463-N-7-40C.
17. Ibid.
18. Memorandum on "The intergovernmental discussions on the Canol development..." 4 February 1944, ibid.
19. Hickerson Memo, 2 February 1944, U.S. Department of State Papers.
20. Richard J. Diubaldo, "The Canol Project in Canadian-American Relations," Canadian Historical Association, *Historical Papers, 1977,* pp. 189-90.
21. Leslie Roberts, *The Mackenzie* (New York: 1949), p. 239.
22. The establishment by both countries of the North Pacific Planning Project in early 1943, to assess the economic potential and general future of the northwestern part of the North American continent, was for some Americans a step in developing "an economy more truly continental in character." "Problems and Possibilities for Canadian-American Collaboration in the North Pacific Area", prepared by James C. Rettie and Roy F. Bessie, U.S. Co-Director of Region X, National Resources Planning Board, 15 September 1942, External Affairs Records, file 4228-40. King feared that the joint study would, or could, lead to Canadian developmental policy resting with the United States. King diary, PAC, MG 26, J13, 30 December 1942. Nevertheless, the study went forward. For a review of the project, see Shelagh Grant, "Search for a Northern Policy, 1940-1950. The Impact of the Canadian Institute of International Affairs," Unpublished Honours Thesis, Trent University, 1981, pp. 66ff.
23. Grant, "Search for a Northern Policy," pp. 7, 32-35.
24. Escott Reid to Norman Robertson, 30 July 1943, PAC, Records of the Privy Council Office, RG 2/18, vol. 21, file A-25-3.
25. Keenleyside to Robertson, 3 March 1943, External Affairs Records, file 463-40C; also, PAC, RG 2/18, vol. 17, file R-16-1.
26. Ibid.
27. Exchange of notes, 17 and 18 March 1942, between the United States and Canada, ibid., file 463-40.
28. "Minutes of Meeting of the Chiefs of Staff with the Canadian Section of the Permanent Joint Board on Defence," 17 March 1943, PAC, Records of the Privy Council Office, RG 2/18, vol. 17, file R-16-1; also, Memorandum of Sir Vice-Marshall N.R. Anderson, 17 March 1943, ibid.
29. LeCapelain to R.A. Gibson, Director, Lands, Parks, and Forest Branch, Mines and Resources, 17 August 1942, External Affairs Records, file 463-40.
30. Ibid.
31. LeCapelain to Gibson, 14 August 1942, ibid.
32. LeCapelain to Gibson, 17 August 1942, ibid.
33. Charles Camsell to J.R. Baldwin, Privy Council Office, 25 August 1942, PAC, Records of the Special Commissioner, RG 36/7, vol. 44.
34. LeCapelain to Gibson, 22 August 1943, ibid.
35. "J.S." (Stewart?) to Gibson, 3 September 1943, External Affairs Records, file 463-40.
36. Keenleyside to King, 29 July 1943, ibid., file 4228-40. Foster, for one, was gratified that a proposed trip, in the summer of 1943, by members of the U.S. Congress had been postponed "as the road itself is not at present available for traffic." Foster to Heeney, 19 July 1943, ibid., file 463-BG-40.
37. Report of J.M. Wardle, Director, Surveys and Engineers Branch, Mines and Resources, to Camsell, 29 October 1943, PAC, Records of the Privy Council Office, RG 2/18, vol. 17, file R-16-1.
38. For example, Edmonton *Bulletin,* 17 August 1943. Camsell to Foster, 31 August 1943, PAC, Records of the Special Commissioner, RG 36/7, vol. 2.
39. Minutes of Third Meeting, Joint Defence Construction Projects Panel, 3 September 1943, External Affairs Records, file 703-40. Present were: Charles Camsell, deputy minister, mines and resources; A.J. MacNamara, deputy minister of labour; H.L. Keenleyside, external affairs; H.F. Gordon, Department of National Defence - Air; J.A. Wilson, Department of Transport; Group Captain W.F. Hanna, R.C.A.F.; W.E. Hunter, Department of Finance; J.R. Baldwin and J.F. Frederickson, Privy Council Office.

40. Report of Wardle to Camsell, 29 October 1943, PAC, Records of the Privy Council Office, RG 2/18, vol. 17, file R-16-1.
41. Meeting of Joint Defence Construction Projects Panel, 3 December 1943, External Affairs Records, file 3874-A-40c. This was confirmed by directions given to the committee by the cabinet war committee, 16 December 1943.
42. For example, Seattle *Post Intelligencer,* 9 May 1944. Article: "Gross Waste in Building Alcan Highway, Magnusson charges Army. Accused of Gigantic Blunder in Route Selection. Still unfit for Military Use."
43. Foster to Heeney, 25 August 1944, PAC, Records of the Privy Council Office, RG 2/18, vol. 18, file R-16-4.
44. Remarks of Maj.-Gen. Guy V. Henry, Senior U.S. Army Member, P.J.B.D., 7 October 1944, ibid.
45. Heeney to Foster, 30 June 1944, Records of the Privy Council Office, RG 2/18, file R-16-4; Keenleyside to R.M. Macdonell, 31 August 1944, and "Memorandum for File" by Macdonell, 2 September 1944, External Affairs Records, file 463-AB-40.
46. The United States Government requested on 28 November 1942 "that the Haines-Champagne cut-off road shall henceforth be considered an integral part of the Alcan Highway" subject to the provisions contained in the original Exchange of Notes of 17-18 March 1942. The Canadian government, anticipating such a request, had assented with a favourable decision of the cabinet war committee, 18 November 1942. "Memorandum of the Alaska Highway", [1947], External Affairs Records, file 463-40.
47. Wing Commander P.A. Cumyn, secretary, Privy Council Office, to Mr. Halliday, 10 October 1944, PAC, Records of the Privy Council Office, RG 2/18, vol. 18, file R-16-14.
48. P.J.B.D. Journal of Discussions and Decisions, Meeting of 6-7 September 1944, ibid., Records of the Special Commissioner, RG 36/7, vol. 47.
49. Report of the Joint Defence Construction Projects Panel entitled "Maintenance of the Alaska Highway" to Cabinet War Committee, 1 September 1944, PAC, Records of the Department of National Defence, RG 24, vol. 2639, file HQS-3487-5.
50. Ibid., italics in original.
51. Decisions of the Cabinet War Committee, 27 September 1944, External Affairs Records, file 463-BS-40.
52. Keenleyside to Hickerson, 10 October 1944, PAC, Records of the Special Commissioner, RG 36/7, vol. 47.
53. Extract of Minutes, Joint Construction Projects Panel, 4 November 1944, ibid.
54. "Continental Defence Value of the Canadian Northwest," Remarks of Major General Guy V. Henry, 8 June 1945, External Affairs Records, file 52-C(s); see also ibid., re: Henry's remarks on "Postwar Collaboration," 8 June 1945.
55. Ibid., file 7.C.W(s), cited in "Preliminary Draft of the Post Hostilities Problems Committee, 6 July 1945.
56. Ibid.
57. Decisions of the Cabinet War Committee, 17 October 1945, ibid., file 3874-A-40. After this decision, officials of the United States would sit down with their Canadian counterparts to work out even the minutest details of transfer, including such items as mail, maintenance shops, machine shop equipment, surplus materials, boundaries, etc. See "Report on visit to Alaska Military Highway by Brigadier General G. Walsh, with a view of taking over by the Canadian Army", [11 or 12 November 1945]; PAC Records of the Department of National Defence, vol. 2426, file HQS-415-9; "Interim Report. Take-over of Alaska Military Highway by Northwest Highway System," 13 February 1946; "Alaska Military Highway. Take-over by Northwest Highway System," [15 April 1946]; "Transcript of Meeting (between officials of Canada and U.S.) Alaska Highway," 13 November 1945, RG 24, vol. 2453, file HQS-631-52-5.
58. "Alaska Military Highway Take-over by Northwest Highway System." [15 April 1946], PAC, Records of the Department of National Defence, RG 24, vol. 2426, file HQS-415-9.
59. Colonel J.H. Jenkins to R.M. Macdonell, 17 December 1945, ibid., vol. 2450, file HQS-631-52-5. See also, "Canadian Northwest Highway System," *Canadian Information Service,* 18 December 1946.
60. J. Allison Glenn, PJBD, to Wing Commander A.M. Cameron, Cabinet Secretariat, Privy Council Office, 4 May 1946, External Affairs Records, file 463-AB-40.

The idea of a highway to Alaska was as old as the Klondike Gold Rush. British Columbia premier T.D. Pattullo (left) tried unsuccessfully in the 1930's to secure federal government support for his dream of a road through northern British Columbia. Though the Canadian government did not agree that the highway was necessary, they gave the United States permission to proceed, signing the Canadian-U.S. agreement (above) in February 1942. Even as construction began, survey crews (below) were still laying out the route for the pioneer road.

U.S. Army bulldozers (left) led the advance through the forests and across the muskeg. The new highway quickly displaced old methods of transportation. Pack trains (above), long used by trappers and prospectors, were used by the initial survey crews but were soon replaced by truck convoys. (Below) Brigadier General William M. Hoge and Colonel Ear. G. Paules, commanding officer of the 18th Engineers Regiment, inspect preliminary road construction near Kluane Lake in the Yukon Territory.

U.S. Army regulations prohibited the use of black troops in northern settings, but the urgency of the project and a shortage of Engineers units resulted in the dispatch of several contingents to work on the Alaska Highway (above left). To speed construction, crews worked north and south along the route from several staging centres. Bulldozers (below) from the 340th, working south, and the 35th Engineer Regiment, working north, met at Contact Creek, north of Fort St. John. Drainage problems plagued highway construction from the beginning. This pull blade (above right) is attempting to dig a drainage ditch to draw water off the road surface.

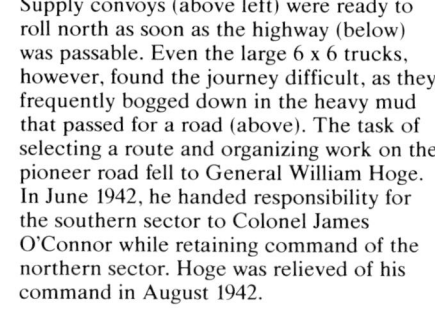

Supply convoys (above left) were ready to roll north as soon as the highway (below) was passable. Even the large 6 x 6 trucks, however, found the journey difficult, as they frequently bogged down in the heavy mud that passed for a road (above). The task of selecting a route and organizing work on the pioneer road fell to General William Hoge. In June 1942, he handed responsibility for the southern sector to Colonel James O'Connor while retaining command of the northern sector. Hoge was relieved of his command in August 1942.

Workers, occasionally reduced to using hand tools because of supply problems (below), pushed ahead on the preliminary work while others, like the 341st Engineers, Company F (above) erected timber bridges like this one over the Beatton River in British Columbia. The completion of the preliminary road did not signal the end of work. From the beginning, civilian contractors (right) working under the Public Roads Administration had begun the less glamourous task of reconstructing and resurfacing the highway.

Temporary pontoon bridges, like this one over the Donjek River in the Yukon (left) allowed work to proceed further along the highway while a more permanent structure (above left) was being erected. This temporary camp at the south end of Kluane Lake (below left) was one of many opened along the highway during the initial construction phase. Less than a year after the decision to proceed had been made, the Alaska Highway was open. Although much work remained to be done, this truck (above right) led the first convoy up the new road in November 1942. Highway engineers soon discovered that the road, built in extreme haste, was far from finished. Scenes like this (below), where run-off had swept away part of a steep grade, were only too familiar along the route.

Working conditions along the highway were less than ideal, as the construction companies were careful to point out (below). So many Americans came to Canada to work on the highway that there were concerns about an American "invasion," and signs such as "Camp Americanada" were commonplace.

Highway workers, most of whom came from the United States or northern Canada, found camp life in winter desolate and uncomfortable (above). Supply problems plagued construction work from the beginning. Despite the best efforts of army and civilian organizers to keep supplies moving, bottlenecks developed in such places as Skagway, Whitehorse, Edmonton and Fort St. John (right). The highway brought dramatic changes to the north, illustrated (below) in the odd mixture of army tents and the buildings of an old trading post and Indian village.

The Alaska Highway was officially opened by Canadian and American representatives at Soldier's Summit, near Kluane Lake in the Yukon, on 20 November 1942 (below). Despite public demands, though, the Alaska Highway was not immediately opened to civilian traffic at the end of the war. Tourists, however, clamoured for the opportunity to travel the highly-touted "Route of '42" from Mile "0" at Dawson Creek to Fairbanks, Alaska.

The wartime highway had not been completed to proper civilian standards. The Canadian Army, responsible for the highway from 1946 to 1964, and Public Works Canada, which took over the road in 1964, faced numerous maintenance problems. Floods and bridge damage were regular occurrences, particularly in 1974 and 1975 when large-scale flooding led to highway closures and costly repairs.

The Alaska Highway continues to be a major tourist route. This collection of sign posts at Watson Lake (above left) was started when a lonesome GI placed his hometown sign there in 1942. Now, room is made each year for more signs. This church in Beaver Creek (left) was built from a quonset hut originally brought from the United States for American soldiers. Whitehorse was transformed by the construction of the highway. In 1942 (inset below), the town was a seasonal transportation centre with only a few hundred residents. Today (below), Whitehorse is the capital of the Yukon Territory and a modern northern city of approximately 15,000 people.

The myth and mystique of the Alaska Highway lingers, drawing thousands of tourists north each year to drive along the famous road. The highway itself has been upgraded considerably, from the dusty, poorly-sited, and winding highway built during the war to a top quality civilian road.

SECTION 4:

The Postwar Highway

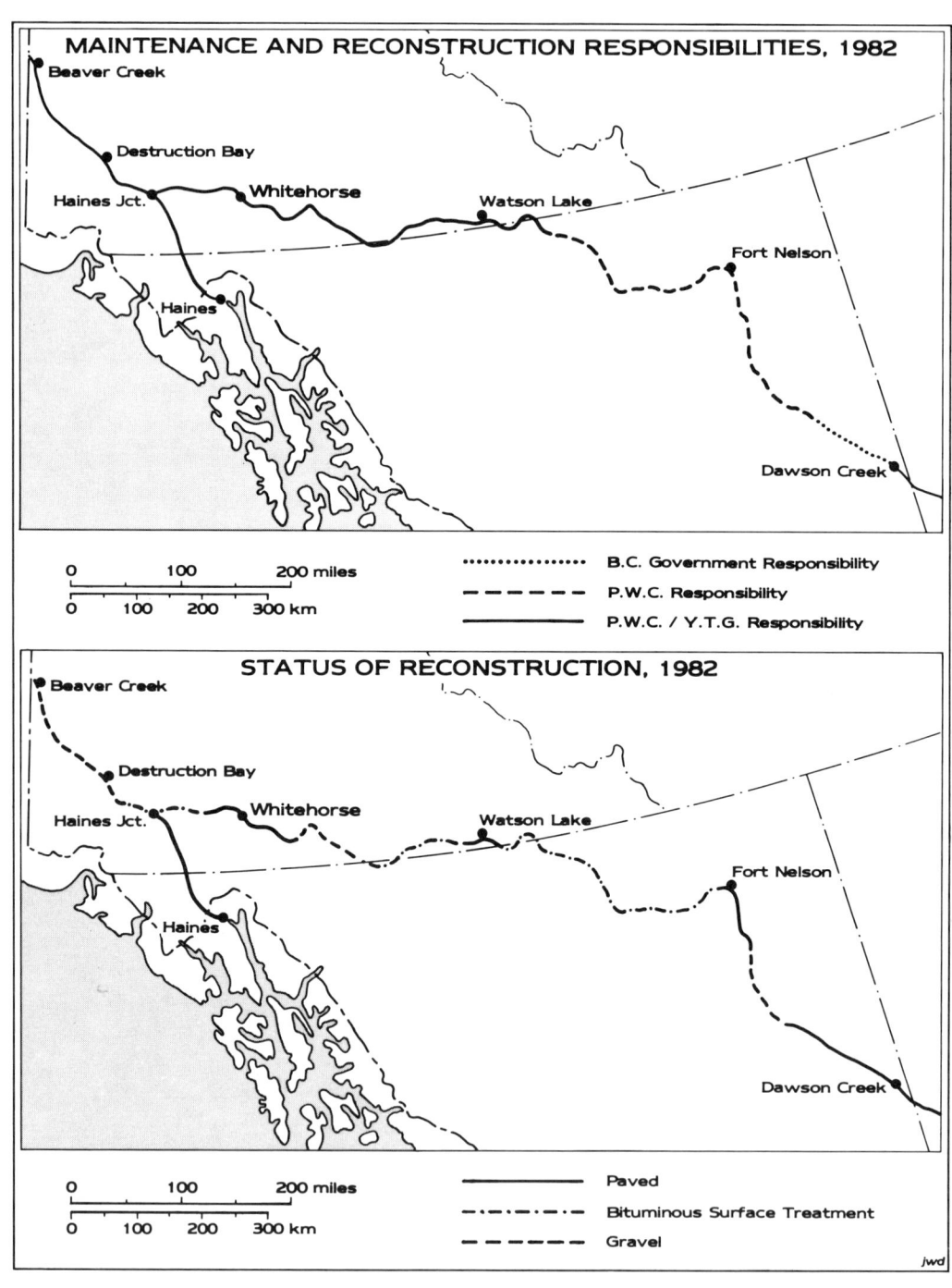

10

"Really a Defile Throughout Its Length": The Defence of the Alaska Highway in Peacetime

STEPHEN J. HARRIS

When Canada assumed responsibility for the Alaska Highway on 1 April 1946, control was passed to the Canadian army for reasons that had little to do with national security. Far from viewing the road as an important strategic supply route to the north or, more fancifully, as a potential invasion route south, the general staff was eager to take up this burden because it would permit the Royal Canadian Engineers to practice road and bridge building and maintenance at negligible cost to the army's disappointingly small share of the defence budget.[1] Even though the general staff actively sought out the task, it chose not to use the highway's potential military value as an argument justifying the army's takeover; instead, army headquarters contended only that soldiers could keep the highway in good repair more efficiently and for less money than any other government department. It was nevertheless conceded that it would be "in the interests of economy to utilize more and more civilian agencies" as the north country developed.[2]

Obviously convinced by this, the government approved the general staff's proposals with virtually no changes. The Alaska Highway would thus be a "military" road commanded by a brigadier, but the forces assigned to it would not constitute a defensive garrison nor have a well-defined operational role in wartime. Why should it have been otherwise? Despite evidence that the Russian brand of communism was inimical to western values and interests, the Soviet Union faced a massive job of reconstruction after the Second World War, and it was almost ludicrous to view it as a direct military threat in 1946. Moreover, Prime Minister Mackenzie King had already decided that if the United States and the U.S.S.R. became rivals, as some predicted they must, Canada would take care not to increase tensions between the two. Among other things, this meant avoiding a large military buildup in the north which the Russians could all too easily claim served American interests only. Finally, there was always the hope that the wartime grand alliance would survive and so obviate the need for defence preparations in the Arctic.[3]

Canada's vision was not shared by all. Having learned the lesson of Pearl Harbor, and somewhat more distrustful than Canada of the U.S.S.R.'s long-term aspirations, political and military leaders in Washington were vitally interested in maintaining "a long polar watch" after the Second World War, preferably with Canadian help. As Canada's chief of the general staff learned only a week after the Northwest Highway System came under his control, the United States still regarded the northern roads and adjacent airfields as defence facilities "of continuing importance"; to the Americans they were the foundations of continental security and the supply/reinforcement lifeline to Alaska.[4]

Other expressions of American concern soon followed. By the end of the year, the U.S. had asked for the construction of weather and radar stations as well as long-range navigation beacons on Canadian territory, regular overflights of the north, practically unhindered sailing in Arctic waters, and bomber bases in Newfoundland and Labrador. In addition, the Americans hoped to maintain a permanent garrison of up to five hundred men at the winter warfare research facility in Fort Churchill, Manitoba.[5]

Initiatives like these had been anticipated even before the end of the Second World War. Geographically, Canada was a buffer state between two of the world's great powers, and it was expected that the Americans would seek to co-operate with the Dominion in continental defence or to use Canadian territory themselves to protect the American heartland. It was also recognized, as Escott Reid of Canada's Department of External Affairs pointed out in 1944, that "a buffer state becomes a client state if it makes bilateral agreements with only one of its great neighbours."[6] Hence, Mackenzie King was disinclined to go too far in accommodating the United States in the immediate postwar period. But the American coin had two sides. Forgetting for the moment any consideration of Soviet intentions, the fact was, as Canada's post-hostilities planners pointed out, that the U.S.S.R. was "strategically in a position to present a serious threat to the Northwest." Moreover, given the American approach to North American defence in the war against Japan, these officials also believed that "failure on the part of Canada to undertake defence measures on a scale considered by the U.S. to be adequate, or to cooperate effectively with the U.S. in its defence, would probably lead to the infringement of Canadian sovereignty by the United States."[7] The Dominion was therefore forced to act earlier and more concretely to protect the north than she might otherwise have wished.

At first, this meant nothing more than participating in discussions about Arctic defence in the Permanent Joint Board on Defence (P.J.B.D.)[8] and in the Canada-U.S. joint Military Co-operation Committee (M.C.C.).[9] But these soon paved the way for more planning and preparation than had been foreseen in the winter of 1945-46. The touchstone document was the M.C.C.'s draft Canada-United States Basic Security Plan, presented to the P.J.B.D. on 5 June 1946 and forwarded to the Canadian government shortly thereafter. Although it gave unquestioned priority to the need for a comprehensive system of air defence for all of North America, it also specified that provisions should be made to defend northern Canada, Labrador, and Alaska against sea or airborne assault. Along with thorough mapping, charting, and air photography, and rigorous testing of equipment and supplies for winter warfare, these were to include "collection of strategic information necessary for military operations," and, most significant of all, "familiarization of appropriate personnel of the armed forces of both countries in military operations under Arctic conditions."[10]

By prior agreement, all P.J.B.D. and M.C.C. proposals were subject to review in Ottawa and Washington, and implementation of the joint defence plan was left to each government. As a result, Canada was not bound by the Basic Security Plan.[11] Nevertheless, the Canadian chiefs of staff and the cabinet had no quarrel with the basic premise of the plan so long as Canadian sovereignty was protected; hence their insistence that Canada take the lead or participate in all exercises and preparations on her soil.[12] The United States agreed, and in the end, one brigade group from the Canadian army was committed to the land defence of North America, with a similar force offered by the United States for the reinforcement of Alaska and the Yukon.

The role of the Alaska Highway in this scheme was crucial. Significantly, the army headquarters in Ottawa had actually begun its assessment of future defence requirements in the area before the M.C.C. had presented its draft plan to the P.J.B.D. The army had agreed that air attack was the paramount concern. However, even though the nearest Russian soil was one thousand miles from Dawson City, close to the extreme range limit of the Soviets' latest transport aircraft and far beyond that of their fighterbombers, the general staff believed that it could not discount the possibility of small-scale enemy raids or lodgements by up to one hundred men on Arctic weather stations, navigation sites, airfields, or the highway itself. These would not constitute an invasion, but only temporary incursions to pin down North American war potential and so divert attention away from Europe, or alternatively, to destroy air defence installations. At most, the enemy would be able to seize bases and facilities that might assist in pushing operations southward.

Still, there was little probability of such attacks because of dismal Arctic flying conditions and difficult land movement. The Soviets would be too lightly equipped, and the general staff doubted whether any lodgement could ever be resupplied or reinforced. None would have close air support unless the Americans had been driven completely out of Alaska and the R.C.A.F. and U.S.A.F. somehow prevented from intervening from the south — all extremely implausible.[13] The Cabinet Defence Committee nevertheless interpreted this assessment to mean that there was a requirement for "garrison forces of reasonable strength to [defend] coastal bases and installations," some of which were in the Arctic.[14]

A general staff officer who surveyed the Alaska Highway in August and September 1946 arrived at the same conclusion. Describing the road as "really a defile throughout its entire length" that could be easily closed by enemy forces of about one hundred men, Lieut.-Col. F. Le P. T. Clifford reasoned that any vital installations would have to be guarded from the outset, otherwise the army would face the long task of having to evict the enemy after it had settled in prepared positions.

Accordingly, Clifford recommended that garrisons strong enough to withstand "a determined and sustained attack" be established at Fort St. John, Fort Nelson, Watson Lake, and Whitehorse, while mobile forces trained and equipped for the job would "sally out and deal with any attempt to block the highway." Col. Clifford thought that the reserve army (or militia as it is known today) could provide the manpower, and he estimated that up to one division (15-20,000 men), about one-fifth of the reserve's planned mobilization strength, should be set aside for this task.[15]

Col. Clifford's report was not a statement of army policy. Indeed, it went far beyond the general staff's accepted appreciation of enemy forms and scales of attack, which did not anticipate that lodgement parties could undertake "determined" and "sustained" attacks. Clifford had nonetheless raised important questions. Given the political requirement to prepare against such lodgements, but mindful too of the very limited nature and the remoteness of threats of this kind, what was the most effective form of defence for the north?

The general staff's bias here was absolutely clear. At the broadest level, consensus held that the best defence would see the army fight as far away from Canada as possible. It followed therefore that there was little to say in favour of creating a large "home army." As far as northern defence was concerned, it was always understood that more than one lodgement could be attempted at any one time. It was thus illogical, if not dangerous, to deploy too large a force in any one region. The appropriate response, then, seemed to be the creation of a centrally located airborne or airportable "mobile counter-attacking force" of brigade size (about 5,000 men) which could eliminate enemy landing parties in short order, within forty-eight hours, and before they could construct strong defensive positions. It was clear that such a force would have to come from the regular army, and that it must be able to operate in smaller combat groups. But if Soviet capabilities increased, it was anticipated that an entire division might have to be earmarked for this role.[16]

Thus, the Mobile Striking Force (M.S.F.) concept was born. What remained was to work out the finer details of organization and equipment, especially as they related to winter warfare, and to fit the M.S.F. into the Canada-U.S. joint defence plan. This was well underway by mid-1947. After one false start, in which the mobile force seemed destined to reinforce army units "normally deployed for defence of principal bases,"[17] Chief of the General Staff Lieut.-Gen. Charles Foulkes presented the essence of the M.S.F. appendix to the joint Canada-United States Basic Security Plan to the Cabinet Defence Committee on 20 October 1947. According to this report, the mobile force would: "provide an immediate and rapid counter to enemy lodgements wherever effected"; it would not serve as a garrison force; and the number of units allocated to the static defence of vital points throughout the Dominion would be kept to an absolute minimum.[18] Most of these locations would, in fact, be guarded by the Royal Canadian Mounted Police, with only a handful of installations on the Atlantic and Pacific coasts having any soldiers assigned to them.

As other writers have remarked, the Mobile Striking Force never lived up to the expectations raised by Minister of National Defence Brooke Claxton when he announced its formation. Indeed, for the next few years, the lack of progress in bringing the government's policy to fruition was attacked strenuously by the opposition during the debates on army estimates.[19] Much of the criticism was well-founded. The units of the mobile force rarely trained together, conversion of the infantry battalions to airborne status proceeded at an apparently leisurely pace, and the development of specialized arctic equipment was slow. The main reason for this, however, which was never fully understood at the time, was that the M.S.F. units were not committed only to the remote prospect of an attack in the north. The units were also expected to practice conventional warfare for the much more likely contingency of a European conflict where they would see action as part of the Active Force Brigade Group. Preparation for this role dominated the training syllabus. Thus, almost from the beginning, there was a lack of clarity about when the M.S.F. would be employed at home and how seriously it should take this task. Such "double-hatting" left the mobile force somewhat formless, while the decision not to form a separate headquarters and staff to study and work out standard procedures for airborne operations in Canada meant that there was minimal development of doctrine. Indeed, it was never entirely clear whether plans should be based on platoon, company, battalion, or brigade-sized actions.[20]

The winter warfare exercises held from 1946 on confirmed many of the shortcomings of the Mobile Striking Force's original organization. The lack of an oversnow vehicle robbed the M.S.F. of much vital mobility, while the R.C.A.F.'s shortage of transport aircraft placed severe limitations on the number of men who could be landed at any one time. In addition, many of these exercises indicated that airborne assaults would require artillery or heavy mortar support to achieve the 4:1 ratio of attack to defence required under arctic conditions, but there were no gunners in the mobile force.[21]

The training exercises conducted on the Alaska Highway went even further to raise doubts about the validity of the original M.S.F. concept of employing lightly-armed, quick-reaction units in the Arctic. Exercise North, a basic route reconnaissance carried out in August and September 1946, suggested that the defence of the highway could be guaranteed only by strong patrols operating from firm bases at Whitehorse, Fort St. John, and Fort Nelson, a deployment of forces contrary to the M.S.F. plan.[22] Exercise Adonis, conducted at army headquarters in 1949, tested the concept against a two-hundred-man lodgement at Port Radium and found that the force would probably need mountain howitzers, recoilless guns, and anti-aircraft artillery, all of which were beyond the planned scale of issue.[23] Exercise Eagle, which involved a parachute assault by the Princess Patricia's Canadian Light Infantry on an enemy-held Fort St. John in August 1949, confirmed this view.[24] There was substantial evidence, therefore, that the defence of the northern highway might be better conducted in a more conventional fashion, especially if a major enemy move south was likely to occur only in conjunction with an attack on Alaska, in which case strong American forces would surely intervene.

This was the scenario for Sweetbriar, possibly the most famous of all northern exercises on account of the large number of Canadian and American troops involved. Here the bulk of the Mobile Striking Force taking part was employed as traditional infantry, advancing up the highway ahead of a larger U.S. force, with only the Princess Patricia's Canadian Light infantry company engaged in a parachute assault to disrupt the opponent's lines of communication.[25] Though the exercise was rigidly controlled, the task of dislodging the enemy proved to be quite difficult and certainly beyond the capabilities of the Mobile Striking Force alone. It appeared that Col. Clifford was correct in thinking that both strong garrisons and mobile forces would be required.

The General Officer Commanding (G.O.C.), Western Command, Maj.-Gen. M.H.S. Penhale, who would direct any battle on the Alaska Highway, certainly agreed with Clifford. Anticipating that the enemy would put in a company or battalion level attack on Whitehorse, Gen. Penhale estimated that he would need an infantry battalion, a tank squadron, field artillery, and anti-aircraft guns ready at thirty minutes' notice to defend the town. This would be much too quick for the Mobile Striking Force, whether or not it had artillery, if the north were attacked in the first few hours of a war that began without any forewarning.[26]

Western Command's appreciation of the threat went well beyond the general staff's understanding of Soviet capabilities, particularly as it related to Russian air power, and so was eventually rejected.[27] "It would be impossible and certainly unwise," explained the director of military operations and plans, "to anticipate the probable scales of attack to the extent of garrisoning [the north] in any strength."[28] The commander-designate of the Active Force Brigade Group, Brig. George Kitching, agreed wholeheartedly. Though he admitted that the maintenance of northern garrisons "might give us a more effective form of defence," he nevertheless argued that they were "unnecessary given the form and scales of attack" expected and, in any event, "would be too costly in both peace and war and would severely restrict our contributions to any allied effort" outside North America.[29] The lessons from Sweetbriar and the other exercises were not entirely ignored, however, as the army planners decided to train engineer and artillery sub-units for airborne operations and to establish a permanent Mobile Striking Force headquarters to develop specific plans of operations, air support, and aerial resupply that would permit the mobile force to participate in the more intensive combat likely to occur on the Alaska Highway.

All this became irrelevant on 12 April 1950. On that date, the mobile force was removed from the defence of the Northwest Highway System, and responsibility for the task was delegated to the General Officer Commanding, Western Command, the very officer who had recently called for the establishment of garrisons in the north.[30] The reasons for this dramatic shift in policy are not entirely clear, but a number of considerations seem to have played a part. The logic of Sweetbriar still left lingering doubts about the efficacy of employing the Mobile Striking Force to defend the highway; the possibility that the airborne regiments might already be embroiled elsewhere before the enemy began his move south down the road system suggested that these units might not be available anyway. In addition, now that the Russians had both the atomic bomb and the means of delivering it on targets in central North America, a good case could be made that they would not waste their own highly trained airborne forces in the Canadian Arctic in the event of a general war. Not only could these troops probably be used to better effect somewhere else — in Europe, for example — but they would have less shock value in North America than the detonation of one nuclear device. Finally, although Canada had not yet committed herself to maintaining a standing army in Europe as part of her NATO contribution, the very existence of the

North Atlantic Treaty Organization suggested that land forces could be deployed overseas. Since this would require a tightening up of commitments at home, particularly for the regular force, withdrawing the Mobile Striking Force from the most remote of all contingencies to be faced made sense.

As things turned out, the expansion of the regular army following the outbreak of the Korean War gave the army enough men to meet all its obligations at home and overseas, despite the subsequent decision to station troops in Europe. Nevertheless, army headquarters was not persuaded to once again allocate the M.S.F. to the defence of the Alaska Highway. Western Command was to plan accordingly, making optimum use of the Canadian Rangers and reserve units at its disposal.[31]

Much time, effort, and confusion could have been saved had this happened, but the G.O.C. in Edmonton remained unconvinced that the task facing him could be undertaken with the conventional forces at hand. Thus, although Gen. Penhale asked permission to earmark one infantry battalion and two regular armoured car squadrons for the defence of Whitehorse and the highway, he also pressed Headquarters to reconsider its stand on the employment of the mobile force. Indeed, the picture he saw was so bleak that he was certain that he would have to call on the M.S.F. to reinforce almost any operation he might undertake.[32]

The authorities in Ottawa refused this last request, complaining that Gen. Penhale had failed to learn the appropriate lesson from Sweetbriar. He was therefore instructed to co-ordinate his plans with those of the American commander in Alaska, presumably to prove to him that sufficient allied forces would be available in the event of an emergency.[33]

This reply did not sit well with Gen. Penhale's successor as G.O.C., Western Command, Maj.-Gen. Chris Vokes. Believing that Whitehorse was likely to be attacked on the first day of war, which itself was likely to begin without warning, Vokes argued that the battle would be over long before the militia had completed its call-out. The enemy would, as a result, achieve its aim with scarcely any losses: North American attention would be diverted from Europe, and in the process the Russians would have secured first-class facilities for continuing their attack southward. The G.O.C. therefore asked for a regular army battalion to be sent to Whitehorse by air as soon as war broke out, and earlier if advance warning were given, where it would remain until the reserve army was ready to take to the field some six months later.[34]

It is a measure of the army headquarters' assessment of the threat to the Yukon that the director of military operations and plans could confirm Gen. Vokes's assessment of when the militia would be fit to fight and still recommend against giving him the Princess Patricia's Canadian Light Infantry. Not only would such a course be a waste of that unit's "airborne and arctic skills," he argued, but it would also unhinge the entire Mobile Striking Force by removing one-third of its combat strength. A small concession was nonetheless possible. Western Command was to be offered a battalion from 25 Canadian Infantry Brigade Replacement Group, the regular army training formation for Canada's Korean force, to augment the units on hand, but these troops would not necessarily be deployed in Whitehorse before hostilities commenced.[35]

Still unhappy, Gen. Vokes continued to press his case, this time pointing out that the United States would undoubtedly take over Whitehorse if Canada failed to respond in a satisfactory manner.[36] Headquarters was again unmoved. Citing higher priorities for the M.S.F., the Deputy Chief of the General Staff Brig. T. G. Gibson worried that acceding to Vokes's wishes would be the " 'thin edge of the wedge' in the development of a 'home army' " such as existed in the Second World War. "We must not drift into a larger commitment [in Canada]," he continued, by creating "isolated precedent. Whitehorse should be considered in company with other localities which may require protection so that we can visualize the whole picture."[37] The chief of the general staff, Lieut.-Gen. Guy Simonds, agreed.[38]

The defence of the Alaska Highway had thus developed into a classic confrontation between the man on the spot, preoccupied with his immediate limited task, and a higher headquarters burdened by farreaching responsibilities. As in most cases, higher authority won out. The G.O.C., Western Command would be sure of having his militia infantry battalion, four additional companies to guard specific vital points, two armoured car squadrons, and the training battalion from the replacement group. But he would not be given any elements of the Mobile Striking Force.

By the end of 1952, even this limited commitment had been reduced. With the formation of 1 Canadian Infantry Division and the conversion of the Lord Strathcona's Horse to a Centurion tank regiment — all for deployment to Europe in the event of war — Vokes lost his armoured car squadron and the infantry battalion from 25 Canadian Infantry Brigade Replacement Group, now part of the division. Furthermore, the consolidation of armoured car holdings throughout Canada left him with only six of these vehicles for the reconnaissance units in Western Command.[39] The G.O.C. was understandably bitter, and even the deputy chief of the general staff at headquarters sympathized with his plight. Accepting Western Command's contention that a "mobilizing [militia] unit" would "not do" because it could not "dominate the Yukon, using Whitehorse as the 'fortress area,' " Brig. Gibson advised the chief of general staff that "the only sound course" was to "earmark" one battalion of the Mobile Striking Force for the task. This was now practical, he added, because the R.C.A.F.'s C119 Flying Boxcars could deliver the unit to Whitehorse at an early stage in the alert and still lift them out for airborne operations elsewhere if that became necessary.[40] The deputy chief of the general staff agreed, but Gen. Simonds did not. As a result, Vokes was authorized only to localize a militia sub-unit in Whitehorse for the town's immediate defence; apart from this, he would have one other reserve battalion to move in when it was ready.[41]

The security of the Alaska Highway was now a militia responsibility entirely, and it remained so for six years. In 1959, however, the reserves were withdrawn from the active defence of Canada and turned over to the task of civilian survival operations after a nuclear attack.[42] This left the regular army as the only organized military force available for deployment to the north. Yet the same set of circumstances that had altered the militia's role provided little justification for planning to use the permanent force in the context of arctic defence. American capabilities to reinforce Alaska by air were improving, thereby decreasing the strategic importance of the northern highways, while the advent of the missile age had reduced the significance of many of the defence installations in the region to the point where there was no real reason for the Soviets to attack them. Nevertheless, the main reason for this shift in policy away from active defence of the north was the simple fact that the potential shock value and threat of either a Russian lodgement or of a Soviet march down the Northwest Highway System had dwindled to almost nothing in comparison with all-out nuclear attack. Hence, the army "abandoned the area as a potential operational theatre," going so far as to close its arctic warfare research facility at Churchill.[43] Then, in 1964, the army happily gave up its responsibility to maintain the Alaska Highway.

Things have changed somewhat over the past decade. The far north has again become an area of concern, and the protection of Canadian sovereignty in the region is once more a problem. Even though the "threat" is generally defined in economic or environmental terms these days, it has led to a significant resurgence of military activity in the north. Northern Region Headquarters has been established in Yellowknife; Air Command flies regular arctic surveillance patrols; the Canadian Rangers organization has been revitalized; engineers are again building roads and bridges; and Mobile Command (the army in the unified armed forces) has reopened Churchill and is conducting a comprehensive series of winter training exercises, in part, admittedly, because of Canada's commitment to reinforce Norway.[44]

All this has reawakened interest in the theoretical problems relating to the defence of Canada's Arctic frontier, and many of the old strategic and tactical concepts have reemerged in the contemporary literature. For example, articles in recent issues of the *Canadian Defence Quarterly* have called for both "a small, highly mobile quick reaction military unit which can not only 'show the flag' but also use coercive force if required,"[45] and for "the establishment of a major base north of the arctic circle" that would "facilitate northern operations and defence of our arctic holdings" against small enemy lodgements.[46] For a time, too, it seemed that there was a modern, up-to-date version of the Mobile Striking Force committed to arctic defence in the Canadian Airborne Regiment based at Edmonton. But when that unit moved to Ottawa in the late 1970's, Chief of Defence Staff Gen. Jacques Dextrase made it very clear that the regiment's change of station would leave no gap in the northwest: the security of the region was primarily the job of 1 Combat Group (now 1 Canadian Infantry Brigade Group), based in Calgary, which would conduct conventional operations if called upon to defend the highway.[47]

From this one could deduce that planning today is premised on a replay of the Sweetbriar scenario. In the event of a lodgement or a more concerted attack, allied forces would move north by road, the Canadians in the lead, with the Special Service Force perhaps intervening on the enemy's flanks or in his rear. That, however, takes us into the realm of conjecture and speculation.

Such uncertainty is inherent in all military planning and in all strategic analysis. It is always possible for soldiers (or, for that matter, politicians and the public at large) to manufacture threats out of extreme enemy capabilities and then rationalize a response to them; hence the fear of and preparations to meet enemy lodgements and incursions in the north. In the period under review, it was almost always possible for the Soviets to land troops in the Canadian Arctic, but only if they were willing to sacrifice the men sent on such a mission. In the early years, Soviet air support would have been non-existent, giving the Allies unquestioned air superiority, so there would be no opportunity for the Russians to withdraw the force, and there was always the chance that the American response would be massive nuclear retaliation, even if by miscalculation. Why the Soviets would wish to risk all this for minimal gains in the Canadian north was a good question.

All these factors had to be taken into account in assessing Soviet intentions, the most difficult aspect of planning. What would the enemy risk? What were its vital interests, its real aims? And what other, more important, capabilities would be jeopardized if it were to become involved in the Canadian north? Although plans were developed to meet this contingency, it should be noted that in Ottawa, at least, they were predicated on the assumption that the threat was remote, if not absurd: the Russians were not likely to take action against the Canadian north.

The reaction of the soldiers on the spot was noticeably different, even though they based their appreciations on intelligence supplied by army headquarters. Why this was so is a complex problem related to the psychology of command. Two explanations may be put forward. The first is that soldiers, like most people, seem to be easily seduced into exaggerating the importance of their task and the difficulties involved in accomplishing it. The second is that commanders need operational forces to justify their existence. In the end, perhaps these two patterns of behaviour explain why the defence of the Alaska Highway became a major planning conundrum.

Notes

1. Funds for the maintenance of the Northwest Highway System would be provided from a separate parliamentary vote, while the 653 personnel required to keep the roads in good repair would not be charged against the manpower ceiling of about 15,000 men placed on the postwar regular army. See NDHQ Circular Leter No. 2, 1946, 26 January 1946, D HIST. 112.21009 (D154).
2. See general staff memorandum, "Maintenance of Alaska Highway by Royal Canadian Engineers," 3 October 1945, in D HIST 314.009 (D17), vol. 3, file HQS 3487-2, and the plan submitted by the deputy quartermaster general (A), 28 November 1945, D HIST, 112.3M2 (D264).
3. For a general discussion of Canadian postwar planning, see James Eayrs, *In Defence of Canada 3: Peacemaking and Deterrence* (Toronto, 1972), pp. 75-167.
4. Director of military operations and plans (Col. John Henry Jenkins) to chief of the general staff, 9 April 1946, D HIST, 112.21009 (D154).
5. See Donald M. Page, comp., *Documents on Canadian External Relations 12:* (Ottawa, 1977), pp. 1617-1712, passim.
6. Quoted in R. J. Diubaldo and S. J. Sheinberg, *A Study of Canadian-American Defence Policy (1945-1975): Northern Issues and Strategic Resources,* ORAE extra-mural paper no. 6: (Ottawa, 1978), pp. 17-18.
7. Ibid., p. 18. See also the Post-Hostilities Planning Committee report on Canada-U.S. defence relations dated 23 January 1945, in Eayrs, *In Defence of Canada,* document 1.
8. Created as a result of the Ogdensburg Agreement of 1940, the P.J.B.D. was a joint Canada-U.S., civilian-military body offering advice to the two governments and their service chiefs, but it had no executive power.
9. Created after the Second World War, the Military Co-operation Committee was a purely military body offering advice to the Canadian and American chiefs of staff, but it too had no executive authority.
10. See Page, *Documents on Canadian External Relations,* document 957: Joint Canadian-United States Basic Security Plan, 5 June 1946, 1623ff.
11. See, for example, the memorandum by the assistant under secretary of state for external affairs, 28 June 1946, ibid., document 961, 1632ff.
12. Chiefs of Staff Committee memorandum to Cabinet Defence Committee, 15 July 1946, ibid., document 964, 1638ff.
13. See the general staff study, "Capabilities and limitations of aircraft in transpolar airborne and air transported operations," 15 May 1946, and deputy chief of the general staff (DCGS) (A) to chief of the general staff (CGS), 18 May 1946, in D HIST 112.3M2 (D232). See also CGS comments on joint appreciation plan, June 1946, in D HIST, 112.3M2 (D325).
14. Extracts of Cabinet Defence Committee meeting, 9 July 1946, sent to DCGS (A), D HIST, 112.3M2 (D125).
15. See Col. Clifford's "Report on visit to Northwest Highway System, 25 August — 9 September 1946," dated 16 September 1946, D HIST, 112.3M2 (D260).
16. "Interim report, Sub-Committee on Army/Air Mobile Striking Force," 21 December 1946, D HIST, 112.3M2 (D138).
17. See Basic Security Plan Canada-United States, appendix: Army/Air Mobile Striking Force, 6 May 1947, revised 27 June 1947, ibid.
18. See Director of Military Operations and Plans (DMO&P), "Operational requirements of airborne forces for the defence of Canada," 29 November 1948, quoting Chiefs of Staff Committee to Cabinet Defence Committee, 20 October 1947, D HIST, 112.3M2 (D369).
19. See Eayrs, *In Defence of Canada 3,* 98ff.
20. This was in part because forms and scales of attack were not always agreed upon, but there was also no consensus about airborne doctrine. See, for example, DMO&P to Brigadier, General Staff (BGS), "Composition of the Mobile Striking Force for the Defence of Canada," 3 December 1948, and DMO&P appreciation of Mobile Striking

Force, 14 May 1949, in D HIST, 112.3M2 (D138); 11th Meeting, Army Plans Committee, 21 October 1948, D HIST, 112.3M2 (D358); and DMO&P memorandum of operational requirements of airborne forces for the defence of Canada, 29 November 1948, D HIST, 112.3M2 (D369).
21. General lessons learned from winter and summer northern exercises, 1945-52, D HIST, 400.033 (D3).
22. See report of Exercise North, 14 September 1946, D HIST, 171.009 (D9).
23. See discussion of Problem 4, Exercise Adonis: "Is the present organization of the Mobile Force suited for the conduct of operations against 200 enemy at Port Radium, 15-35 enemy at weather stations." Discussion was led by Col. Pangman. D HIST. 1212.3M2 (D372).
24. See GOC's preliminary report, Exercise Eagle, sent to Vice Chief of the General Staff (VGCS), 20 August 1949, D HIST, 169.009 (D187), and General Staff, Western Command, outline, 3 March 1949, D HIST, 169.009 (D186).
25. See reports on Exercise Sweetbriar in D HIST, 327.009 (D211), and the final report prepared by the GOC, Western Command, May 1950, in D HIST, 491.033 (D1).
26. See "Appreciation of the situation by Commander 15 Infantry Brigade and GSO 1, Western Command, for the point of view of the GOC, Western Command," 27 August 1948, D HIST, 327.009 (D94).
27. The Soviets still had no fighterbombers capable of flying from the U.S.S.R. to the highway unless airfields had already been secured in Alaska. See the study entitled "For 'The Mobile Striking Force,'" dated March 1950, in D HIST 112.3M2 (D400) which estimated that the TU4 Russian transport might be able to penetrate deep into North America in 1951, but which confirmed that at present airborne operations would be limited to areas west of Fairbanks, Alaska.
28. See the DMO&P's appreciation on the Mobile Striking force, 14 May 1949, D HIST, 112.3M2 (D369).
29. Brig. George Kitching to Maj. K. L. Campbell, staff officer with Active Force Brigade Group, 28 November 1949, D HIST, 112.3M2 (D400).
30. Brigadier General Staff (Plans) (Brig. T. G. Gibson) to Active Force Brigade Group: Employment of the Mobile Striking Force, Part I, 12 April 1950, D HIST, 112.3M2 (D401).
31. The Canadian Rangers were a northern counterpart to the coast-watching organization of the Second World War. Part of the reserve army, these units were located in various northern communities and were aimed at using indigenous peoples and their expertise in the north to provide an early warning network, guides for army operations, and, as a last resort, to supplement the fighting power of more conventional formations.
32. See Western Command's "Appreciation of the defence of the Northwest Highway System and the Yukon," November 1950, and covering letter to BGS Plans, 30 November 1950, D HIST, 112.3M2.009 (D267).
33. See minutes on above, and BGS to DMO&P, and Acting Chief of the General Staff (Maj.-Gen. H. A. Sparling), to GOC, Western Command, 20 December 1950, ibid.
34. GOC Western Command to BGS Plans, 28 March 1951, ibid.
35. DMO&P to Director of Staff Duties (DSD), 5 May 1951, and DMO&P to BGS (Plans), 11 April 1951, ibid.
36. GOC Western Command to CGS, 26 April 1951, ibid.
37. CGS to GOC, Western Command, 22 May 1951 and DCGS to DMO&P, 17 January 1952, ibid.
38. CGS to GOC Western Command, 7 March 1952, ibid.
39. MO(2) (Subordinate staff officer in Directorate of Military Operations) to DMO&P, 23 October 1952, and DMO&P to DCGS, 12 May 1953, ibid.
40. DCGS (Brig. T. G. Gibson) to VCS (Maj.-Gen. H. A. Sparling), 11 June 1953, ibid.
41. Gibson to Sparling, 16 June 1953, ibid.
42. See *Defence 1959* (Ottawa, 1959), 11. All equipment not required for survival operations was to be withdrawn from the militia.

43. Maj. Kenneth Charles Eayre, "Custos borealis: the military in the Canadian North," unpublished Ph.D. thesis, King's College, University of London, 1981, p. 180.
44. See *Defence in the 70's* (Ottawa, 1971), passim.
45. Col. W. N. Russell, "Airborne or heliborne?" *Canadian Defence Quarterly,* 7,3 (Winter, 1977-78): 39.
46. Maj. L. Bowen, "Winter Warfare: Are We Prepared?" *Canadian Defence Quarterly* 9,1 (Summer, 1979): 42. Floyd Low, "Canadian airborne forces, 1942-1978," unpublished B.A. graduating essay, University of Victoria, 1978, p. 67.

11

The Civilian Highway: Public Works Canada and the Alaska Highway, 1964-83

KENNETH COATES

Under the terms of the British North America Act, responsibility for highway construction and maintenance rests with provincial governments. For reasons of short-term necessity or long-term design, however, the federal government entered the highways field on a number of occasions and assisted with the development of the Canadian transportation infrastructure. Of the various programmes involving federal participation, few share the profile of the Alaska Highway. This route, built in 1942-43 to provide military access to Alaska, was handed over to the Canadian authorities in 1946. The Department of National Defence (D.N.D.) assumed responsibility for what was then primarily a military access route. The D.N.D. soon appealed to have the government transfer control of the road to a different department. Almost twenty years were to pass before the long-sought-after transfer took place, with Public Works Canada assuming responsibility for the highway on 1 April 1964.

Federal involvement in highway construction and maintenance has traditionally concentrated on providing access to frontier areas of known resource potential. Undertakings such as the Department of Energy, Mines and Resources' Mine Access Roads Program (a cost-shared arrangement with the provinces) and the more renowned Roads to Resources Program, along with the Department of Indian Affairs and Northern Development's Northern Roads programme, were clearly designed to stimulate industrial activity in otherwise inaccessible areas. On an even grander scale, the construction of the TransCanada Highway, a joint federal-provincial project, was to provide a single highway link from coast to coast. Public Works was actively involved in the entire twenty-one year construction period of this, the most significant federal incursion into the field of highway construction.[1] Before Public Works's takeover of the Alaska Highway in 1964, the federal government had considerable experience across the country in highway construction and, most importantly, had repeatedly indicated a willingness to participate in highway programmes deemed to be of "national interest."

While the Alaska Highway was still being administered by D.N.D., there were indications that the route was serving a purpose far beyond that originally intended. Civilian traffic increased rapidly between 1946 and 1964 and a number of industrial and service businesses opened up to take advantage of the opportunities provided by the highway. Conflicting government jurisdictions, however, stood in the way of any quick or logical reassignment of control of the route to a non-federal authority. It was clear that many people expected that the national government would not only maintain the Alaska Highway but would also answer ever-increasing demands for the reconstruction and paving of the road.

When the decision was made in 1963-64 to transfer responsibility for the Alaska Highway from D.N.D. to Public Works, the latter department was able to call upon a lengthy, if not intensive, association with northern transportation. Beginning in 1942-43, Public Works was responsible for assessing bridge plans and issuing appropriate permits during the Alaska Highway construction phase and was actively involved in highway construction in the northwest. When the Conservative administration of Prime Minister John G. Diefenbaker introduced its highly touted Roads to Resources Program in 1958, Public Works was once again called upon, this time to provide the engineering services during the construction of a number of northern access routes.[2]

A more direct association with the Alaska Highway actually began several years before the Roads to Resources Program. With the war, and the urgent need for the road, over, D.N.D. found itself in control of a highway of little strategic importance. With the route now opened to public traffic, pressure mounted to have the road paved, or at least reconstructed, a task D.N.D. felt exceeded its mandate.[3] Public Works assigned an investigative team in the late summer of 1954 to assess the need to rebuild the highway and the necessity of transferring responsibility within the government. The federal cabinet had agreed in principle earlier that same year that Public Works should take over maintenance duties; the team's main duty was to develop an orderly plan for the transfer. Even though their studies demonstrated that a civilian agency, paying market wages for staff, would incur significantly higher costs than had D.N.D., the team nonetheless agreed that Public Works should assume administrative responsibility for the highway. One note of hesitation was sounded. The investigators pointed out that at least one year's lead time was required before the transfer could be affected, during which time Public Works personnel would be required to work together with the Northwest Highway System management to ensure an orderly passage of control.[4]

The recommendations were not acted upon, however, and D.N.D. reluctantly retained responsibility for the Alaska Highway. But the 1954 inquiry did not end discussion of a transfer, as questions continued to be raised about the possibility of Public Works assuming control of the highway.[5] Pressure on the federal government to commence reconstruction and paving increased with each passing year. The Department of National Defence was hardly enthusiastic about undertaking a major redevelopment programme, limiting itself instead to maintenance, resurfacing, bridge replacements and renovation of drainage systems. As civilian traffic continued to increase, particularly along the southern sections, interest in redevelopment picked up. Members of Parliament for Cariboo and the Yukon continued to raise the issue in the House of Commons, arguing that paving be given top priority.[6] The government responded in part, proceeding in 1958 with the realignment and paving of the heavily travelled segment of the highway between Fort St. John and Dawson Creek.[7] That year, the Diefenbaker government implemented the Roads to Resources Program, and northerners took it as a sign that highway construction in their area had been given some measure of priority. At the same time, there were signs that the American government was considering a cost-sharing arrangement whereby monies required for reconstruction and paving would be provided by both countries.[8]

Public demands for paving received a major boost with the release of a report prepared by the Batelle Memorial Institution in 1961. The Batelle study was a major examination of northwest North America, focusing primarily on Alaska, and offering a series of recommendations designed to stimulate economic and demographic growth in what was viewed as America's "last pioneering frontier." One suggestion in particular caught the northern public's attention: pave the Alaska Highway! The Batelle report argued that the estimated cost of improvements, $102.3 million, would be more than offset by a subsequent increase in tourist traffic and by improved access to resources. Prepared for the Alaska International Rail and Highway Commission, the report did not represent official government policy. It was, however, the first sophisticated study of the connection between transportation and economic development in the northwest and hence carried considerable weight.[9] Supported by the Batelle study, proponents of paving the Alaska Highway intensified their lobbying efforts. Over the next three years, numerous representations from politicians, business groups, and private citizens reached federal officials, requesting that the Canadian government proceed immediately with reconstruction and blacktopping.[10]

It was in the midst of this heated political debate that federal authorities decided to proceed with the oft-discussed transfer of responsibility for the Alaska Highway. Encouraged by the Public Works report of 1954, D.N.D. had been disappointed when the transfer was postponed. In 1959, yet another attempt was made to free the army of its duties in the area, but that also failed.[11] When the Royal Commission on Government Reorganization recommended that maintenance and redevelopment of the highway be placed in part with the private sector through the use of government supervised contracts, the minister of defence tried once again. On this occasion the suggestion was accepted, and on 25 October 1963, the Honourable Paul Hellyer, minister of national defence, rose in the House of Commons to give public notice that the Department of Public Works (as it was then called) was to assume control of the Alaska Highway as of 1 April 1964.[12] Negotiations were quickly concluded between D.N.D. and Public Works concerning the transfer. Public Works agreed to accept all civilian personnel and to take control of all maintenance operations and equipment.[13] Importantly, the government also decided that Public Works would attempt to pass on maintenance duties to the appropriate territorial or provincial jurisdiction as soon as possible. For the Yukon section, the department would retain responsibility for finance, design and construction.[14]

From the date of transfer, Public Works viewed its maintenance function on the highway as only temporary. In the end, the federal department retained control of maintenance operations in the Yukon sector until 1972, despite repeated attempts from 1964 on to secure an earlier transfer. Changes in territorial administration, and problems ranging from wage differentials between federal and territorial civil services to equipment breakdown conspired to retard negotiations. The proposed transfer, initially slated to coincide with Public Works's takeover, was postponed until 1967, called off at that date, and not accomplished until 1972.[15] The department had intended to avoid responsibility for routine highway maintenance at the start but, through force of circumstances, retained that task for eight years. While under Public Works control, the maintenance infrastructure was significantly renovated. Maintenance camps were modernized, equipment upgraded, and the number of employees engaged in highway upkeep reduced.

Both the 1964 and 1972 transfers went smoothly, somewhat surprisingly given the possibility for conflict and dissension attending major departmental reorganizations. Public Works, as noted, accepted all civilian employees attached to the highway operations of D.N.D. and could also call on any military personnel required to assist in the transfer.[16] Similarly, in 1972, the Yukon territorial government agreed to make positions available for most persons wishing to remain in the Yukon. The Yukon government agreed further that terms and conditions of employment for individual employees would be comparable and that they would retain service benefits after the handover. While most of the employees went willingly, not all accepted positions with the Yukon government. Public Works retained a limited number of employees and attempted to locate positions for those wishing to stay with the federal government. The few remaining individuals either retired or were declared surplus and laid off.[17]

Maintaining the B.C. section of the highway required a separate set of negotiations and procedures. Shortly after the first fifty miles of the highway were paved, and while the highway was still in D.N.D. hands, the federal and provincial governments negotiated the transfer of that segment of road to the province. On 26 January 1961, the federal authorities confirmed the transfer of the first eighty-four miles of the highway, with a provision that the section would be paved before the transfer became effective.[18] After assuming control from the army in 1964, Public Works called for tenders for a contract to maintain miles 84 to 300 of the highway. In August 1965, a three-year contract for highway upkeep was started, and on 1 April 1967, a similar arrangement was in place for miles 300 to 496. The final section, mile 496 to the B.C./Yukon border (mile 626.6), remained under direct Public Works supervision until a third contract was awarded in 1968.[19] In this manner, Public Works was able to provide for adequate highway maintenance while restricting its direct role to planning and the supervision of contracts.

By 1972, Public Works had partially accomplished its stated goal of delegating maintenance responsibility to regional governments. Before the 1964 takeover, the province of British Columbia had assumed responsibility for the first 84 miles of the highway. Attempts to pass total control of the B.C. section to the provincial department of highways, however, were unsuccessful. In what was clearly a second-best alternative, maintenance of the remainder was placed in private hands, with Public Works retaining only a limited staff on site to supervise the work. Similarly, the 1972 agreement with the Yukon government meant that the federal government, through Public Works, retained financial and supervisory responsibility for the Yukon section of the Alaska Highway, but left the routine maintenance of the road with the territorial authorities. The department's remaining responsibility for the highway included the important tasks of financing, roadway design and construction. Indeed, it was the prospect of reconstruction and the affiliated debate over paving that has served as the focus for Public Works's association with the Alaska Highway from 1964 to the present.

The public discussion that had followed the publication of the Batelle report in 1961 never subsided, and in the years after the Public Works takeover, calls for paving and reconstruction increased in frequency and intensity. The fact that Public Works, a branch of government associated specifically with federally funded construction, was now in control of the highway augured well for the possibility of meaningful action. The federal government's initial response was to call for a study of the feasibility and necessity of highway redevelopment.[20] Tied closely to this was the ever present possibility of a U.S.-Canada agreement to pave the highway as a joint venture, a proposal that stimulated no end of political debate on both sides of the border and an endless run of speculation and false hopes.[21] At one point, technical meetings between American and Canadian highway officials were held, but both sides agreed that a cost-sharing programme could not be justified. The possibility of a unified paving effort faded.[22]

Anxious to resolve the issue of redevelopment and, equally important, to provide a study of its own on the costs and benefits of paving the highway, the federal government proceeded in 1964 with a major economic analysis of proposed improvements. The Stanford Research Institute was commissioned to provide the report, which was submitted in 1966.[23] The final product lacked the scope of the Batelle report, primarily because of the limited time allocated for the study, a restraint which forced the researchers to rely on previously generated projections of economic growth and impacts. These weaknesses notwithstanding, the Stanford report offered firm policy recommendations that proved of greater import than those of the more detailed Batelle study. The main argument of the 1966 report was that there was no economic justification for paving the Alaska Highway. Tourism, it suggested, was the only area that would gain significantly from a paving programme, and even then not on the scale claimed by proponents of blacktopping. Other economic ventures, such as mining and lumbering, were not dependent upon the provision of a paved access route.[24] Public and political response to the Stanford report was uniformly negative, in direct contrast to the wave of enthusiasm for the Batelle study. Yukon Member of Parliament Erik Nielson noted that the conclusions were, in his opinion, "completely unjustified" and that the single-minded purpose of the report had been to "justify a further delay in the government coming to some kind of decision with respect to the paving of the highway."[25]

While arguing that paving the entire length of the highway was not required in the immediate future, the Stanford report did suggest that "a very significant proportion of all projected cost savings benefits would be realized by a partial improvement program that concentrates on those stretches of the highway where traffic densities are higher than average." The authors claimed that those regions, particularly the southern third of the highway and the immediate environs of major population centres, should be reconstructed and paved. According to the data collected, extensive work on the remainder of the route could not be justified on the grounds of anticipated economic benefit.[26]

At the same time as the Stanford Research Institute was undertaking its studies, Public Works was in the midst of an internal engineering investigation of the Alaska Highway and alternative northern access routes. In the study, five possibilities were examined: retention of the status quo; reconstruction and pavement with minor diversions; reconstruction and pavement with major diversions; development of a new route if the Liard River Power development was to proceed; and improvement of existing roads between Hazelton and Watson Lake. The projected costs of redevelopment and maintenance over a twenty-year period ranged widely for the five options, from a low of $143,137,000 for maintenance only to $231,882,000 for reconstruction with major diversions. The latter alternative offered a net user benefit of almost $150,000,000 over the same period, while the former promised no such positive return.[27]

With these studies in hand, the federal government finally had the documentation needed to proceed with a responsible redevelopment of the Alaska Highway. The two reports, a departmental cost estimate and an independent examination by an American consulting firm, clearly pointed to the fact that a full-scale paving programme was too costly, unnecessary and, more to the point, unjustified. While anticipating considerable negative reaction from residents, businessmen and politicians in the north, it was nonetheless decided to heed the warnings offered by the Stanford Research Institute and proceed cautiously. Instead of an all-out reconstruction programme, the government would commence with a Limited Improvement Programme targeted at the areas of highest traffic density: the strip of road between Fort St. John and Fort Nelson and the approaches to Whitehorse.[28]

After considerable internal discussion and public debate, the federal government proceeded with a phased improvement programme. Suggestions that the government consider a cost-sharing agreement with the United States did not cease, nor did calls for an accelerated paving programme. But with substantial evidence that the enthusiasm of the Batelle Institute had been misplaced, the government felt confident of its decision to proceed at a more controlled pace.[29] One component of a limited construction programme was already underway. Beginning in 1964, funding had been arranged for the gradual replacement of all temporary and substandard bridges along the route, with $19 million approved, subject to the annual availability of funds, to cover the ten-year programme. The remaining details of the programme were filled in following the release of the Stanford study. In October 1968, the federal government finally set the redevelopment of the highway in motion. A budget of $5 million was granted for the reconstruction and paving of 43 miles of highway over a five year period. As had been suggested, the money was directed to high traffic density areas, with initial paving slated for 25 miles north of the end of pavement at mile 84, and three miles on each approach to Watson Lake.[30] This "Paving Through

Settled Areas" programme was designed to upgrade driving conditions where traffic warranted while other components of the programme, most noticeably bridge replacement, were intended to improve the general standards of the road.

This procedure, first made public in the Stanford report and given official sanction with cabinet's 1968 decision, turned the highway into something of a patchwork. Until 1968, the road had been in essentially the same condition from the end of pavement to the Alaska/Yukon border. Under the Limited Improvement Programme, areas with the greatest traffic volume and stretches of the road in worst condition were to be reconstructed and in some instances paved, while the remainder of the highway remained in its pre-1968 condition. The ultimate goal was the eventual reconstruction and paving of the entire route. But that end occasionally fell from view as funding problems, environmental difficulties (most notably flooding), and policy changes often diverted the development programme from its course. As often happens to government programmes left vulnerable to the political process, the federal government's plan to redevelop the highway "as necessary" quickly became a programme to proceed "as possible," with the speed and intensity of construction determined by political and budgetary considerations.

While the government had a programme it felt it could live with — and paving the Alaska Highway was fairly low on any government's list of priorities — the travelling public, many local residents, and even officials within Public Works were unhappy with the improvement scheme. The department experienced increasing difficulties maintaining (and financing) a twenty-five-year-old highway suffering under an ever-increasing traffic load. As early as 1970, Public Works's Pacific Region requested a major expansion of the improvement programme with the money to be directed to seriously weakened sections of the road, particularly south of Fort Nelson, and an accelerated bridge replacement programme. To substantiate departmental claims, it was pointed out that traffic was not only increasing more rapidly than forecast in the Stanford report; it also included a larger than anticipated number of large vehicles, including heavy trucks and personal camping units.[31]

Public criticism increased in the early 1970's, although it did subside temporarily when reconstruction of fifty miles south of Fort Nelson began. Clearly, however, a pattern had been set. Consideration of an overall plan for the development of the Alaska Highway was set aside and both Public Works and the federal Treasury Board proceeded solely on the basis of a limited renovation of the system. The department's 1972 proposal, for example, followed the same line, encouraging additional paving around settled areas, continued bridge replacement, and consideration of a more effective dust control programme.[32]

Throughout this period, the federal government adhered closely to the spirit if not the word of the Stanford Research Institute study and devised their Alaska Highway policy accordingly. Increasing economic activity in the Fort St. John-Fort Nelson corridor, and the proposed construction of an additional route from Fort Nelson to Fort Simpson led to even greater interest in the southern section of the highway. Beginning in 1973, the department began discussions with the federal Treasury Board for the requisite funding to reconstruct and pave miles 93 to 317, the junction of the proposed new road. With an estimated cost of $43,200,000 and an expected time frame of five years, this proposal represented the Department of Public Works's largest request for reconstruction along the Alaska Highway. The programme received cabinet approval but was not completed in the form outlined.[33]

A major component of the plan to finally pave the highway as far as Fort Nelson was the expectation that, once completed, the road would be turned over to the B.C. government. All future responsibility for maintenance and renovation would then rest in provincial hands. Provincial reluctance to accept the increased costs soon ended negotiations, leaving the highway with the federal government. Faced with this abrupt change in plans, the government revised the reconstruction programme. Redevelopment was not completely shelved, but whereas the 1973 proposal had called for paving from miles 93 to 317, the new project included only those sections from miles 93 to 115 (near the settlement of Wonowon) and miles 230 to 291 (the new Muskwa River Bridge, completed in 1976 and connected by paved road to Fort Nelson). The idea of turning the B.C. sections of the highway over to the provincial authorities was not abandoned, but without an agreement in hand, the federal government was reluctant to proceed with the full-scale reconstruction of the British Columbia segment of the road.[34]

British Columbia had backed away from its earlier position whereby it would assume control of any paved section of the Alaska Highway. The demand now was that full compensation be paid by the federal government for any costs incurred. From the federal viewpoint, the possibility of divesting itself of maintenance responsibility had always been a major positive factor. The provincial change of heart clearly interrupted Public Works planning. The department continued its consideration of the future of the highway and in 1977 turned to the possibility of reconstructing the entire route, a proposal that had not been closely examined since 1968. Public Works still urged that the redevelopment be phased in slowly, a choice based both on a consideration of the logistics of a major paving programme and a realistic assessment of the willingness of the federal government to provide funds. The 1977 capital programme called for the expenditure of $18 million a year for five years, a significant increase over the previous half decade which saw an average annual spending of $11.3

million (adjusted to 1977 dollars). The proposal fell far short of meeting the total costs of paving, estimated to exceed $380 million, but was designed to "provide a reasonable level of service on the highway and should satisfy the local inhabitants that a continuing program is underway."[33] The focus of redevelopment remained the region south of Fort Nelson, slated to receive $8 million of the annual allotment. However, a significant amount was also earmarked for bridge replacement and for reconstruction of segments of the road between Watson Lake and Haines Junction.

The federal government still tried to transfer responsibility for paved sections of the highway to the B.C. government.[36] At the same time, the construction of the Alaska oil pipeline and the proposed construction of a gas pipeline alongside the Alaska Highway held the possibility that ever increasing numbers of automobiles would be travelling over the outdated highway. Public Works was willing to proceed with redevelopment at an even faster pace, and the federal government was prepared to fund the reconstruction, although not at the level requested by the department.[37] By 1980, the department was administering a programme that was designed to reconstruct and pave major segments of the Alaska Highway. As had been the case since 1966, however, priority was once again given to the first 300 miles of the route. This section of the highway, indeed the entire road, was something of an engineering oddity, with sections of pavement sandwiched between the familiar gravel surface. In addition, much of the road surface not slated for reconstruction was treated with a new substance called bituminous surface treatment, which possessed many of the characteristics of a paved road, including a virtually total suppression of dust.[38] The continued emphasis on the southern third of the Canadian section of the highway did not mean that the remainder of the road went unnoticed, however. Sections between Fort Nelson and Haines Junction, particularly near Whitehorse and other population centres, were selected for improvement. More importantly, attempts to reopen discussions with the United States government over a cost-sharing programme to pave sections of the Alaska Highway had finally been successful.

The negotiations between the two countries about the highway would have remained unresolved were it not for the desire of the American authorities to provide paved access to Alaska. Faced with an enormous cost for renovating the entire route, the United States government instead proposed that the section from Haines Junction to the Alaska/Yukon border be paved, with a similar project to be undertaken on the Haines Road. This accomplished, it would then be possible for travellers to reach Fairbanks and Anchorage from Haines, Alaska (and, through a tie in with the Alaska Ferry System, from the Alaskan Panhandle and points south) without exposing their automobiles to the rigours of a gravel road. With this end in sight, in 1973, the United States government offered to provide an initial sum of $58.67 million to finance the project. Commencement of the project was conditional upon reaching a suitable agreement with Canadian authorities.[39]

The project was designed to encompass a total of 322 miles of highway, including 52 miles of the Haines Road in British Columbia, 65 miles in the Yukon, and 205 miles of the Canadian section of the Alaska Highway. Though such reconstruction had the lowest priority of any section of the route, the Canadian government was reluctant to discourage the American offer, and negotiations proceeded. Initial meetings, however, turned up a potentially fatal stumbling block. Because the United States funded the entire project, American negotiators suggested that control of the reconstruction and all contracts should be administered by American supervisors and, further, that special tax exemptions should be granted to U.S. residents and corporations involved with the project. The Canadian position called for much greater Canadian participation, and its government was unwilling to participate in a project of benefit primarily to the Americans without negotiating a guarantee of a substantial role for Canadian workers and contractors. While the initial bargaining positions revealed a potential for great division, both sides expressed a willingness to continue discussions towards a suitable accord.[40]

Negotiations proceeded, with debate focusing on the right of American contractors to bid on associated projects and the Canadian demand that the reconstruction agreement not infringe on Canadian sovereignty by allowing the slightest suggestion of American control of the highway.[41] By January 1975, Public Works officials and other federal negotiators had reached an agreement they felt they could recommend to cabinet. The meetings had led to an acceptable compromise. The U.S. government backed down on its demand that the reconstruction be an entirely American project, and in return, the Canadian negotiators were prepared to recommend that American contractors be allowed to bid on construction contracts on an equal basis with their Canadian counterparts. The Canadian government stood firm concerning the future of the highway, rejecting an American request that the right of way "shall forever be held inviolate as part of such highways for public use." Viewing this as an unacceptable encroachment upon national territorial rights, the Canadian government instead agreed to guarantee the right of way for 25 years, with an indefinite extension for as long as both parties agreed the route was required. The Canadian authorities were generally pleased with the accord, for the American undertaking promised to improve a stretch of the Alaska Highway and the Haines Road — a project near the bottom of the Public Works priority list — while at the same time providing greatly improved access to the recently opened Kluane National Park.[42]

Even as negotiations closed, however, there were still several outstanding problems. The original congressional bill called for the appropriation of only $58.6 million, well short of the estimated $200 million needed to complete the project. Similarly, there was no commitment on the part of the American authorities to a specific starting date. One further Canadian problem concerned Public Works officials. With construction expected to proceed in the 1975-76 season, the department was concerned that it would spur an inflationary spiral in construction costs in the northwest. A number of major projects, including development elsewhere on the Alaska Highway, Dempster and Mackenzie highway construction, and a few northern railway undertakings, competed for the limited number of available northern contractors and tradesmen. The concern was expressed that if the Haines Road-Alaska Highway programme was not carefully phased in, it would either push general Canadian contracting costs even higher, or leave the majority of the work for American contractors.[43]

Enthusiasm for the project from governments on both sides of the border was far from overwhelming. Canadian authorities were aware of the many benefits to be derived from the American offer but had significant reservations about the timing of the project. More particularly, federal officials were concerned about whether funds were available to carry the work through to its conclusion. From the American perspective, the entire project was something of a luxury although it did have sustained support in parts of Alaska and among businessmen associated with the Pacific Northwest tourist industry. The Canadian cabinet agreed to proceed with the project in May 1975, but not without requesting that several obstacles, particularly the securing of an agreement with British Columbia regarding reconstruction of the provincial segment of the Haines Road, be cleared before an accord could be signed.[44] This proved to be more difficult than expected, with the B.C. government expressing some concern that the project would hinder plans for further paving of the Alaska Highway in the province. The federal government, anxious to preserve what many viewed as a "windfall gain," pressed the provincial authorities to agree to the accord.[45]

With several matters still unresolved, most notably Canada's inability to secure a guarantee that the work would be completed, the two governments ratified an agreement on 11 January 1977, calling for the immediate commencement of the Shakwak (named after the valley east of the St. Elias Mountains) project.[46] In accordance with the agreement, and in recognition of public concern over the physical, biological and social impact of the reconstruction, an environmental impact study was carried out, and a Shakwak Review Committee was established to oversee the work.[47] Initial plans augured well for the future success of the project, with an eleven-year construction schedule drawn up extending to 1989, and with unofficial assurances from American authorities that the required $200 million would be forthcoming.

Unfortunately, the funding arrangements called for biannual submissions to the U.S. Congress, a process which left the project entirely dependent upon the electoral success of the major proponents of the project. Accordingly, the Shakwak Project was on a precarious political footing from the outset. When Alaskan Senator Mike Gravel, a key supporter of the programme, was defeated in the primaries for the 1980 elections, there was immediate concern that the project would flounder. The financial arrangements not only made it difficult to plan with any degree of certainty, but it also made it hard to maintain staff and contractors on site. Fearing the imminent closure of the programme, many left for more secure employment elsewhere.[48]

The worst fears were realized. Funding for the 1981 construction season did not make it into the U.S. federal budget and the highway project slowed abruptly. Enough money was provided to continue work already in progress, but the grand design of a paved road from Haines to the Alaska/Yukon border faded from view.[49] A meeting was called in December 1980 to assess the project. American officials noted that under the budget-conscious Reagan administration, additional funding was unlikely. Canadian representatives, recalling yet again the low priority assigned this sector, held out little hope of financial assistance from Ottawa. With such a pessimistic but realistic forecast, it was agreed to wind down the programme, leaving only a few minor projects to be completed.[50]

The Shakwak Project was all but over by 1981. Several minor works were slated to continue through the 1983-84 construction season, utilizing the last of the $37 million provided by the United States for the project. With the completion of these programmes, Shakwak will be officially on hold, with reactivation possible whenever funding becomes available. The administrative and construction infrastructure has been withdrawn, however, adding time and cost to any future work on the programme. This second attempt at Canadian-American co-operation in the northwest was decidedly less successful than the first undertaking over 35 years earlier, an indication more of the perceived urgency of the project than of the ability of the two governments to work together.

When Public Works inherited the Alaska Highway in 1964, it assumed control of a hastily built, often poorly located, military road that had undergone only minor improvements in its first twenty years of existence. While the initial goal of delegating maintenance responsibility to local governments was realized only for the Yukon section and is still the focus of negotiations with the B.C. government, the federal government has undertaken a substantial reconstruction of the route. The Stanford Research Institute Report of 1966, which recommended a limited improvement programme, has served as something of a guiding light for Public Works policy since that date. Apart from the apparent validity of its conclusions, in stark contrast to the buoyant enthusiasm of the earlier Batelle study, the document had the welcome advantage of offering a politically flexible programme.[51] Unwilling to accept and unable to justify the need for the immediate paving of the Alaska Highway, the government opted instead for an "as required" reconstruction of the worst or most heavily travelled sections of the road, with a decided emphasis on the first three hundred miles. Such a programme addressed the more serious problems quickly, while still allowing the federal government to adjust funding on an annual basis to suit changing budgetary conditions. The Shakwak Project, funded by the American government, temporarily brightened hopes for the redevelopment of the Alaska Highway north of Haines Junction, but that programme has since been put on hold.

For twenty years, the future of the Alaska Highway has been one of the most contentious issues in the Canadian northwest, promoting continued discussion and debate at the local, territorial, provincial and national levels. The peculiar balance of responsibility for highways in the region, with overlapping and often poorly defined jurisdictions, has only served to confuse an already complex situation. Recently, additional problems have arisen, such as the possible upgrading of the Stewart-Cassiar Road and a proposed dam along the Liard River, which pose different questions about the future status and importance of the route. These questions have yet to be answered.

To the casual observer, the highway between Dawson Creek and the Alaska/Yukon border, with its varied and apparently inconsistent design and construction, must appear somewhat unusual. The once standard dusty and winding road remains only in sections, sandwiched between upgraded and paved segments of the highest quality. This visually haphazard situation is, however, the best possible reflection of the political and financial realities of federally funded northern highway development. More directly, it indicates Public Works Canada's best attempt to carry out a logical redevelopment scheme in the face of ever-changing regional and national priorities.

Notes

1. Canada, Transport Canada, Transportation Development Agency, *Canadian Highway System Study: Federal Interest in Highways,* by V. Setty Pendakur and D.L. Burke (Montreal, 1972).
2. Public Works Canada, Design and Construction Branch, Pacific Region, "Public Works' Role in Transportation: Past, Present and Future," March 1979.
3. Canada, Parliament, Debates (hereafter cited as Debates), session 1953-54, vol. 1, 19 November 1953, p. 180.

4. "Summary of Information Obtained and Observations Made by Department of Public Works Team on Northwest Highway System, August 25, 1954 - September 1, 1954," Public Works Canada, Design and Construction Branch, Ottawa (hereafter cited as PWC, Ottawa), File 91-0-0.
5. Debates, session 1953-54, vol. 5, 13 May 1954, p. 4675; ibid., session 1955, vol. 1, 14 January 1955, p. 185; ibid., 19 January 1955, p. 330.
6. Ibid., session 1956, vol. 7, 2 August 1956, p. 6901; ibid., session 1957, vol. 1, 15 January 1957, p. 269. For an example of mounting business pressure, see D. Phillips, Dawson Creek Chamber of Commerce to E.D. Fulton, Minister of Justice, May 27, 1959, PWC, Ottawa, file 91-0-0, pt. 1.
7. Debates, session 1957-58, vol. 3, 4 January 1958, p. 2859.
8. The main indication was the introduction of bill S4097 to the U.S. Senate, proposing a cost-sharing arrangement. The federal government, in the wake of this proposal, announced that talks were underway. Ibid., session 1958, vol. 3, pp. 2287-88; ibid., session 1959, vol. 3, 7 May 1959, p. 3414-45.
9. Batelle Memorial Institute, *An Integrated Transport System to Encourage Economic Development of Northwest North America*, Columbus, Ohio, 31 October 1960.
10. PWC, Ottawa, file 91-0-0, pt. 1, pt. 2 and pt. 3 contain a number of petitions and resolutions, the latter mainly from Chambers of Commerce in B.C., Alberta, Yukon and Montana.
11. Memorandum to Cabinet, 30 August 1963, PWC, Ottawa, file 91-0-0, pt. 3.
12. Ibid. Canada. *Royal Commission on Government Reorganization: Report*. (Ottawa: Queen's Printer, 1962), vol. 2, p. 357; Cabinet approval was granted on 3 October 1965.
13. Army Headquarters: Handover of N.W.H.S., January 8, 1964, PWC, Ottawa, file 91-0-0, pt. 3.
14. Notes on Procedures and Programme for Inspection of the NWHS, October 1963, PWC, Ottawa, file 91-0-0, pt. 2.
15. Koropatnick to Clarke, 28 August 1964, PWC, Ottawa, file 91-2-0, pt. 1.
16. Public Works Canada, Whitehorse Office (hereafter cited as PWC, Whitehorse), Northwest Highway Command Brief, 1964.
17. Department of Public Works, Pacific Region, Yukon District, *Report on the Northwest Highway System Handover*, 1 April 1972.
18. Gaglardi to Pearkes, 20 July 1960, PWC, Ottawa, file 91-1-0, pt. 2; ibid., 91-6-4, pt. 1, Privy Council Minute 1961-102.
19. Canada. Advisory Committee on Northern Development, *Government Activities in the North, 1968* (Ottawa, Queen's Printer, 1969); Millar to Deputy Minister, DPW, 3 February 1967, PWC, Ottawa, file 91-0-0, pt. 5; "Public Works' Role in Transportation."
20. Debates, Session 1964, vol. 9, 16 November 1964, p. 10097.
21. Ibid., vol. 2, 1 May 1964, p. 2819; ibid., session 1964-65, vol. 11, 14 February 1965, p. 11695; ibid., session 1969, vol. 9, 5 June 1969, p. 9764.
22. Technical Talks on the Question of Paving the Alaska Highway, 22 January 1965, PWC, Ottawa, file 2209; memorandum to the minister, DPW, 16 February 1965, ibid., file 91-1-0.
23. Authorization to Enter into a Contract with Stanford Research Institute, 27 August 1964, PWC, Ottawa, file 91-0-0, pt. 1.
24. Stanford Research Institute, *Improvement Program for the Alaska Highway: An Analysis of Economic Benefits*. (Ottawa: Queen's Printer, 1966). The deficiencies in research design were willingly acknowledged by the report's authors.
25. Debates, session 1966, vol. 7, 18 November 1966, p. 10087.
26. Stanford, *Improvement Program*.
27. Department of Public Works, Development Engineering Branch, *Preliminary Engineering Study: Alaska Highway*, August 1965.
28. Memorandum to Cabinet: Question of Paving the Alaska Highway, 16 March 1966, PWC, Ottawa, file 91-0-0, pt. 5.
29. Debates, session 1966, vol. 6, 6 June 1966, p. 6027-8; ibid., session 1969, vol. 9, 5 June 1969, p. 9764; ibid., session 1972, vol. 2, 13 April 1972, p. 1291. Meetings were held, but concluded with an agreement that a mutual effort on this project was unwarranted. See

Report on Negotiations Concerning Reconstruction of the Alaska Highway, PWC, Ottawa, file 1230-1, supp. A.
30. D.P.W., Pacific Region, A Report on the Northwest Highway System, October 1970, PWC, Ottawa, file 2008.
31. Ibid.
32. Koropatnick to Binks, 24 October 1975, PWC, Ottawa, file 1230-4, vol. 6; A Limited Improvement Program - Northwest Highway System (draft copy), July1972, ibid., file 2009.
33. Project Approval: To reconstruct and pave approximately 225 miles of the Alaska Highway in British Columbia, PWC, Ottawa, file 2002; Marchand to Drury, 19 November 1973, ibid., file 1230-1, vol. 9.
34. Alaska Highway - Project Approval Amendment, 26 March 1975, PWC, Ottawa, file 2002.
35. Project Approval: "To initiate a project which provides a rational approach for reconstruction, paving and bridge replacement on the Alaska Highway....," 1977, PWC, Ottawa, file 2268; Project Feasability Report - Alaska Highway Reconstruction, Mile 93 to Mile 1016, 1977, ibid., file 1230-1, vol. 9.
36. MacKay to Minister, D.P.W., August 21, 1978, PWC, Ottawa, file 1230-1, vol. 11; Lang to MacEachen, June 13, 1979, ibid., vol. 13; Cosgrove to Fraser, n.d. (1980), ibid.
37. O'Toole to Machay, April 21, 1978, re Treasury Board item 755925, PWC, Ottawa, file 1230-1, vol. 11.
38. One section, Mile 317 to 635 (Watson Lake), received very little attention for the simple reason that B.C. Hydro is currently considering damming the Liard River, which would in turn flood sections of the Alaska Highway and force a major relocation. Limited reconstruction is, however, being undertaken on substandard sections.
39. Alaska Highway and the Haines Road: Background Papers, 22 October 1974, PWC, Ottawa, file 1230-51, vol. 3.
40. G.B. Williams to minister, D.P.W., 30 August 1973, ibid.
41. MacDonald to minister of public works, 19 June 1974, ibid.
42. Memorandum to Cabinet: Construction of the Haines Road (Canadian Section) and the Alaska Highway from Haines Junction to the Yukon/Alaska Border, 29 January 1975, ibid.
43. MacDonald to minister, D.P.W., 9 January 1975, ibid.
44. MacEachen to Drury, July 21, 1975, ibid.; Williams to Crerar, Environmental Land Use Secretariat, Victoria, 7 August 1975, ibid.
45. Cameron to Binks, 16 August 1976, PWC, Ottawa, file 1230-51-5.
46. Signature of agreement between Canada and the United States on Haines Road/Alaska Highway Reconstruction, 10 February 1977 (Date of press release), PWC, Ottawa, file 1230-51-5.
47. Mitchell, Director, Public Relations and Information Services to Binks, 31 January, 1975, PWC, Ottawa, file 1230-51, vol. 3; Public Relations, General Plan, ibid.; MacEachern to Drury, 21 July 1975, ibid.; Public Participation in the Planning and Assessment of the Shakwak Project, 3 March 1976, ibid., vol. 4; Minutes of a Meeting of Haines Road/Alaska Highway Environmental Assessment Panel, 3 March 1975, ibid.
48. Federal Environmental Assessment Review Office, *Report of the Environmental Assessment Panel: Shakwak Highway Project,* is the title of the impact study. Shakwak Review Commitee Report, 1979/80 Construction Season, PWC, Ottawa, file 1230-105-5, vol. 1.
49. Bilawich to Roberts, 27 October 1980, ibid.
50. Shakwak Policy Committee Meeting, December 2, 1980, ibid. The American decision not to proceed was reiterated in 1981. See Lande to Lee, 12 February 1981, PWC, Ottawa, file 1230-51-6.
51. These conclusions were supported by two further studies, one by N.E. Lee and Associates in 1970 and Ministry of Transport, *The Northwest Transportation Plan, 1972.*

SECTION 5:

The Impact of the Alaska Highway

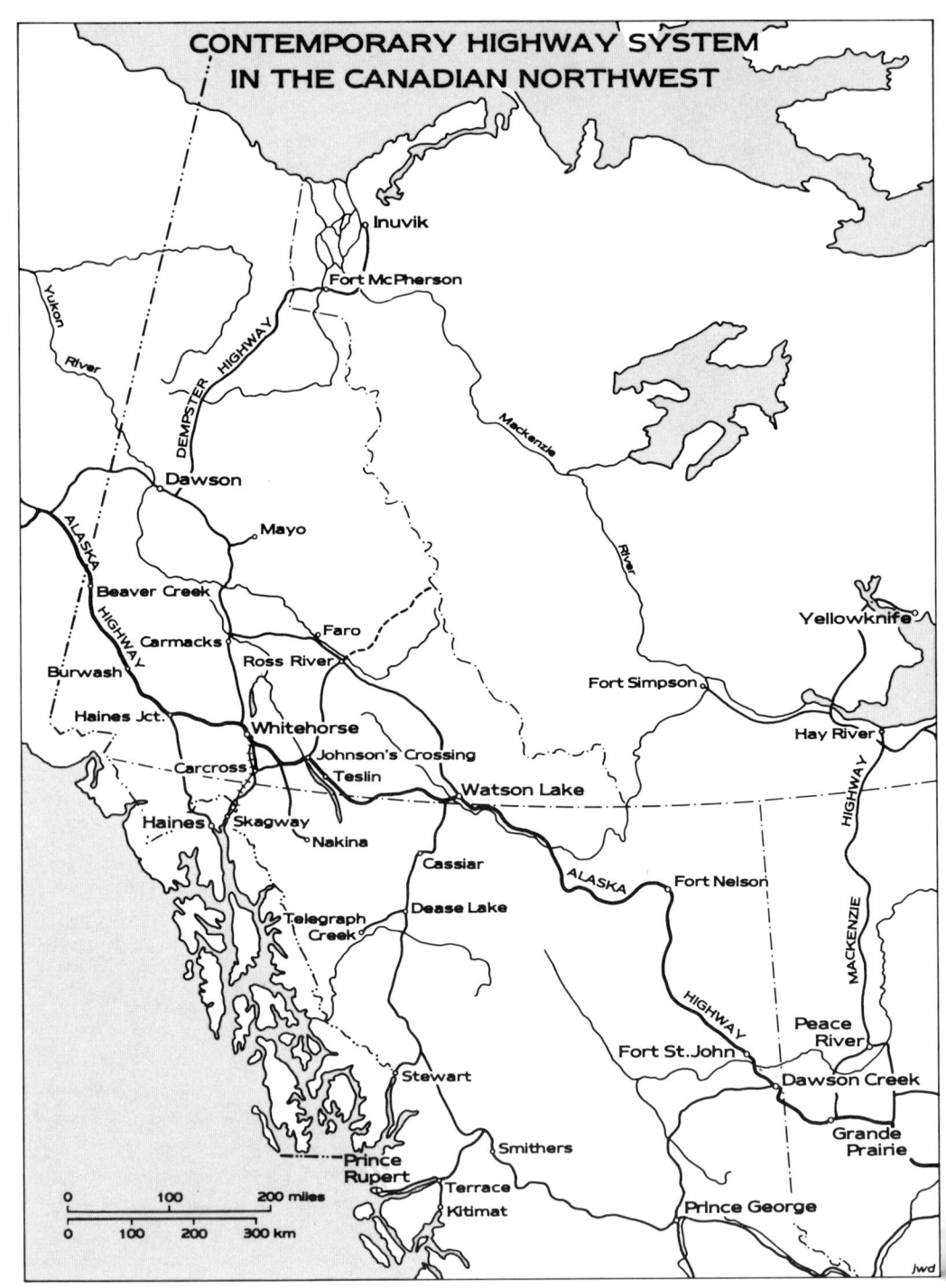

12

The Alaska Highway and the Indians of the Southern Yukon, 1942-50: A Study of Native Adaptation to Northern Development

KENNETH COATES

The invasion of more than 20,000 soldiers and construction workers into the sparsely populated Yukon Territory in 1942-43 was of a magnitude matched only by the Klondike gold rush of 1896-1904. The road they built, the Alaska Highway, cut a swath through the southern reaches of the territory, opening up vast expanses long the preserve of native hunters and a few white trappers and traders. Most contemporary writers paid scant attention to the natives, seeing them only as casual observers of the construction process, somewhat awed by the plentitude of mechanical might. Others, more familiar with the toll exacted on native health from diseases introduced by outsiders, offered a decidedly pessimistic assessment of the consequences of construction.[1] In recent years, writers have expanded on the negative perspective and have suggested, somewhat unconvincingly, that the highway had immediate and severe implications for natives in the area.[2] That the initial construction and subsequent opening of the road had a significant effect on the Indians is obvious; less clear is the precise nature of the social, economic and demographic consequences of the Alaska Highway construction on the natives of the southern Yukon.

Highway construction between 1942 and 1950 raised important questions about the role of the natives in the region's economic order, Indian demography and health, interracial relations, native crime and alcohol use, and the expansion of government programmes for Indians. The intention is to place the Indians in the context of the existing Yukon social, economic and administrative order and, in particular, to assess the manner in which the building and completion of the Alaska Highway altered patterns in the Yukon. By restricting the focus to the immediate post-construction years, it is hoped to better separate changes directly attributable to the highway from those caused by other, post-construction, factors.

The construction of the Alaska Highway promised economic opportunity to residents of the Yukon, white and Indian alike. Highway employment, increased requirements for provisions, and work in related service industries seemed to offer readily available and remunerative positions to all interested. The natives' response to the alleged opportunities was, however, far from unbridled enthusiasm. Instead, they opted in large measure for a continuation of past practices, hunting meat for personal and market consumption and trapping furs for trade. There were, of course, a number of individuals who found work with the highway crews, usually on a casual basis as guides, packers or labourers. In very few instances were native workers hired for more skilled positions. The Indians' limited role was not entirely a result of restrictive hiring practices by contractors. Of far greater importance in determining native employment decisions was the Indians' established role in the Yukon economy.

From the first years of gold mining in the Yukon River valley, the natives had, by both choice and circumstance, been slotted into a peripheral economic position. Unlike the fur trade period, when the Indians' importance placed them in a central and vital role, the mining era saw them relegated to a more marginal status.[3] Their efforts as packers, hunters, trappers, woodcutters and labourers remained valuable to the territorial economy, but otherwise they served primarily as a casual labour pool. Drawn into the mining economy only when labour shortages dictated, and then only at unskilled levels, the natives chose to maintain their harvesting existence. Under this economic order, the natives were not tied to the disciplined, time-oriented workplace of the mines and were instead able to follow the seasonal, migratory patterns of wild game harvesting.[4] At the same time, regular requirements for seasonal labourers provided those living close to the Yukon River with an opportunity to supplement their earnings. This economic system was well-adapted to the cyclical requirements of the mines and the seasonal lifestyle of the natives. Thus, while permanent work at the mine sites was rarely available to Indians, few natives were attempting to break away from the hunting-gathering routine and into the industrial system.[5]

The opportunities associated with the highway readily fit into this pattern. Short-term work as a guide or labourer was consistent with past experience as a hunting guide, woodcutter or packer and allowed for an easy and annual return to the trapline. As well, most construction work was undertaken in the short summer months, a period when the natives were away from traplines and hunting grounds and were available for casual work. In several instances, more substantial alterations to past practices were made in an attempt to take advantage of perceived employment prospects. Dr. John Marchand, affiliated with the Public Roads Administration work crews, observed in 1942 that the Teslin Indians had remained in the community throughout the winter, hoping to find work, a deviation from the usual routine of leaving for the band's hunting grounds each fall. This change was of short duration, however, and it was noted shortly thereafter that the Teslin natives had reverted to their former seasonal cycle.[6]

The natives opted for bush over highway because of a cultural preference for the former. The choice also had a solid economic rationale. While the hunting-trapping economy offered a pursuit closely attuned to the natives' lifestyle, it also provided reasonable financial returns. Those close to population centres and construction camps could sell meat (usually caribou and moose but occasionally sheep). Even more importantly, the fur trade continued to offer a viable, remunerative living to those with the requisite skills. Fur prices were high during the two-year construction phase and remained so for much of the 1940's. It was only after 1947 that a sizeable decline in the market value of furs occurred, and even then the short-term fall was not dramatic (Table 1).

TABLE 1

FUR PRICES — FIVE YEAR AVERAGES, 1920-49

	Beaver	Lynx	Silver Fox	Marten	Mink	Muskrat	White Fox
1920-24	17.81	21.38	152.91	24.47	9.78	1.56	38.12
1925-29	23.85	31.69	94.38	24.72	15.11	1.49	41.47
1930-34	13.12	23.86	44.17	14.57	9.15	.70	22.98
1935-39	11.35	30.60	27.73	22.10	11.05	1.05	13.75
1940-44	26.15	42.89	23.76	38.47	12.12	2.01	22.80
1945-49	33.93	27.16	19.37	35.99	20.19	2.40	38.47

Source: *Canada Year Book, 1920-1950*

There are abundant signs that the natives maintained their trapping and hunting operations largely uninterrupted throughout the 1940's, as illustrated by the limited appearance of Indians in the road crews, and the virtual absence of native participants in Alaska Highway lore.[7] As well, the activities were never mutually exclusive, and the natives were often able to combine both enterprises. An Anglican missionary at Champagne in 1949 noted that the natives were continuing to trap and fish, with a few accepting occasional, seasonal work along the highway.[8] Such a pattern was widespread, with local highway authorities calling on the Indians as season and need dictated and the natives accepting part-time employment providing it did not conflict with trapping, hunting or fishing. By and large, the trapping efforts of the Yukon Indians continued and even increased despite the reported availability of alternative employment. The increasing value of furs traded and number of pelts offered for sale suggests that trapping retained its attractiveness, giving the Indians few reasons to look for other permanent work (Table 2).

TABLE 2
YUKON FUR RETURNS, 1940-54

	Number of Pelts	$ Value of Pelts
1940-41	70,953	373,399
1941-42	66,700	398,132
1942-43	52,897	338,035
1943-44	78,005	467,188
1944-45	85,292	669,217
1945-46	107,252	677,495
1946-47	58,777	373,176
1947-48	131,227	230,117
1948-49	151,969	143,810
1949-50	153,574	199,086
1950-51	228,616	361,969
1951-52	171,274	173,252
1952-53	246,379	247,001
1953-54	176,338	182,238
1954-55	213,515	242,944

Source: K. Rea, *The Political Economy of the Canadian North* (Toronto: University of Toronto Press, 1968), pp. 386-87.

There were, however, some natives who made a more complete transition, leaving the pursuit of game in favour of more structured employment. A number of men moved from the long-standing native practice of cutting wood for the steamships to providing fuel logs for townsfolk and military establishments.[9] Similarly, a few found work with local mines and road maintenance crews. While it is easy to assert that some natives were pursuing different economic activities while the majority continued to trap and hunt, it is difficult to quantify the relative importance of the two groups, a task made even more onerous by the fact that many followed both paths. Census figures are not entirely useful, particularly given the questionable definition of job categories in the Yukon. (The 1951 census, for instance, has no listing for woodcutters.) Employment statistics in the national census indicate a steady decline in the number of trappers and hunters. The 1931 report listed 449, both Indian and white, thus employed. The number dropped to a territorial total of 427 in 1941 and to 271 ten years later.[10] The census data probably overstates the decline; government officials, unlike the Indians themselves, tended to emphasize industrial or skilled work, even if it was only of short duration. Agents thus downplayed the numerical significance of hunting and trapping. Native birth registration forms provide another means of assessing native occupational pursuits. This data base, while biased in favour of young males near population centres, as a result of the nature of the registration process, offers a way of examining male occupations as indicated by the men themselves.[11] The results from a sample of these returns (Table 3) provide a further indication of the continued occupational importance of hunting and trapping.

TABLE 3
FATHER'S OCCUPATION AS LISTED DURING THE REGISTRATION OF INDIAN BIRTHS, 1930-50

Occupation	1930-35		1936-41		1942-50	
Trappers	40	(87%)	63	(85%)	113	(75%)
Labourers	4	(9%)	6	(8%)	14	(9%)
Section-Hands	—		—		4	(3%)
Woodcutters	—		2	(3%)	12	(8%)
Not Given/Dead	2	(4%)	3	(4%)	7	(5%)
	46	(100%)	74	(100%)	150	(100%)

Source: Random Sample (Approximately 30% of total cases) from Native Birth Registrations, Vital Statistics Branch, Yukon Territorial Government.

From initial construction through the first seven years the Alaska Highway was in use, the economic activities and expectations of the Yukon Indians changed very little. Hunting and trapping continued to be of primary importance. The fundamental role of trapping was given administrative expression in the latter part of the decade when, led by Yukon Indian Agent R.J. Meek, government officials began to argue for the registration of traplines. Afraid that the increase in white population attending the construction would lead to the displacement of native trappers, Meek and others in the Department of Indian Affairs sought a means of protecting those leading "the hunting life."[12] The expected encroachment by white trappers was a matter of some concern for officials and, reportedly, for Yukon Indians, but action was slow to come.[13] Throughout the debate over the implementation of a registration system, it was accepted without question that the principal goal remained the necessity of preserving native access to game resources.[14] In theory, registration was designed to entrench an economic order, to keep the Indians in the bush and to reserve for them traditional and valued hunting areas. The vitality of national fur markets before 1950 were such that the natives did not protest, but rather encouraged, the government's obvious effort to typecast them in a permanent role as trappers and hunters. With unfortunate timing, however, trapline registration finally came into effect in 1950, just as fur prices began a serious decline.[15]

While Alaska Highway construction did not quickly or irrevocably alter the occupational pursuits of the natives of the southern Yukon, it did have a noticeable impact on wild game resources near the road. In the Yukon, unlike the Northwest Territories, American soldiers and construction workers were allowed to secure licences to hunt big game and game birds.[16] In addition to this legalized hunting, allegations were made that "Yankee" personnel engaged in wanton destruction of game, and stories circulated about carcasses abandoned by zealous American target shooters.[17] Further pressure on southern game stocks came from increasing demands for wild meat in the towns, especially Whitehorse, and in the construction camps.[18] Government officials were worried about the possible depletion of game, a concern shared by their American counterparts. They tried to encourage native hunters to restrict their harvests.[19] Similarly, officials refused licences to any operation, such as a proposed commercial fishery on Teslin Lake, which threatened to undermine native access to resources.[20] The construction and subsequent traffic undoubtedly forced game away from the immediate environs of the highway, while improved access to difficult to reach areas exposed more game to the guns of meat hunters and sportsmen. However, following an extended study of the development of wildlife legislation in the Yukon, Robert McCandless has concluded that the impact of the highway on game stocks has probably been exaggerated, and that the depletion of resources was not on the scale alleged by both contemporary and later commentators.[21] For the period before 1950, when highway traffic remained light, this analysis appears to be correct.

In one region, the Kluane Lake district, the highway had a more direct impact. Encouraged by similar action in Alaska, the federal government decided in 1942 to close off a major block of land, later to become the Kluane National Park, to future development.[22] Four months later, the Yukon government declared the designated area a game sanctuary, suspending all hunting activity including that by local Indians.[23] Protests were registered on behalf of the natives by Eugene Jacquot, a resident game guide, who attempted to get the region reopened.[24] The efforts were partially successful: the government agreed to redraft the boundaries to exclude a ten-mile section along the highway near the White River. According to government officials, this change was unfortunate as it enabled hunters and game guides to enter the sanctuary and hunt with impunity far from the view of enforcement officers.[25] In 1949, the section was returned to the sanctuary. The debate over the appropriate boundaries was not easily settled, as officials wrestled with the issue of balancing problems of enforcement with the often contradictory attempt to ensure native access to adequate supplies of game.[26] Although sympathetic to the Indians' plight,[27] the Yukon and federal governments concluded that the sanctity of the preserve had to be maintained.[28] They did, however, give special consideration to a proposal to allow a few Indians limited access to muskrat trapping areas.[29] In this one instance, the coming of the Alaska Highway had more serious consequences than elsewhere in the territory, as it resulted in the closure of a substantial tract of land along with the reduction of accessible game in the southern Yukon.

A few new avenues of employment opened up as a result of the development activity. The influx of thousands of outsiders to the small town of Whitehorse placed inordinate demands on the town's service capacity. Consequently, sizeable incomes could be gained by whites and natives alike from such routine chores as washing laundry, cleaning, and supplying wood. Temporary Indian Agent J.E. Gibben tried to encourage the Indians to take advantage of such opportunities. He believed in particular that native handicrafts would find a ready market among the white population, and he attempted to establish a distribution network for a variety of products produced by native women. Problems securing the requisite materials, particularly beads, frustrated his efforts. Even more important, Gibben found the natives rather uninterested in the enterprise. As he noted, "it appears that most of the work is done by the older women and it seems difficult to interest the younger generation in their traditional handicraft."[30] The programme was not without its successes; the women of Moosehide (near Dawson) earned over $1,300 from the proceeds of one shipment to Whitehorse.[31] While this particular undertaking collapsed through lack of interest, many native women resident near assembly points or construction camps could find a ready source of income providing domestic services.

The short-term economic consequences of Alaska Highway construction were rather limited. With few exceptions, the natives did not move from the marginal position ascribed them in the territorial economic order, preferring the still remunerative pursuit of game. Their entry into the construction-based economy was, as had been the case since the 1890's, largely confined to casual and seasonal work. Hunting and trapping retained their economic and cultural importance; with those activities remaining viable to the 1950's, the natives found little rationale for a greater association with the mining and defence-based territorial economy.

While the economic consequences of Alaska Highway construction were limited, the same cannot be said of the demographic impact. Traversing large areas that had previously seen only sporadic encounters between whites and natives, the highway served as the conduit for the introduction of a variety of diseases into the southern Yukon. Dr. J.F. Marchand noted in 1942-43 that the native community at Teslin Lake suffered successive attacks of measles, dysentery, jaundice, whooping cough, mumps and meningococcic meningitis.[32] The outbreaks of these and other diseases were not confined to the Teslin area and in short order spread along the construction route. Measles and influenza epidemics were particularly serious, reaching into virtually every native settlement in the southern Yukon.

Death records scratch only the surface of the actual incidence of epidemic disease. The impact of measles and influenza was particularly widespread, affecting a majority of the native population in the diseases' path and having harmful effects far in excess of the number of deaths attributable to the illnesses.[34] Nonetheless, mortality highlights the personal and demographic consequences of the epidemics. The total number of native deaths in the territory rose from an average of less than 30 per year before 1942 to 64 in that year and 54 and 48 in 1943 and 1944 (Table 4).

TABLE 4

RECORDED NATIVE BIRTHS, DEATHS AND NATURAL INCREASE, 1940-50

	Births	Deaths	Natural Increase
1940	32	20	12
1941	35	26	9
1942	45	64	(19)
1943	37	52	(15)
1944	57	48	9
1945	36	35	1
1946	50	35	15
1947	77	28	49
1948	81	42	39
1949	65	35	30
1950	67	32	35

Source: *Canada, Vital Statistics, 1930-1950.*

The Yukon native mortality rate was significantly higher than in neighbouring British Columbia and than among the national native population. The B.C. mortality rate in 1942, for instance, was approximately 24 per 1,000 population, while the national figure that year was 23 deaths. Importantly, the rate for the Yukon natives remained higher than preconstruction figures after the highway was completed, suggesting that the general health of the population did not quickly improve after the epidemics of 1942-43. Deaths attributable to epidemics were, for the most part, limited to the construction years, with the main exceptions being outbreaks of meningitis in 1944, influenza in 1946 and whooping cough in 1948 (Table 5).[35]

While general death rates are significant in their own right, even more illustrative is the astonishingly high mortality among infants and youths. Between 1940 and 1950 from 27 per cent to 58 per cent of all native deaths were children under the age of ten, far higher than comparable figures for the Yukon's white population (Table 6).

TABLE 5

CAUSES OF DEATH AMONG NATIVES, 1940-50

	TUBERCULOSIS	DIPHTHERIA	CIRCULATORY	WHOOPING COUGH	VIOLENT DEATH	INFLUENZA	RESPIRATORY	MEASLES	INFANT DEATH	MENINGITIS	OLD AGE	OTHER	TOTAL
1940	4		1		8		3		1			3	20
1941	11				1		6		1		1	6	26
1942	18			2	3	3	7	13	2		2	14	64
1943	14		2	2	4	2	9	1			4	14	52
1944	22		1		4	2	1		2	5	6	5	48
1945	15		1		4		5				5	5	35
1946	17	2			3	5	1					7	35
1947	17				2		3					6	28
1948	11			3	1		8		5		3	11	42
1949	14		2	1	2		3		2			11	35
1950	12		1		2	1	7		1	1	4	3	32

Source: *Canada, Vital Statistics Reports, 1940-1950*

TABLE 6

DEATHS OF YUKON INFANTS AND YOUTHS, 1940-50
(PER CENT OF TOTAL DEATHS)

	NATIVES		WHITES	
	Under 1 Year	Under 10 Years	Under 1 Year	Under 10 Years
1940	40.0	55.0	5.5	5.5
1942	32.8	57.8	2.3	6.8
1944	8.3	27.0	3.8	3.8
1946	14.0	40.0	4.4	8.8
1948	45.2	54.7	12.8	12.8
1950	21.8	34.3	15.1	22.7

Source: *Canada, Vital Statistics Reports, 1940-1950.*

The infant mortality rate provides an even better indication of the devastating impact of the 1942-43 epidemics on the children. In 1942, when a series of diseases were prevalent in the territory, there was a mortality rate of 47 per cent among infants less than one year old. While the general Indian populace was highly susceptible to the illnesses, the younger members were especially vulnerable. One can speculate with considerable confidence that the social impact of the numerous infant deaths was particularly devastating.

The net impact of the infant deaths was exacerbated by a comparatively low birth rate. Although the Yukon Indians' birth rate in the decade exceeded the national average, it was significantly lower than comparable figures for Canadian Indians. The Yukon Indians were clearly experiencing a demographic crisis of significant proportions, as witnessed by a population decline from a recorded 1,563 in 1939 to 1,531 five years later and even further to 1,443 in 1949.[36] This decline came when the national native population increased 16 per cent over the course of the decade. It would be erroneous to attribute all of the ills to the construction of the Alaska Highway; the incidence of endemic diseases such as tuberculosis and common respiratory ailments including pneumonia and bronchitis contributed to native mortality and to widespread medical debility. Before 1942, however, the Yukon Indians had enjoyed comparative good health, and the highway epidemics were largely responsible for the malaise of the Yukon Indians in the 1940's.

The medical implications of construction were not entirely negative, and attending the opening of the highway was an expansion of treatment facilities and a wider availability of medical services. Before 1942, the natives of the southern Yukon had enjoyed a government-funded health care system, with the federal Department of Indian Affairs assuming the costs of hospitalization and medical attendance. The major drawback with the system was a woefully inadequate delivery network. Indians in such remote settlements as Teslin, Upper Liard and Burwash enjoyed few of the benefits available to those closer to the Yukon River. Residents of the Carcross-Whitehorse region came under the care of a Whitehorse-based physician who visited out-settlements as need dictated. As well, any ill native who could reach town had access to the hospital, although admittance was far more restricted than for white residents. Obviously, many of the natives in the southern reaches of the territory fell outside the rather narrow cast of the government's medical assistance net.

The highway changed conditions radically. Whitehorse and the best medical facilities in the territory were now accessible to most residents in the region. As well, physicians attached to the Canadian and American armed forces and Public Roads Administration made their services available to natives on an emergency basis.[37] But, the extension of military health services to the Yukon Indians was not without complications. Attempts by territorial authorities to protect private medical practices by requiring any military physicians treating civilians to secure licences resulted in a threat by Canadian military officials to withhold their own doctors' services.[38] Similarly, arrangements were reached early in 1947 to allow natives to use the Whitehorse army hospital, with the provision that access was restricted to non-tubercular patients.[39] With that disease endemic among the Indians, the exclusion was a significant one.

The opening of the highway also allowed federal authorities to deal more effectively with tuberculosis. Beginning in 1947, a major anti-tuberculosis campaign was launched. Personnel from the Charles Camsell hospital in Edmonton undertook an x-ray survey of all residents of the territory between 1947 and 1949. Existing legislation allowed for the compulsory hospitalization of any persons deemed infected[40] on the grounds that they represented a threat to the community.[41] In the wake of the survey, a number of natives were singled out for treatment. The results illustrated the need for closer attention to the problem. Of the over 900 natives tested in July 1949, 49 per cent showed signs of a tubercular condition and sixteen were placed in the newly opened T.B. wing of the Whitehorse hospital.[42] The results in this instance revealed a higher incidence of infection than in earlier tests, but on each occasion a number of cases were identified and subsequently treated.[43] As important as the immediate results of the anti-tuberculosis campaign was the indication of the government's willingness and, as a result of the opening of the highway, improved ability to offer the Yukon natives extended medical care.

The introduction of epidemic diseases and medical debility represented only one example of the changes in the territory. One of the major alterations was a substantial shift in the Yukon's racial balance. Before 1942, the natives, while not in a majority, constituted a substantial minority of the populace. The arrival of tens of thousands of mainly white soldiers and construction workers, and a dramatic rise in the permanent population, tipped the scales decisively away from the Indians. The concentration of newcomers in the south was of particular importance to the natives in that region. While racial relations were consistently peaceful, there was an underlying current of separateness which kept the groups socially apart. The barriers, especially noticeable in Whitehorse but evident in most construction and maintenance camps, were erected by persons anxious to prevent overly familiar contact with the natives. Public schools, for instance, were generally closed to Indian students, making it necessary to open a missionary school in Whitehorse in 1947 for native, Métis and "poor" white children.[45] Similarly, when white and native residents in the town were asked to use the same medical gowns during the tuberculosis survey, the former refused to participate for fear of being infected with "native" diseases.[46] The prevailing attitude, not disputed by doctors or sanitary inspectors, was that the Indians were "dirty," unsanitary and disease-ridden.[47] This belief provided the justification for a continuation of the practice of social segregation long characteristic of life in Yukon towns, which generally kept the natives outside of community life.[48] Some efforts were made, particularly by Indian Agent R.J. Meek, to break down "barriers of prejudice which [were] unfortunately very prevalent in the past." But having native boys compete in Boy Scout meetings and athletic events was only a preliminary step, and a tenuous one at that, towards eliminating the distance between white and Indian.[46]

While social relations generally featured separation and exclusiveness, the same was not true for contact between army and construction workers and native women. Miscegenation had been a fact in the territory since the arrival of the gold miners in the 1880's, but never before on the scale of the war years. Even the gold rush of 1896-1904 saw a much lower rate, largely because of the foresight of a large number of prostitutes who followed the prospectors northward.[50] While there were 'ladies of the evening' in the southern Yukon in the 1940's, supply was decidedly lower than demand and was not adequately distributed to serve a dispersed clientele. There were reports from along the highway of promiscuity among the native women; in Whitehorse, several incidents involved Indian prostitutes, some alleged to be as young as fifteen years old.[51] A further indication of an increase in interracial sexual relations was a growing government concern over the status of children from such alliances.[52] The significant increase in native births after 1942 (Table 4), can be attributed in some measure to miscegenation. There is no doubt that the arrival of the soldiers and workers was greeted with some enthusiasm by a number of young Indian women. Relations between these men and women stands in stark contrast to a general attitude of racial segregation, a pattern not at all uncommon in interracial situations elsewhere in North America.

Sex provided one meeting place between natives and whites; another came through alcohol. Liquor had been an important feature of Yukon life from before the gold rush and had served as an important point of contact, drawing Indians and whites together in a mutually enjoyable setting. There has been considerable debate over the role of alcohol in northern native communities, with analysts suggesting consumption was to "show respect,"[53] for spiritual release,[54] and to reduce anxiety.[55] While these suggestions are valid, they do not offer a completely satisfactory explanation for native drinking patterns before 1950. It is now generally accepted that alcohol does not have a set physiological impact on all peoples. Instead, it has been forcefully argued that response to the intoxicating effects of alcohol is a learned behaviour.[56] Natives, without the dubious benefits of alcohol before the arrival of the white men, had to learn their reaction to the drink. As a result, early native drinking habits originated primarily in the social context of white drinking. In the Yukon, from the 1880's to 1942, alcohol consumption was long associated with "parties," often interracial in character and including excessive drinking and boisterous, though seldom violent, celebration. The frequent appearance of whites and Indians in the same parties was owing primarily to the fact that the natives were legally interdicted from purchasing, making, possessing or consuming alcoholic beverages, which forced them to rely heavily on white bootleggers to supplement their supplies of "homebrew." From the limited evidence available, it seems that this pattern remained intact to 1950.

The principal source for assessing native drinking habits is the records of the Royal Canadian Mounted Police, particularly court records. Such materials are, of course, fraught with problems, especially regarding "crimes" of social control. The recorded incidence of such breaches of law usually owes more to the size and zeal of the police force and prevailing public attitudes than it does to actual occurrences. This phenomenon is amply demonstrated in relation to native drinking in the Whitehorse region during and following Alaska Highway construction. Superficially, the increase in average yearly convictions from 17 in 1940-44 to more than 53 in the next five years suggests a marked rise in alcohol consumption. However, when the size of the police force (which shifted its territorial headquarters from Dawson City to Whitehorse in 1943-44) is taken into account (Table 7), it is far more likely that the increase is attributable to changes in enforcement than to breaches of law.

TABLE 7

NATIVE ALCOHOL-RELATED CONVICTIONS[1] AND POLICE MANPOWER, SOUTHERN YUKON, 1940-49

	Convictions	*Police Force*
1940	3	4
1941	9	4
1942	28	4
1943	27	15
1944	34	25
1945	51	25
1946	75	30
1947	82	27
1948	61	21
1949	55 (32)[2]	22

[1] Supplying, Possession, Drunkeness, Breaches of Indian Act.
[2] Records to July 1949. 55 equals rate of convictions projected over the entire year.
Source: Whitehorse Police Court Register, PAC, RG 18.

The pattern of alcohol-related convictions, which involved both whites and Indians, suggests that the established system of liquor as a medium for interracial contact remained intact. That many of the "parties" were arranged by whites to gain the sexual favours of native women seems clear, but that does not represent a deviation from past practice. While a few individuals appeared before the court on a regular basis, their number was small and, as far as police records allow one to generalize, it does not seem that native alcohol consumption adopted a new pattern in the 1942-50 period or that "boozing" was removed from its party setting. Indeed, ethnographer John Honigman noted, following extensive studies of Indians along the highway in 1943-44, that natives rarely drank individually, preferring the social function of alcohol to any physiological or psychological release.[57] While alcohol constituted a major problem for enforcement officers, even more among whites than Indians, there is no indication that the natives' approach to booze altered during the construction of the various northern defence projects. Instead, liquor use, based on behaviour learned from contact with miners, remained essentially as before.

Perhaps the most surprising result of an analysis of the Whitehorse court records is the virtual absence of non-alcohol-related crime. When the Indians broke the law, which they did at a comparatively modest rate, they confined their transgressions to liquor offences. There were remarkably few incidents of violence involving Indians and alcohol, a marked departure from the standard stereotype and from the expectations of most government officials, police officers and clergymen in the area. In addition, there were only a few other charges against natives in the Whitehorse area (Table 8).

TABLE 8
NATIVE CONVICTIONS, WHITEHORSE COURT, 1930-49

	Supplying Liquor	Drunk	Possession	Theft	Assault	Other
1930-34	7	24	2	3	1	6
1935-39	4	32	2	—	1	3
1940-44	5	86	6	3	4	10
1945-49	5	265	31	—	1	15

Source: Whitehorse Police Court Register

The natives were clearly law-abiding and found little difficulty accepting and heeding the parameters set by the Canadian legal system. Most of the offences, including the alcohol-related convictions, were against laws designed to control social or moral behaviour. There were, for instance, seven native women apprehended between 1942 and 1944 under a Venereal Disease Protection Ordinance which allowed the court to order the confinement of any infected individual to a hospital to ensure treatment and prevent further spread of the disease.

The courts were generally lenient with the natives who appeared before them, especially in contrast to whites charged for similar offences. The standard punishment for native intoxication was from $5 to $30, depending on the number of times the offender had visited the court, with an option of a jail term of from ten days to a month. Particularly frequent offenders were not given the option of paying the fine. Those whites accused and convicted of supplying liquor to Indians faced a minimum fine of $100 or two months, with harsher penalties for subsequent offences. The high penalties were, in part, a reflection of the high returns available to bootleggers.

In sum, the natives' encounter with the legal process was generally uneventful, although the regulation of alcohol use was emphasized. The influx of population and increased availability of liquor associated with the opening of the Alaska Highway provided far more occasions for drinking, and there is little doubt that native consumption did increase. At the same time, however, the R.C.M.P.'s decision to shift their Yukon headquarters to Whitehorse and to expand police operations in the southern territory ensured "better" enforcement of alcohol regulations and resulted in more convictions for liquor infractions.

The expansion of police operations was only one of the government services available in the heretofore poorly served area. As already mentioned, medical services were extended, and now included occasional dental clinics and, in 1949, the appointment of a public health nurse to deal with native health problems along the highway.[58] Educational opportunities also expanded. The Carcross Residential School was installed in larger quarters, and more day schools were opened, including a combination residential/day school operated by evangelist Rev. H. Lee which was erected in Whitehorse in 1947 to serve the town's growing native population.[59]

By far the most important government move in the decade was the 1944 decision to establish a universal family allowance system. Under the programme, parents were to receive a set amount of money each month for each child of school age. The money was targetted for the children's needs; the programme required that, if facilities existed, the children were to attend school on a regular basis. Failure to conform to the regulations, particularly the educational requirement, resulted in a suspension of payments. Not surprisingly, one result was an increase in the number of native students in school (Table 9).

TABLE 9
DAY SCHOOL ATTENDANCE, YUKON INDIANS, 1935-54
(YEARLY AVERAGES)

	Schools	Total Enrolled	Average Attendance (Per Cent)
1935-39	6	124	52
1940-44	4	71	60
1945-49	7	178	71
1950-54[1]	6	230	90

[1] An average of 47 students per year enrolled in territorial public schools are included in the tabulation.

Source: Department of Indian Affairs, *Annual Reports, 1935-1955.*

As well, the number in attendance at the Carcross Residential School increased. The expansion of educational offerings was not without difficulties, however, as the Catholic and Anglican missionaries in the region fought, often bitterly, for the right to teach individual students and, even more important, the right to establish schools at key locations.[60]

Although the national family allowance programme was based on regular cash payments, the Yukon Indians did not receive such disbursements. Instead, the government issued the monthly allotment "in kind," meaning that traders and storekeepers throughout the territory gave native parents foodstuffs and clothing for their children in the amount designated by the government. Fear that the natives' nomadic lifestyle would lead to profligate waste each summer when the families returned to the trading posts provided the rationale for this departure from standard practice. In an even more paternalistic vein, payment in kind also allowed the government to dictate precisely what the natives received, ensuring that such products as canned milk and tomatoes and prepared baby foods came into wide use among the Indians. In addition to changes in diet and material culture fostered by the programme, the family allowance encouraged, and eventually required, natives to reside near schools on a permanent basis or else send their children to a residential school. The alternatives forced harsh and difficult choices between seasonal patterns of movement and a more sedentary existence calculated to ensure a continuation of the payments. In the short term, however, the government was not unduly harsh in enforcing the regulations among the Yukon Indians. In 1948 for instance, over 480 children were registered in the programme while school attendance in the territory totalled only 130 in day schools and 62 at the Carcross Residential School. Those natives who had access to the appropriate facilities were expected to make use of them, and the government did not hesitate to enforce the requirements in such situations.[61]

The establishment of the family allowance with its accompanying social dislocations obviously had nothing to do with the construction of the Alaska Highway or the economic condition of the Yukon Indians. Rather, it originated with a desire to provide a nation-wide, universal social assistance plan. While the building of the highway did ease delivery problems somewhat, the fact that the government relied on traders already on site to dispense the allowance ensured that the impact of the programme was generally even throughout the territory.

A similar relationship existed between federal expenditures on the Yukon Indians and the construction of the highway. Before 1948, expenditures increased very slowly. The surge in expenditures in 1949-50 was primarily a result of the decision to build a residential school at Lower Post and improve the Carcross Residential School. It is apparent that the coming of the highway did not in itself usher in a new era in government-native fiscal relations (Table 10).

The noticeable increase in welfare expenditures in 1949-50 again cannot be traced solely to the highway, but was owing instead to a precipitous decline

TABLE 10
FEDERAL EXPENDITURES ON YUKON INDIANS, 1930-49
(YEARLY AVERAGES)

	Administration	Day Schools	Residential Schools	Welfare	Total[1]
1930-34	2,789	2,872	20,972	8,836	44,541
1935-39	1,011	4,366	15,459	9,950	42,358
1940-44	665	4,844	11,145	11,719	41,682
1945-49	7,227	23,988	17,884	18,287	67,386

[1] Includes other expenditures not listed.
Source: Department of Indian Affairs, *Annual Reports, 1930-1955.*

in fur prices at that time. The government was far more active than before, but the vitality was largely a reflection of a wider government commitment to aid the northern Indians. This increased activity resulted in the establishment of such programmes as the family allowance, allowances for aged Indians, and the decision to intensify participation in job placement, health care and education.[62]

It is difficult, if not impossible, to separate the impact of expanded government programmes and declining fur markets from the construction of the Alaska Highway. The juxtaposition of these events has resulted in a blurring of distinctions, with the result that the more high-profile activity has been singled out as responsible for the changes and difficulties of the time.[63] Attribution of responsibility is, of course, a futile practice, but there is nonetheless a noticeable tendency to see the Alaska Highway as the root cause of the problems currently being experienced by the Indians of the southern Yukon. Current concern over the impact of such projects as the Alyeska Pipeline and the proposed Mackenzie Valley and Alaska Highway Pipelines has unquestionably spurred interest in what is perceived as an older but related example of "corridor development."[64]

The Alaska Highway construction did not pass without noticeable impact on the Yukon Indians. The consequences, however, were much more ambiguous than have usually been asserted. Economic and social relations between the natives and the wider Yukon community continued to conform to patterns established in the gold rush era, although miscegenation and alcohol consumption increased in relation to the larger white population in the region. Unquestionably, and at a level greater than normally believed, the highway construction had catastrophic demographic implications, with the diseases and epidemics introduced by the soldiers and workers wreaking havoc on the native population and contributing to a staggering infant mortality rate and an overall decline in population.

The legacy of the construction and opening of the Alaska Highway, however, with the exception of the medical consequences, does not provide evidence for an indictment of northern construction projects. It seems that the social and economic order in the 1942 to 1950 period fell within long established patterns and points more to the entrenched peripheral role of the natives in the Yukon than to any standard impact of development in areas occupied by nomadic Indians. The past, to alter an old saying, is not always prologue.

Notes

1. In the first group fit such pamphlets as *The Alaska Highway: A Saga of the North,* (Edmonton: Stuart Douglas, 1943); "Alcan: America's Glory Road," *Engineering News-Record.* 17 December 1942, 31 December 1942, 14 January 1943. Also, a recording of 1942 CBC radio broadcast originating along the highway can be found in the National Film, Television and Sound Archives, PAC. Examples of the second set of commentators include, C.K. Le Capelain to R.A. Gibson, 17 July 1943, PAC, RG 91, vol. 9, file 1490, part J; Dr. John Marchand, "Tribal Epidemics in Yukon," *Journal of the American Medical Association,* 123 (1943): 1019-20.
2. David Remley, *Crooked Road: The Story of the Alaska Highway,* (Toronto: McGraw-Hill, 1976), pp. 205-12; Julie Cruikshank, "Alaska Highway Construction: A Preliminary Evaluation of Social Impacts on Yukon Indians," unpublished paper presented to the Mackenzie Valley Pipeline Inquiry.
3. Ken Coates, "Furs Along the Yukon: Hudson's Bay Company-Native Trade in the Yukon River Valley, 1830-1893," unpublished M.A. thesis, University of Manitoba, 1980.
4. For an interesting comment on the non-oppressive nature of the hunting-gathering economy, see Marshall Sahlins, "Notes on the Original Affluent Society," in *Stone Age Economics* (Chicago: Aldine/Atherton, 1972).
5. One small group — male graduates of the Carcross Residential School — stood as an exception to this general statement.
6. Marchand, "Tribal Epidemics"; Geddes to Gibben, 11 January 1945, PAC, RG 10, vol. 6477, file 928-1, pt. 1.
7. Hiring practices of companies involved in highway construction in the Whitehorse district are outlined in Corpl. Allen to Officer in Charge, R.C.M.P., Whitehorse, 24 March 1943, PAC, RG 91, vol. 62, file 35411. Indians are not mentioned. See also *The Alaska Highway: A Saga of the North.*
8. Report to the Diocese of Yukon upon the present state of the Champagne (Y.T.) Mission Field, Summer 1949, by Anthony Guscoyne, Yukon Territorial Archives (YTA), Anglican Church Records, Champagne file.
9. Department of Indian Affairs, *Annual Report 1949,* p. 195; *Annual Report 1950,* p. 63.
10. *Census of Canada,* 1931, 1941, 1951.
11. With almost no exceptions, women were listed as housewives.
12. R.J. Meek report, 28 February 1947, PAC, RG 10, vol. 6761, file 420-12-2-2; R.A. Gibson to J.E. Gibben, 17 December 1947, PAC, RG 10, vol. 6742, file 420-6-1-1.
13. R.J. Meek to Indian Affairs Branch, 3 July 1947, PAC, RG 10, vol. 6761, file 420-12-2-2.
14. Meek to Indian Affairs Branch, 17 November 1947, PAC, RG 10, vol. 6761, file 420–2-RT-1.
15. Meek to Indian Affairs Branch, 17 January 1950, ibid. The downturn in the market led to a number of requests that the annual $10 licence fee be waived for Indians. Meek to Gibson, 17 September 1950, YTA, YRG 1, series 3 (Game Branch), vol. 11, file 12-23B; Petition of Teslin Indians, 7 July 1950, ibid.; Old Crow Petition, 24 July 1950, ibid.; Kjar to Gibson, 5 October 1950, ibid.
16. Gibson to P.J. Hoffmaster, 23 January 1943, YTA, YRG 1, series 3, vol. 10, file 12-20B; Gibson to LaForest, 30 April 1949, ibid.

17. D.A. Macdonald to Commissioner, R.C.M.P., 11 December 1944, YTA, YRG 1, series 3, vol. 10, file 12-20A; See also Testimony of Joe Jacquot, 21 April 1976, PAC, RG 126 (Records of the Mackenzie Valley Pipeline Inquiry), vol. 37. No substantive evidence of such destruction was found. Gibben to Gibson, 17 December 1942, YTA, YRG 1, series 3, vol. 10, file 12-20A.
18. C.H.D. Clarke to M. Cumming, 3 November 1942, PAC, RG 85 (Northern Administration Branch), vol. 944, file 12743, pt. 1; Gibson to Jeckell, 3 June 1943, YTA, YRG 1, series 3, vol. 10, file 12-20B; Gibson to Jeckell, 9 September 1942, ibid., file 12-20A.
19. Jeckell to Gibson, 13 January 1944, YTA, YRG 1, series 3, vol. 10, file 12-20C; for American comments, see Albert Day to R.A. Gibson, 19 January 1943, ibid., file 12-20B, W.E. Crouch to R.A. Gibson, 3 February 1943, ibid.
20. Gibson to Jeckell, 6 October 1943, YTA, YRG 1, series 3, vol. 17, file 28798.
21. Robert McCandless, "Yukon Wildlife: A Social History," unpublished manuscript, March 1981, ch. 4, copy in YTA.
22. Ibid.; Privy Council order 11142, 8 December 1942, PAC, RG 91, vol. 71, file 32.
23. Gibson to Finn, 9 June 1943, ibid.
24. Jacquot to Jeckell, 28 November 1943, ibid.
25. Privy Council order 7101, 15 September 1944; F.H.R. Jackson to Jeckell, 19 November 1945; Gibson to Jeckell, 8 December 1945, ibid.
26. F.H.R. Jackson to Gibson, 12 September 1946, YTA, YRG 1, series 3, vol. 11, file 12-21A; Privy Council order 3518, ibid.; Jackson to Gibben, 17 September 1947, PAC, RG 91, vol. 71, file 32; Jacquot to George Black, 30 March 1947, ibid.
27. See Jackson to Gibben, 17 September 1949, ibid.
28. Ibid.; Meek and Kendall to H.R. Conn, 20 June 1950, PAC, RG 10, vol. 6761, file 420-12-2-RT-1; Gibson to Simmons, 22 April 1950, YTA, YRG 1, series 3, vol. 11, file 12-23B; Morriset to Indian Affairs Branch, 11 April 1950, ibid.; Morriset to Simmons, 13 April 1950, ibid.
29. Gibben to Gibson, 19 June 1950, YTA YRG 1, series 3, vol. 11, file 12-23B; Conn to Meek, 22 May 1950, PAC, RG 10, vol. 6761, file 420-12-2-RT-1; Meek to Indian Affairs Branch, 16 May 1950, PAC, RG 10, vol 8865, file 1/18-11-12 pt. 1; Jackson to Gibben, 17 September 1949, PAC, RG 91, vol. 71, file 32; Kjar to Gibben, 15 June 1950; ibid.; Meek to Indian Affairs Branch, 15 March 1950, PAC, RG 10, vol. 6761, file 420-12-2-RT-1.
30. Gibben to Indian Affairs Branch, 10 April 1943, P.A.C., RG 10, vol. 7553, file 41-166,1.
31. The programme, such as it was, is documented in ibid. See especially Lowe to Noey, 15 June 1943.
32. Marchand, "Tribal Epidemics in the Yukon." Interestingly, ethnographer John Honigman noted that further to the south, in the Fort Nelson area, the epidemics witnessed by Marchand seemed to have bypassed the native population. J. Honigman, letter to the editor, *Journal of the American Medical Association,* 124 (1944): 386. Re the Teslin epidemics, see also S. Webb to Bishop, 9 July 1943, YTA, Anglican Church Records, Champagne File.
33. Department of Indian Affairs, *Annual Report 1943,* p. 148, and *Annual Report 1944,* p. 153.
34. Disease spread throughout the territory, as had happened on many occasions in the past. In 1945, a major influenza outbreak was reported at Old Crow, affecting 70 out of 130 residents. E. Kirk to O.C. Whitehouse, s/d, R.C.M.P., 1 September 1945, PAC, RG 85, vol. 609, file 2657.
35. Death records, particularly among natives in remote areas, are not always accurate and tend to emphasize Indian populations near towns or access routes. With the territorial registrar able to rely on clergy, R.C.M.P. officers and Indian agents for information, however, the Yukon data base, while not perfect, appears to be fairly comprehensive.
36. Department of Indian Affairs, *Annual Reports* for 1940, 1945 and 1950.
37. Marchand, "Tribal Epidemics in the Yukon"; Honigman, letter to the editor; C.K. Le Capelain to R.A. Gibson, 17 July 1943, PAC, RG 91, vol. 9, file 149B, pt. J.
38. Lawrence to W.W. Foster, 24 November 1944, PAC, RG 36/7, (special commissioner on northern defence projects), vol. 15, file 28-12; Foster to Gibbon, 28 November 1944, ibid.
39. R.A. Gibson to J.A. Gibben, 5 February 1947, PAC, RG 91, vol. 9, file 1490, pt. J.

40. P.E. Moore to R.A. Gibson, 5 April 1946, ibid.
41. See Gibben to Indian Affairs Branch, 1 March 1946, ibid.
42. Summary of X-Ray Survey, Indian Residents, Whitehorse, Yukon, July 1949, PAC, RG 91, vol. 65, file 813. The figure for the white population was only 11 per cent.
43. See results of the following surveys: Carmacks-Dawson, June 1948; Old Crow, December 1948; Whitehorse, February 1949; Lee's School and Carcross School, 21 February 1949, PAC, RG 91, vol. 65, file 013.
44. For details on the survey, see Gibben to Keenleyside, 4 September 1947; Gibben to Meltzer, 10 March 1949; Report on a Tuberculosis Survey in the Yukon Territory, (1949), ibid.
45. Meek to Indian Affairs Branch, 24 November 1949, PAC, RG 10, vol. 647B, file 929-11, pt. 1; Meek to Indian Affairs Branch, 25 October 1947, ibid., vol. 6477, file 929-1, pt. 1.
46. Report on Tuberculosis Survey in the Yukon Territory (1949), PAC, RG 91, vol. 65, file 813.
47. Ibid.; J. Locke to J.E. Gibben, 28 September 1949, YTA, YRG 1, series 2, vol. 44, file 36496H.
48. The standard argument, that the natives and whites lived in harmony and friendship before 1942, is not supported by the evidence of frequent and consistent expressions of racial feelings in Whitehorse, Dawson and Mayo which began in the gold rush era. Barring natives from hospitals and schools was standard practice, as was the setting of curfews to keep Indians out of town in the evenings. For an expression of the other view, see McCandless, "Yukon Wildlife: A Social History."
49. Extract from report of R.J. Meek, 9 April 1948, PAC, RG 10, vol. 6479, file 940-1, pt. 2; Meek to Indian Affairs Branch, 8 February 1950, p. 6, ibid., vol. 8762, file 906/25-1-005, pt. 1.
50. For a description of prostitutes' activities during the gold rush, see Hal Guest, "Dawson City," unpublished manuscript prepared for Parks Canada, 1981.
51. See, in particular, J. Honigman and I. Honigman, "Drinking in an Indian-White Community," *Quarterly Journal of Studies on Alcohol*, vol. 5 (March, 1945): 575-619. Prosecutions under a territorial Venereal Disease Protection Ordinance were aimed at keeping sexually active women, often prostitutes, out of commission while the disease was being treated. See PAC, RG 18, Yukon Records, Whitehorse Police Court, 1900-50; also, H.J. Sparten to Commissioner of Y.T., 9 December 1949, PAC, RG 91, vol. 62, file 35411.
52. Meek to Gibben, 28 May 1947; Gibben to Hoey, 4 June 1947; Gibben to Hoey, 20 June 1947; Superintendent, Reserves and Trusts to Gibben, 19 August 1947, all in PAC, RG 91, vol. 9, file 1490, pt. J.
53. Cruikshank, "Alaska Highway Construction."
54. Submission of Hugh Brody to Mackenzie Valley Pipeline Inquiry, PAC, RG 126.
55. Honigman and Honigman, "Drinking in an Indian-White Community."
56. Robert Edgerton and C. MacAndrews, *Drunken Compartment: A Social Explanation*. (Chicago: Aldine, 1969). For the best available review of the subject, see W. Taylor, *Drinking, Homicide and Rebellion in Colonial Mexican Villages* (Stanford: Stanford University Press, 1979).
57. Honigman and Honigman, "Drinking in an Indian-White Community."
58. Meek to Indian Affairs Branch, 8 February 1950, PAC, RG 10, vol. B762, file 906125-1-005, pt. 1.
59. Meek to Welfare and Training, Indian Affairs Branch, 15 January 1947, ibid., vol. 6477, file 929-1, pt. 1.
60. The battle can be followed in a variety of Anglican Church files and in Department of Indian Affairs records. See YTA, Anglican Church, Carcross Property file; PAC, RG 10, vol. 6482, file 942-1, pt. 1; file 942-5; vol. 8762, file 906/25-1-001.
61. Department of Indian Affairs, *Annual Reports* for 1945 to 1950; Rowat to Jeckell, 4 June 1945, YTA, YRG 1, series 4, vol. 33, file 689; in particular, see R.J. Meek to Indian Affairs Branch, 8 February 1950, PAC, RG 10, vol. 8762, file 906/25-1-005, pt. 1.
62. See Department of Indian Affairs, *Annual Reports* for 1940 to 1950 for indications of the

increased activity. Each report contains a short comment on conditions and undertakings in the Yukon.
63. See in particular Cruikshank, "Alaska Highway Construction," also Remley, *Crooked Road.*
64. The Cruikshank piece was prepared for the Berger Inquiry into the proposed Mackenzie Valley Pipeline. See also Julie Cruikshank, "The International Highway Commission and the Building of the Alaska Highway," submitted to the same inquiry, PAC, RG 126, vol. 37.

13

The Gravel Magnet:
Some Social Impacts of the
Alaska Highway on Yukon Indians

JULIE CRUIKSHANK*

Popular accounts of Alaska Highway construction emphasize heroic themes: "man against the wilderness," "North American defence," "triumph of technology," "bringing civilization north," and so on. They stress the speed with which the road was built and the overall efficiency of the operation in the face of wartime constraints. More serious investigation, on the other hand, indicates that building the highway was a process which began well before 1942 and continued after the road was in place. Scholars have begun to consider construction in a variety of contexts: military, political, industrial and social.

One context worth examining is that of the social impact of the Alaska Highway on Yukon Indians, through whose territory the road passed. In a preliminary attempt to evaluate that impact, this paper begins by outlining some aspects of the native economy and society before the construction of the road. Secondly, events surrounding the construction in the southern Yukon are summarized, followed by a discussion of short-term and long-term effects of the highway on Indian people living close to the route. Such effects include changes in the annual cycle, settlement patterns, sources of subsistence and cash income, social organization, values, education, health conditions and alcohol use. The analysis is based on church, government and military records available in the Yukon archives, and also draws on oral accounts I have recorded since 1974.[1] In these accounts, people rarely single out the construction as an event; rather they mention the highway in passing in discussions of how life has changed during the twentieth century.

Ethnographers have repeatedly documented the ability of Athapaskan Indians to adapt to the changing conditions of life, and nowhere is this clearer than in the southern Yukon.[2] Native people living there were aboriginal hunters and fishermen who developed technology, social customs and a subsistence lifestyle admirably suited to a subarctic environment. Since resources varied cyclically, families migrated over large areas of land in the course of a year to obtain food, clothing and shelter. They fished for and dried salmon in summer, hunted game animals and dried the meat in fall, stayed relatively immobile in winter to conserve energy, and began trapping and fishing again in spring. Because animal migration patterns might change, the Indians were always prepared to modify their movements when necessary.[3]

Social organization was also flexible, though structured by the matrilineal descent groups (moieties), Wolf and Crow, which were sometimes further subdivided into "sibs" or clans. It was fundamental Indian law that a Crow person must marry a Wolf and vice versa; marriage within one's own moiety was treated as incest. Such marriage rules reinforced alliances between kin groups, guiding proper behaviour at birth, puberty, death, and other occasions.

Division of labour reflected age, sex, and kinship. Generally men provided and women prepared the food, clothing, and shelter within the domestic household, although each was capable of performing the other's roles when necessary. A man was responsible for supporting his wife's parents until their deaths. Old people were well cared for and were respected for their knowledge and experience, which they were expected to pass on to the young. Children were encouraged to take responsibility early in life and to work with and learn from adults.

Political leadership was not institutionalized apart from kinship. A "chief" was the ranking male representative of his lineage, and his influence depended on his abilities to acquire and manipulate wealth. He did not exercise absolute power but earned respect on an ongoing basis.

A rich mythology stressed the need for harmony with all beings in the natural world, particularly respect for animal species on which life depended.[4] Irresponsible hunting and trapping were deplored.

Native people in the north have long adjusted not only to changes in wildlife cycles but also to changes in human history. Trade between coastal Tlingit Indians and interior Athapaskans began at least two centuries ago. The Tlingit imported trade goods from European traders on the coast and exported valuable furs. Some Tlingit moved inland to be closer to the source of furs, and they brought their language, social customs, clans and crests with them and blended into the local culture.

More dramatic change came with the Klondike gold rush of 1896-98. More than thirty thousand immigrants arrived within a few years. Some

Indians along the way became involved in packing, guiding, and providing food for prospectors; a few years later others were deck hands on riverboats. The Tagish who were involved in the initial gold discovery, and the Han at the mouth of the Klondike were most directly affected. Most other Yukon natives were observers of rather than participants in the rush. The greatest effects for them included the breaking of the Tlingit fur trade monopoly;[5] the impact of forest fires on wildlife along the Yukon River;[6] the arrival of independent white traders;[7] the expansion of missionary activity;[8] the building of the White Pass and Yukon Route railway from Skagway to Whitehorse; and the running of a riverboat fleet between Whitehorse and Dawson. Some early trading post sites later became villages along the Alaska Highway.

Most whites left the country soon after the beginning of the century. In 1900, the total population of the Yukon Territory had climbed to over 27,000, of whom 3,000 were Indians. By 1912, it had declined to 6,000 Indians and whites and by 1921 to just over 4,000. The population remained relatively stable for the next twenty years: 4,230 in 1931 and 4,914 in 1941.[9]

Fur prices remained high well into the 1930's.[10] By then, a family's annual cycle included one or more trips to a trading post, and some families built log cabins near posts to use when they visited. There was some seasonal wage work on riverboats, at wood camps, with game guides, and on the White Pass railroad. More children were attending residential schools. Yet basic social organization and coherence of the traditional lifestyle remained.

Before the Second World War, there were no major roads and almost no mechanized vehicles in the Yukon. A few wagon trails remained from the flurries of mining activity near Kluane Lake and Carcross in the early 1900's. A winter road parallelled the Yukon River from Whitehorse to Dawson City. The White Pass railroad brought freight from the coast to Whitehorse and carried out gold and other ore brought upstream from Dawson and Mayo. Generally, however, people travelled by foot, dog team or boat, and were separated from each other by several days of travel.

Then in April 1942, three regiments of American soldiers arrived in Whitehorse with orders to build the Yukon section of the Alaska Highway. Between April 1942 and December 1943, more than 34,000 men were employed, constructing the road through British Columbia, the Yukon, and Alaska. Once again, native people were overwhelmed by large numbers of outsiders with radically different lifestyles.

The second "rush," as older people call it, marked the beginning of another new era. Its consequences were substantially more disruptive than those of the first rush, testing native adaptability to the limits, often at great personal cost. Although the Alaska Highway was not the only factor involved in altering old ways, its construction and use can be seen as a central thread in changes which began to take place after 1942.

Discussions between the governments of Canada and the United States about a Yukon-Alaska-Pacific Highway began as early as 1929. In 1931, a joint United States-Canadian committee was set up to consider such a project. On 29 December 1938, Prime Minister Mackenzie King announced the appointment of a five member Canadian commission which was to parallel a commission already appointed by Roosevelt.[11] Although the commission held hearings to secure first hand data about the feasibility of proposed routes and even travelled to some Yukon communities, the final decision was made under the pressure of war.

The Alaska Highway itself was built in two phases: first, the pioneer road was constructed by the U.S. military and some civilian contractors: then a permanent road was built by the United States Public Roads Administration (P.R.A.) and the War Department, using Canadian and American civilian workers. The pioneer road was built by seven regiments of the U.S. Army Engineer Corps, including 394 officers and 10,765 enlisted men. As well, 47 contractors under the supervision of the Public Roads Administration employed a further 7,500 men. Three regiments worked in British Columbia; one worked in Alaska. Three other regiments reached Whitehorse in April 1942.[12] From there, one worked north to Alaska while another worked south to Teslin; the third regiment was sent to Teslin by boat and worked south to Watson Lake. Construction camps or "line camps" were located at 10- to 15-mile intervals along the route and at every major bridge site. Each camp housed between one hundred and two hundred men. Main camps were at Fort St. John, Fort Nelson, Whitehorse and Tok.[13] Overnight, the population of Whitehorse rose from 754 to 20,000, and an array of army buildings, supply depots and warehouses appeared around the city.[14] The pioneer road was completed on 20 November 1942, eight months after construction began.

The building of the permanent road along the approximate path of the pioneer road was completed in 1943. The work consisted of straightening and upgrading the original road. For this job, the P.R.A. employed 81 contractors who in turn employed 14,000 men. They were assisted by 1,850 employees of the P.R.A. itself. The work was done by dividing contractors into two shifts, each working ten to twelve hours a day with equipment working twenty-two hours a day. This permanent road was completed on 31 October 1943, although twenty bridges remained to be finished.[15] Within a year and a half, a total of 34,637 men came to a relatively isolated part of the world where only a few thousand people made their homes.

Related projects accompanied the building of the Alaska Highway, opening up an entire communications system. In the winter of 1940-41, Canada had released funds to build a chain of airfields across northern British Columbia and the Yukon — the Northwest Staging Route. A series of airfields were built at Fort St. John, Fort Nelson, Watson Lake and Whitehorse, extending to Northway, Big Delta and Fairbanks, Alaska. Construction of the Haines Road to Alaska, begun in December 1942, further increased road access to the southwest Yukon. The Canol, or Canadian Oil, Project, funded by the United States and built by the United States Army and Canadian labour, pushed through a short-lived road and pipeline from the Alaska Highway to Norman Wells, Northwest Territories. A refinery was built at Whitehorse. Started in 1943, the project was abandoned in 1945, soon after it was completed.

On 1 April 1946, the Canadian government took over the Alaska Highway, and the Canadian army began administering the Northwest Highways System. At first, camps were strung along the highway at places like Brooks Brook, Canyon and Koidern. But by the late 1950's, there was an increasing tendency to concentrate workers and their families in centres such as Haines Junction and Whitehorse and, ultimately, in the Camp Takhini enclave at Whitehorse.

With transportation routes clearly shifting away from the river, a new road connecting Whitehorse, Mayo and Dawson City was begun in 1951 and was completed and upgraded in 1953. When it was finished, the Yukon's capital was transferred from Dawson City to Whitehorse. Subsequent roads, such as the Robert Campbell loop from Watson Lake to Faro to Carmacks, were built to accommodate the mining industry.

A project the size and scope of the Alaska Highway has a range of consequences, some anticipated, others entirely unforeseen. The impact of the highway on Indian subsistence patterns and social institutions falls in the latter category, partly because these were not issues considered particularly important in the context of the Second World War, and partly because the real consequences were long-term rather than short-term and can only be appreciated in hindsight. In order to analyze a range of interrelated consequences, one must examine: the overall impact of the highway on the subsistence pattern; its influence on employment patterns and cash income; the effects of government programmes on family life; the effects on demography and health; and finally, the effects on native values.

Consequently, native elders say that in 1942 fur prices were lower than they had been for years. Many native families who traded at posts near the new highway route (Teslin, Champagne, Burwash Landing) decided, for the first time, not to trap that winter but rather to remain at the post or go to Whitehorse to seek employment related to highway construction. After the highway was completed, many of these people continued to live year-round along the highway, where they were joined by other natives from more distant areas. A steady drift of natives from all over the Yukon to the margins of Whitehorse has continued ever since.

Once the road from Whitehorse to Mayo and Dawson was built, and the riverboats no longer ran, Indians began to abandon river communities such as Upper Laberge, Lower Laberge, Big Salmon, Little Salmon, and Fort Selkirk. They moved closer to the roads with the intention of getting wage work to supplement an unstable income based on deteriorating fur prices.

A similar population decline at traditional native centres of Hutshi, Aishihik and Kloo Lake followed road construction. The creation of new permanent villages, such as Watson Lake, Haines Junction, Beaver Creek and Pelly Crossing, and the growth of older villages such as Teslin, Carmacks and Burwash Landing, can be attributed directly to road construction.

Most natives who moved to the highway or to Whitehorse from other areas could no longer maintain their old subsistence patterns. The land adjacent to the highway was limited, and earlier residents resented the competition of newcomers from elsewhere, especially as game and fish supplies dwindled.

Additional competition for resources came from highway workers. In 1942, the commanding officer of the United States Engineer Corps requested from the Yukon territorial government special hunting privileges for the United States Army and for Canadian civilians working on the highway.[16] After considerable correspondence on the subject, United States Army personnel and civilians working on the road were granted resident hunting licences while they were working in the Yukon. Indian people have stated repeatedly that some soldiers shot moose and other large game animals for sport and then had to return to work before they could get the meat out. Similarly, soldiers reportedly caught fish on their days off and left behind what they could not consume. This kind of waste ran counter to native ethical codes and directly affected Indians who relied on animal resources for food.

Perhaps the most obvious result of this sport hunting along the highway was the establishment of the Kluane Game Sanctuary. Its creation eliminated Indian hunting rights in an area where they had formerly hunted and trapped. In December 1942, the Governor-General of Canada signed an order-in-council placing about 10,000 square miles in reserve. During the summer of 1943, a team of specialists (a mammalogist, a forester and the controller of national parks) examined the southwest Yukon and reported that it was seriously depleted of game because of the new accessibility provided by the Alaska Highway and the Haines Road.[17] That same year, an amendment was made to the existing territorial game ordinance giving the Commissioner of the Yukon power to declare a two-mile wide "no shooting" zone along the Alaska Highway and creating the Kluane Game Sanctuary.[18] Hunting and trapping by Indians and whites was prohibited within the sanctuary.

Yet according to the fur supervisor for Indian affairs in Ottawa at the time:

The limited correspondence on our files concerning this sanctuary would indicate that the decimation of the big game resources in the area was the direct result of too intensive big game hunting by whites generally and particularly by U.S. Army personnel of the Alaska Highway construction crews. The Indians, therefore, who from time immemorial had hunted and trapped over the area without decimating the supply of big game animals have now to bear the brunt of rehabilitation.[19]

After considerable discussion, the area was later opened by special permit to Indians for "supervised" muskrat hunting between the White and Donjek Rivers and for hunting of bull moose. But Indian people at Kluane Lake, whose livelihood was seriously disturbed by the restrictions on their traditional hunting territory, continued to blame the highway for troubles caused by the game sanctuary.

Indians who had formerly fished at Dalton Post and Klukshu found their lands arbitrarily bisected by the Haines road. New regulations cut them off from what were once their chief resources at a time when they had few other ways of procuring either food or cash.

The highway left another legacy. Publicity generated by the media and by the thousands of people who passed through the territory during construction created the image of the Yukon as a desirable place to hunt big game trophies. A "Director of Game and Publicity" was put in charge of wildlife management. A new perception of wildlife as an export commodity came into vogue.[20]

The introduction of registered traplines shortly after the highway was built further complicated the economic picture. The government-imposed plan did not take into account the natives' matrilineal social organization, which had formerly regulated use and inheritance of land.

All these factors, including new transportation routes and new methods of travel, low fur prices, availability of seasonal work in highway communities, increased pressure on wildlife and new government regulations about hunting and trapping, combined to limit the ability of families to provide for their basic needs as they had in the past. By the late 1940's, only a few families spent entire winters on traplines or engaged in extensive summer meat hunts. More and more it became necessary for men to earn cash income by new kinds of seasonal labour, often at low wages.

Very marked changes in annual cycle and settlement patterns then directly followed construction of major roads. As an elderly Teslin native explained, "Before the highway came and split us all in different ways, we used to feed ourselves good from this country."

The Alaska Highway also affected native employment patterns, cash income, and technology. Initially, some Yukon Indians benefited from opportunities for wage employment brought by highway construction. A few men got jobs doing slashing, general construction work, and guiding. The guides were invaluable because they knew the country best; in fact, they determined much of the actual ground route the pioneer road took.

Indian women earned money taking in laundry, cleaning maintenance camps, and sewing mukluks, jackets and mitts to sell to construction workers. A number made considerable incomes during the construction period: a Carcross woman says she made $900 sewing during the summer of 1942, while another in Whitehorse made $3,500 taking in soldiers' laundry between April and November 1942. Still another sold mukluks and mitts to soldiers and saved enough money to buy her family a truck. She enlisted the help of her husband and son-in-law who took boxes of items to the airport and sold them to departing soldiers. One time her son-in-law came back without a coat; someone had offered him eighty dollars for it. Another time her husband was wearing a caribou coat trimmed with beaver which she had made for him. A soldier asked if he could buy it. How much? Five hundred dollars, the son-in-law suggested hopefully. The soldier produced five one hundred dollar bills.

There was a certain amount of euphoria at first; times looked good and certainly interesting. One native man described how, in 1942, the army bought dogs to train for dog teams needed for construction work. Fur prices were low, and dogs were expensive to feed. Indians who had jobs did not expect to need the dogs again, so no one objected greatly to selling the animals. Later, when they had to return to trapping as a chief source of income, the natives who lacked dogs were seriously handicapped. What had seemed a small thing at the time came to make a great difference.

The sudden influx of cash meant a chance to experiment with new technology. While they were earning money in the spring of 1943, some people were able to buy cars to take advantage of the opening of the road to civilian traffic. They travelled extensively that summer, but by the fall, the cars began to break down, and most owners decided not to fix them. Those who had cars were frequently asked to lend them, making maintenance expensive. More importantly, many people were injured or killed in accidents.

Most of the jobs held by natives in 1942 and 1943 were short-term. Once the boom was over and the construction workers had left, many Indian families were less clear about their economic futures than ever before. Employment as pilots, deckhands and cooks on the riverboats disappeared in the early 1950's, when riverboats were withdrawn from service and replaced by road transport. Some Indians had worked for white contractors for decades cutting wood for boats during summer. Often they developed relationships not unlike those with fur traders, getting supplies each year and going into debt to the contractor.

Still, people continued to move out to the highway or to the subsequent branch roads looking for work. That they considered the move temporary was indicated by the large number of possessions they left behind in their old homes. When they returned they sometimes found their houses had been thoroughly looted.

Once in Whitehorse or in one of the smaller settlements along the highway, women sometimes found work in laundries, cafes, or hotels. Some wives brought in larger incomes than their husbands, since temporary jobs were usually the only kind of work available to Indian men. Thus many Indian men found themselves no longer able to provide for their families. Increasingly, native families were forced to rely for their livelihood on the more readily available government subsidies. These government programmes had a wide-ranging effect on Indian families.

The postwar expansion of government legislation and administrative agencies across Canada was facilitated in the Yukon by the new communications corridor. Government agents could now travel north, and Indian families could be relocated at settlements if they wanted access to schools, medical facilities, or social assistance programmes.

The 1944-45 Family Allowance Act made special provision for Indian families, but cheques were not issued directly to them. Rather, benefits were administered by the Indian Affairs Branch of the Department of Mines and Resources, which greatly increased its Yukon activities after the completion of the highway. By 1946, 165 Yukon Indian families with 483 children were registered.[21] Family allowances were offered as a direct inducement to register children in schools.

The 1952 Revised Act to Provide Old Age Assistance brought another small source of income directly to Indian families with members over seventy years of age.[22] As a result, the former close ties between old and young sometimes became strained when younger natives, unable to find work themselves, began to exploit the old as an easy source of cash. And, as English became the dominant working language, many young people could no longer communicate easily with their grandparents whose way of life and values they could not fully understand.

Sketchy statistics from the annual reports of the Indian Affairs Branch during the 1940's show the growing emphasis placed on Indian education in the Yukon. The number of students attending day schools increased as new schools were constructed in highway settlements. Once native children were integrated into the territorial school system, parents who wanted their children to live at home while they attended school had to move to settlements where schools were located. This meant that women with children could no longer accompany their husbands on traplines. Men found it difficult to trap for extended periods of time when they had to take on the additional burden of women's work in the bush. From 1942 to 1949, the number of schools rose from two to eight and the Indian students from 26 to 227.[23] During the same time period, welfare expenditures by the Indian Affairs Branch doubled.[24]

As government activities expanded, a host of new agencies began to operate in these villages, usurping the former functions of kin groups by providing economic support, social control, health care, and education. Many agencies dealt primarily with women who now remained in the villages with their children while their husbands left to seek work in Whitehorse or elsewhere, to hunt, to trap, or to accompany big game hunting parties. In many cases, mothers were directly eligible for various forms of family assistance and could have their own independent incomes. As one husband put it, "The government became my wife's old man. She didn't need me any more."

In the short term, many of the government services obviously benefited those Indians who had no other resources, but the cumulative effect of living in government-administered communities with no solid economic base also meant social breakdown in many families. A sense of frustration set in. Older people identify "the highway" as the time when traditional institutions began to break down.

The highway also had an effect on demography, health, and alcohol use. Although native villages were officially off limits to the army, the arrival of so many men from "outside" could not help but affect Indian-white relationships and particularly male-female relationships. Soldiers and construction workers were attractive to some women because they represented a life which seemed exciting and different, and because they seemed to have a lot of money. A few whites married Indian girls and took them home, thus reducing the chances of marriage for young Indian men, especially for those who adhered to moiety rules. Many white men formed short-term liaisons with native women whom they later abandoned. Older people describe the tragedies of girls who froze to death after drinking parties or who died in other violent ways because of their association with the men.

The army maintained relatively tight control over its personnel, but there were abuses. Records describe an incident at the Carcross Residential School in which two soldiers were discovered making regular overnight visits to the girls' dormitory. They were court-martialled the following spring and were given a sentence of eight months hard labour and a dishonourable discharge.[25] Police records also refer to alcohol related incidents such as "two American soldiers procuring liquor for an Indian man in an attempt to obtain the services of his two daughters."[26]

As early as 1943, there were a number of birth registrations with father listed as "unknown," and three letters from Indian mothers to the Yukon territorial government asking the government to locate white men who had abandoned their daughters with children.[27] By 1944-45, the government was discussing plans for an ordinance to provide for the maintenance of the children of unmarried parents. By 1947, the government became concerned about the status of "illegitimate" children with white fathers and Indian mothers. After much debate, it was decided that these children should be recognized as Indians.[28]

The net result of an influx of restless, dislocated males was to expose the native people to a new and distorted pattern of social behaviour in which promiscuity was no longer condemned, as it was in their traditional code. The moiety system began to lose its significance, and this caused great confusion about expected social obligations and support. The old rules ceased to work as they had in the past, yet it was difficult to adjust them readily to a rapid barrage of unexpected new regulations or freedoms which Indians themselves had not created.

Among the most immediate and horrifying results of the coming of the highway were the epidemics brought to settlements along the route. Any discussion of genealogies or old family photographs leads to commentary on people who "died in '42" or people who became ill during or after the construction. A doctor described how families remained at the Teslin post in the winter of 1942-43, hoping for jobs. During that winter they were overwhelmed by measles, dysentery, jaundice, whooping cough, mumps, tonsillitis and meningitis. Only the Indian population was affected.[29] During the winter, the same report notes, diphtheria took three lives at Ross River on the Canol Road, and pneumonia caused many deaths in northern British Columbia.

Many people are said to have died at McDame, just south of the Yukon border in British Columbia, and survivors fled to the new village of Lower Post. At Telegraph Creek on the upper Stikine River, the route used to transport men and materials to Watson Lake, sickness reportedly caused the deaths of most of the old people in the community.[30] Anglican Church records mention a dysentery epidemic at Champagne in 1942.[31] The same report notes that at Klukshu, then away from any highway, there was "very little sickness."[32] An Anglican missionary at Champagne in the summer of 1942 wrote that the epidemic began when "some Indians arrived from Whitehorse and brought the dysentery with them. Nearly all the Indians caught the disease one after another during the next three weeks ... (we) obtained medicine from the Army camp nearby." He recorded two deaths at Champagne.[33] For good reason, a government agent wrote to Ottawa in 1943 of his grave alarm about health conditions all along the highway.[34]

Indians remember these epidemics most vividly when discussing the highway. They grieve especially the deaths of children. One woman who lost a daughter in 1942 recalled a family who tried to leave Whitehorse to return home to Champagne. One of their children died eight miles from Whitehorse. In panic, they hurried back to Whitehorse. Another child died that afternoon. By evening they had lost a third. Another woman living near Ross

River in 1943, on the route of the Canol Road to Norman Wells, described how her mother was able to save some children by swabbing their throats with iodine. She remembers the army construction workers stopping work to build caskets for all the children who died.

Efforts to improve health care did eventually follow the construction of the Alaska Highway. A massive tuberculosis X-ray clinic toured the full length of the Alaska Highway between 1947 and 1949, bringing people in from their camps for tests.[35] The roads also provided better access to the hospital at Whitehorse, and health services improved significantly. However, one reason government agents urged families to move to the highway was so they could avoid expensive medical flights to isolated bush camps and villages. Although long-term hospitalization in Edmonton and Vancouver often meant survival for natives who might otherwise have died, the patients, especially young ones who had been away from their families for long periods of time, found readjustment to the Yukon very difficult.

A major change in the use of alcohol also accompanied the soldiers and construction crews. In the 1940's, it was still illegal for Indians to purchase alcohol. Alcohol had actually been used since the time of the gold rush, but usually in well-defined public contexts, "to show respect" to those of the opposite moiety. People say that in the 1920's and 1930's, it was used mainly to celebrate specific occasions, privately and infrequently, and by adults only. If parents planned to drink, they say, they made sure their children were safely cared for in another home. When soldiers and construction workers came, they brought alcohol to Indian homes openly and often. In some cases it was a genuine gesture of friendship; in other cases, it was clearly used to take advantage. Younger Indians began to drink, some of them heavily.

R.C.M.P. statistics show an enormous increase in liquor-related offences during and after the construction of the highway. Records of the twelve-year period from 1936-48 document this dramatically. Charges against Indians rose from 11 to 106, increasing more than tenfold.[36] In this context, though, it is significant that in 1943-44, at the height of the highway development, Indians were still far in the minority of persons charged. For example, in 1944, a total of 401 charges were laid by the Royal Canadian Mounted Police; only 44 of them were under the "Indian Act."[37] While increased numbers of charges may simply reflect increased police personnel or zeal, the exposure to the courts was simply a further intrusion of government authority into an area formerly regulated by family and community.

Older natives overwhelmingly maintain that the highway brought alcohol abuse and an alarming amount of violence, grief and further social disruption. Some Indians became enfranchised and gave up other government benefits so that they might purchase liquor without legal discrimination. Not until 1967 was legislation changed, giving Indians the same rights as other

Canadians to purchase liquor in the Yukon and the Northwest Territories.[38] But by then, alcohol abuse had become the serious problem that it is today for both natives and whites in the north.

Dramatic changes in demography, in health conditions and in alcohol abuse directly accompanied the construction phase of the highway. Once the road was completed, the problems it brought continued over the years as people moved from the bush to new communities. In these communities, traditional social institutions were less able to deal with the new problems.

Some of the most obvious effects that the highway has had on Indian customs and values have already been touched upon, but Indians who experienced the building of the highway and who have tried to assess the current state of their culture cite still other changes, some of which are also reflected in government records. For example, the older natives frequently refer to the fact that the soldiers stole, taking valued personal items from the traditional gravehouses or fences, or necessary equipment or irreplaceable ceremonial items from cabins. These things were taken as souvenirs, not because they were needed, and the Indians found this behaviour impossible to understand. The whites apparently got away with stealing from the Indians without serious consequences. There were major problems involved in policing the civilian camps, but troublemakers were usually given a free ride home under an international agreement.[39] Faced with such examples, a few Indians began to commit similar violations. R.C.M.P. files show that in 1950, thirteen Indians were charged with theft: of articles in caches, store goods, furs, liquor, and other items.[40] These violations would have been neither necessary nor tolerated in traditional native society.

To make matters worse, and in contrast with the treatment of soldiers and construction workers, Indians were severely punished, often out of all proportion to the violations. Considerable correspondence concerns one case where a white man gave an Indian man liquor. The Indian man went "joy riding" in a truck and was sentenced to one year in jail.[41] Another case is documented where a young native man, convicted of theft, was sentenced to one year in jail. Months later, it was discovered that he was only twelve years old.[42] Similarly, two teenage Indian girls convicted of shoplifting were each sentenced to one year in jail.[43]

These kinds of convictions had a noticeable impact on native communities. Discipline, always the prerogative of the family, began to fall to outside authorities: teachers, police courts, medical specialists, and later, to a whole host of government agencies.

Another pattern of behaviour introduced by the highway which ran directly counter to the native ethic was the incredible waste of army and construction camps, and the ruling that food and materials had to be destroyed or abandoned rather than distributed when personnel left the area. This was because the government felt distribution would constitute unfair competition to local businesses. The Indians recall "potholes filled with hams," "bags of flour dumped in the garbage," and so on. Such behaviour was repugnant to people who had always made maximum use of their environment. Such waste, which the older Indians have never forgotten, seemed a betrayal of man's obligation to share. All these events and attitudes, as well as others, steadily eroded the traditional value system without offering acceptable alternatives.

In conclusion then, the economy and society of the region now known as the Yukon has twice undergone dramatic metamorphoses: first in 1896-98 with the Klondike gold rush, then in 1942-45 with the construction of the Alaska Highway. Each event has generated a literature which describes it as adventure. Yet each was also part of a more prosaic process, the expansion of the Canadian state into the margins of northern North America and the establishment of an infrastructure which has continued to shape the Yukon's economy and society.

The Alaska Highway can be considered a classic example of corridor development. It was built at tremendous capital cost to serve "national interests." It was constructed by a large imported labour force through an isolated area inhabited mostly by native people. The construction phase was extremely rapid; short-term jobs were created for a few local people. Once the construction phase was over, the boom ended. However, the new road created new villages and opened a communications system which continued to change the lives of nearby residents. It also changed the ethnic balance, making Indians a decided minority in the Yukon.

It can be argued that these changes were initiated during the construction phase of the highway; however, the institutionalization of those changes came in the years following construction when a dramatically increased government presence in the north was facilitated by the establishment of the communications route. Government departments placed restrictions on trapping and hunting, effectively altering the native mode of production. Federal and territorial agencies armed with new legislation began to usurp social roles and institutions formerly under the authority of kin groups. The new communications corridor facilitated the arrival and effectiveness of these programmes and agencies. In the years during and following construction, irreversible changes occurred in the lives of Indians living along the route. Such changes occurred in two broad areas: first, in the relationship between Indians and their land, and second, in longstanding social institutions associated with kinship.

The highway was a decisive factor bringing Yukon Indians to the marginal position they have in the present Yukon economy and society. Development has continued to take place independently of Yukon Indian communities ever since, and frequently the natives have borne the social costs.

Forty years later, as celebrations of the anniversary of the Alaska Highway construction get underway, it is these same issues which concern Yukon Indian leaders negotiating their land claims settlement: their relationship to the land, their relationship to the economy, and their social institutions. In 1982, we have just passed through a decade of investigations into the potential social and environmental impact of large-scale development projects in the north. The Alaska Highway might serve as a case study of how seemingly short-term projects can have long range, far-reaching effects.

Notes

* This paper is a revised version of evidence presented by Dr. Catharine McClellan and myself at the Mackenzie Valley Pipeline Inquiry on 5 May 1976. Although we prepared the testimony together I take full responsibility for any errors in this revised paper.
1. Dr. Catharine McClellan has worked as an anthropologist in the southern Yukon periodically since 1948 and is the author of a number of ethnographic studies including a two volume work *My Old People Say*, (National Museums of Canada, 1975). The author has worked as a researcher in the Yukon and Alaska since 1968, and the oral accounts used for this study were recorded while I was compiling genealogies, biographies, family histories, photographic histories and traditional stories in the course of my work with the Yukon Native Languages Project. Over the years Dr. McClellan and myself have each been involved in discussions with people who experienced the coming of the Alaska Highway.
2. Catharine McClellan, "Introduction" to Special Issue: "Athapaskan Studies," *Western Canadian Journal of Anthropology* 2, no. 1, (1970): vi-xix; J. Vanstone, *Athapaskan Adaptations*, (Chicago: Aldine Publishing Co., 1974).
3. Catharine McClellan, *My Old People Say*, Publications in Ethnology No. 6 (2 vols.). (National Museum of Man, National Museums of Canada, Ottawa, 1975), passim; Julie Cruikshank, *Through the Eyes of Strangers*, (Yukon Territorial Government and Yukon Archives, 1974).
4. Julie Cruikshank, *When The World Began*, (Whitehorse: Department of Education, 1978); Julie Cruikshank, comp., *My Stories Are my Wealth*, by Angela Sidney, Kitty Smith and Rachel Dawson, (Whitehorse: Council for Yukon Indians, 1978); Angela Sidney, *Tagish Tlaagú*, recorded by J. Cruikshank (Whitehorse: Council for Yukon Indians and Department of Education, 1982).
5. Catharine McClellan, *Culture Change and Native Trade in the Southern Yukon Territory*. Ph.D. diss., Department of Anthropology, University of California, Berkeley, 1950.
6. Robert McCandless, *Trophies or Meat: Yukon Game Management 1896-1976*. (Yukon Territorial Government, 1977), p. 32.
7. Adrian Tanner, *The Structure of Fur Trade Relations*, M.A. thesis, Department of Anthropology, University of British Columbia, 1965.
8. Leslie Bullen. *An Historical Study of the Education of the Indians of Teslin, Yukon Territory*. M.Ed. thesis, University of Alberta, 1968.
9. *Canada Yearbook, 1973-1974: Historical Statistics of Canada*, ed. M.C. Urquart (Toronto: MacMillan, 1965), p. 304.
10. Adrian Tanner, *Trappers, Hunters and Fishermen: Wildlife Utilization in the Yukon Territory*, Yukon Research Project No. 5, Northern Co-ordination and Research Centre (Department of Northern Affairs and National Resources, 1966) pp. 8-10. Tanner writes that fur prices were high until 1914, dropped between 1914-17, rose until 1929 and again after 1935, but began to fall again after 1946.
11. *Whitehorse Star*, 6 January 1939, p. 1.
12. The 35th, 95th and 341st regiments worked in British Columbia; the 97th worked in Alaska; the 18th, 93rd and 340th were sent to the Yukon.
13. House of Representatives, *The Alaska Highway: An Interim Report from the Committee on Roads*. #2255, (1946), pp. 4, 53.

14. Jim Lotz, *Northern Realities,* (1970), p. 54.
15. Arthur E. Buckley, *The Alaska Highway,* M.Sc. thesis, University of Alabama, 1956, pp. 29-50.
16. Letter dated 30 April 1942, government records, YTA, file 466.
17. Letter from Mr. Gibson, director, Department of Resources and Development, 3 May 1948, to George Black, M.P. for the Yukon; on file, YTA.
18. Ordinance, Yukon Territory, ch. 4.
19. Letter from H.R. Conn, Fur Supervisor, Indian Affairs Branch, Ottawa, to R.J. Meek, Superintendent of Indian Agency, Whitehorse, 22 May 1950; on file, YTA.
20. McCandless, *Trophies or Meat,* pp. 53-54.
21. Indian Affairs Branch, Department of Mines and Resources, *Annual Report, 1946.*
22. The former "Old Age Pension Act," 1927, specifically excluded Indians.
23. From Indian Affairs Branch, *Annual Reports* from 1942 to 1949. Figures come from "Statement of Ordinary Expenditures, Education."
24. Figures from Indian Affairs Branch, *Annual Reports* from 1942 to 1949, from "Statement of Ordinary Expenditures, Welfare."
25. YTA, RG 10, vol. 6479, file 940-1, pt. 2.
26. R.C.M.P. Files, 1949-50. Prosecutions under the Indian Act, Section 135 or 128, YTA.
27. Government records, YTA, box 65, file 518.
28. Ibid., box 9, file 1490.
29. John Marchand, "Tribal Epidemics in the Yukon," *Journal of the American Medical Association,* 123, (1943): 1019-20.
30. Mrs. Eva Callbreath, formerly of Telegraph Creek, identified a number of people in old photographs taken in that community by ethnologist James Teit in 1912 and 1915. Her comments suggest that a significant number of people in the photos died in 1942.
31. *Northern Lights,* 31, no. 3, (November 1942).
32. Klukshu is still a summer fish camp on the Haines Road.
33. Anglican Church records, letter on file, YTA.
34. Letter from C.K. Le Capelain, liaison officer, to R.A. Gibson, Department of Mines and Resources, 19 July 1943:

> The Indians of the Teslin and Lower Post bands until the advent of this new era, have been almost completely isolated from contacts with white people and, have had the least opportunity of creating an immunity to white peoples' diseases. Consequently they have been distressingly affected by the new contacts. No doubt a contributing factor has been the fact that to a considerable extent the adult males have abandoned their normal nomadic pursuits and have accepted work on various construction projects, both American and Canadian.
>
> The band at Teslin suffered epidemics of measles and whooping cough, which in some cases developed into pneumonia, last year, and now are plagued with an epidemic of meningitis and have suffered three deaths so far from the latter. The bands at Lower Post were devastated last spring with an epidemic of influenza which caused 15 deaths among a total population of about 150 of all ages. There is no doubt in my mind that if events are allowed to drift along at will, but what the Indian bands at Teslin and Lower Post will become completely decimated within the next few years. The problem is how to prevent this, or at least to ameliorate conditions as far as possible.

35. Government records, YTA, box 65, file 813.
36. Police court records, Whitehorse, 1901-51, YTA, file 33937-8-D.
37. Ibid.
38. Decision of Mr. Justice Morrow in the Joseph Drybones case, June 1967.
39. Government records, correspondence, Gibben, 3 October 1942, YTA, file 466.
40. R.C.M.P. files 1949-50, Prosecutions Under the Indian Act, Section 128 or 135, YTA.
41. Government records, YTA, box 9, file 1490.
42. R.C.M.P. files, 1949-50.
43. Ibid.

14

The Impact of the Alaska Highway on Dawson City

RICHARD STUART

I regret that the route chosen for the highway and the railway are not through Dawson....

I hope someday a road connecting Dawson with the highway will be built. Meantime, we can carry on satisfactorily as we have done for so many years, relying on the good old gold paystreak that has, after all, been the backbone of the whole Yukon Territory.[1]

When George Black, the Yukon's member of parliament, addressed the residents of Dawson on Discovery Day, 1942, he probably expressed a common view: that the Alaska Military Highway was of ephemeral significance, while gold mining based in the Dawson district would continue to be the "backbone" of the Yukon's economy. In this Black was mistaken. The highway transformed the Yukon as dramatically as had the 1896 gold rush, increasing the pace of economic activity in the territory, opening up for exploitation areas hitherto inaccessible, and creating a city where the village of Whitehorse had stood. The construction-based boom passed quickly, but Whitehorse endured. It was transformed, while Dawson, the Yukon's metropolis since the gold rush, could not escape the weight of its past.

Between 1941 and 1951, the economic and political centre of gravity in the Yukon shifted three hundred miles south, from Dawson to Whitehorse, transforming the former from the major community and territorial capital to a village dependent upon gold mining and tourism. During this period, Whitehorse's size and prosperity undermined Dawson's entrepôt and service function, helped weaken its gold mining activities and eventually attracted the seat of government.

There is no simple causal link between the building of the Alaska Highway and the reduction of Dawson from territorial capital to village. The city's economic base had been eroding for years, and it was vulnerable to assault by a more dynamic community. Had the Yukon continued at the low level of economic and political activity of the 1930's, there would have been no justification for moving the capital. But the Alaska Highway transformed Whitehorse, and most of the territory, without benefiting Dawson.

A century before the Alaska Highway was built, the Yukon was drawn into the world economy by fur traders, particularly those of the Hudson's Bay Company. The fur trade period in Yukon history was short, but it was important as it set a value upon the resources of the territory for the outside world. From the 1880's to the present, however, the Yukon's value has been determined by its mineral resources. Gold was the first, and for years, the most important resource, attracting labour and capital to the territory at the time of the Klondike gold rush. The rush established a primary extraction economy, initially of gold, later of base metals, and determined that the dominant group in Yukon society would be white immigrants who brought with them the skills and capital necessary for the efficient operation of such an economy.

Many communities sprang up at the time of the gold rush, but only two significant ones survived: Dawson and Whitehorse. Dawson was an urban service centre, the Yukon's major port and entrepôt, and the administrative centre of the territory. It was established because of and was dependent upon gold mining. Its other urban functions, service, commercial and administrative, were secondary. Whitehorse, on the other hand, was sustained by its location on a river-rail transportation system extending from tidewater at Skagway to the markets of Dawson and the Klondike district. It was merely the breaking point between the rail and river systems. Though it shared some of Dawson's functions, the "Terminal City" on the Whitehorse rapids was subordinate to the "City of Gold" at the mouth of the Klondike.

Inevitably, the gold rush ended, resulting in a decline in economic activity and population. The Yukon did not relapse entirely to its pre-1896 state because it possessed a commodity, gold, for which there was a constant demand, and it had the necessary infrastructure to facilitate its extraction. Dawson suffered from the collapse of the gold rush, but it survived as mining changed from labour- to capital-intensive, and its promoters looked to many years of profitable exploitation of the Klondike.

By 1913, after the economic dislocations associated with the transition to capital-intensive mining were over, the territory seemed set to achieve the prosperity the gold rush had promised, albeit at a lower level. The First World War blighted this promise. It drove costs up and drew labour away from the Klondike. Dawson shared wartime costs, taxes, and inflation with the rest of Canada but none of the compensatory war work. Gold production collapsed in the early 1920's, dragging a territory totally dependent upon this one commodity down with it. The Yukon's population, which fell from 25,000 in 1901 to 8,500 in 1911, was halved again, to 4,100, by 1921. Dawson was built for 10,000 people. By 1921, it had barely 1,000 inhabitants, although the Klondike district still contained almost 20 per cent of the territory's population.[2]

The postwar decline in mining activity meant the reduction of Dawson to a small town, and "the withering away of the state in a way which Marx never envisaged."[3] Klondike gold mining could not generate sufficient tonnage on its own to keep the White Pass and Yukon Route rail and steamer system in operation, yet without the railway, mining could not function. Fortunately, in the early1920's, rich silver-lead ore bodies were developed near Mayo. The exploitation of these provided the White Pass with sufficient tonnage to continue to serve Dawson.

During the 1920's and 1930's, Mayo's silver-lead mines supported the Yukon. However, although it was the economic basis of the territory, it was no more than a mining camp, and posed no threat to Dawson's preeminence. At the same time, Mayo was economically subordinate to Whitehorse, not to Dawson, subtly altering the relationship between the latter two communities.

In the late 1930's, there were three main centres of population in the Yukon: Dawson, the capital and centre of the Klondike gold fields; Mayo, the economic base of the territory; and Whitehorse, the transportation hub. The territory was dominated by three monopolies, whose activities formed a "tripod" based upon gold extraction by the Yukon Consolidated Gold Company in Dawson, silver-lead mining by the Treadwell Yukon Company in Mayo, and transportation by the White Pass railway based in Whitehorse. With the increase in the price of gold in 1934, and the efficient exploitation of the Klondike placer deposits by the Yukon Consolidated Gold Company, Dawson contributed its share to Yukon's modest prosperity. However, the territory's society and economy were based totally upon resource extraction and evacuation, with no internal development.

Simplicity in economic activity was reflected in administration, which was minimal in the extreme during these "always afternoon years."[4] After the First World War, the Yukon's constitutional development towards self-government went into reverse, as the federal government slashed its annual grant and the size of the civil service, reduced the assembly from ten elected representatives to three, and eliminated the office of the chief executive, the commissioner, by combining its functions with those of a lesser official, the gold commissioner. This position was, in turn, abolished in 1932, and its responsibilities transferred to a lower level official, the territorial comptroller (or controller), George A. Jeckell, who was the Yukon's chief executive officer. Some indication of the narrow range of territorial government can be seen by identifying Jeckell's consolidated functions: comptroller (from

1913); agent for public works (1914); income tax inspector (1918); *ex officio* mayor of Dawson (1926); chief registrar of land titles; and senior territorial executive upon the abolition of gold commissioner (1932).[5] The Yukon had a curious system of government, under the control of this one man from 1932 to 1947. Liquor sales profits and federal grants enabled this tiny administration to function with under $200,000 in revenue as late as 1937.[6]

In 1941, Dawson was the major community in Yukon, but its population remained around one thousand. At that it still contained 20 per cent of the territory's population, the same proportion as in 1921.[7] It remained the service and administrative centre for Yukon, as well as the port and supply depot for the Klondike district. The major employer in the district was the Yukon Consolidated Gold Company, which employed a labour force of up to seven hundred men, paid an annual wage bill of over one million dollars, and spent several hundred thousand dollars a year for supplies, transportation and contracts.[8]

However prosperous Dawson was in 1941, it laboured under severe disabilities. The "city" had a vast aging infrastructure of wooden buildings, many of them derelict; it was isolated at the end of a river transportation system; extremely expensive to live or invest in; and although the capital, it was primarily a company town, dependent upon the profitable depletion of one non-renewable resource.

The Second World War began in 1939, but the impact was not immediately felt. For the next two years, both the Yukon Consolidated Gold and Treadwell Yukon companies maintained production. As had been the case in the First World War, however, the war eventually eroded the Yukon's economic base. Both mining companies were affected as materials and labour grew more difficult to obtain. The price of gold at least remained constant, but when the silver market weakened, Treadwell Yukon shut down in November 1941. This disrupted the fragile, if profitable, "tripod" economy, leaving only the Yukon Consolidated Gold company in Dawson and the White Pass and Yukon Route railway.

The Yukon Consolidated did not close down, but it operated with difficulty. The depression no longer drove men north; they were drawn off to the armed forces or to obtain more remunerative war work elsewhere. In 1941, the company faced its first employees' strike. The firm granted a cost of living allowance, which cut into profitability, but even with this, the company was unable to attract sufficient labour.[9] The labour force fell from 700 in 1941 to 470 in 1942.[10] Wartime income taxes were a major disincentive for workers able to earn more elsewhere and live more cheaply than in Dawson.[11] As a result, the number of workers fell to a low of 174 in 1944, the number of dredges working dropped from 10 in 1940 to 3 in 1944. Gold production declined proportionately. The 1944 figure was a quarter that of 1940.[12]

As was the case in the First World War, the decline in gold production hurt the Yukon's economy, but history did not repeat itself. The slack was taken up by a second Yukon "rush": a second influx of capital and labour comparable to 1896, which was to create an entirely new economy, one functioning at a higher, more stable level of activity, and independent of placer gold mining. This was a result of three defence projects in the Yukon: the Northwest Staging Route, the Canol Pipelines, and the Alaska Highway, all of which gave the Yukon a new "value" to the outside world. The new status originated in its geographical position, not its natural resources nor its population. Of these three, the most important was the Alaska Highway. Had conditions permitted consultation, residents would have supported a road which brought some benefit to the mining areas around Dawson and Mayo, not one which merely cut across the territory.

Yukoners had long considered both a road link with the "outside" and an internal network desirable. The territory's distance from the populated regions of North America resulted in high mining and living costs. The Yukon was not isolated, but the White Pass and Yukon Route's river-rail system remained its one transportation route to the outside world. This was efficient and reliable, but it was a costly monopoly, and its operations north of the railhead at Whitehorse were only seasonal. Most importantly, it could not move large amounts of goods as cheaply or efficiently as could a road.

Before the First World War, the territorial administration had attempted to develop an internal road system. Dawson's isolation after the close of navigation was mitigated somewhat by a winter road to Whitehorse which was maintained until 1937. George Black, while commissioner from 1912 until 1916, apparently began upgrading this to an all-season road, but his initiatives were not sustained.[13]

In 1929, the International Highway Association was formed to push for a road link between Alaska and the rest of the continent.[14] The initiative came from Alaska, but gained support in British Columbia and Washington state, and in the Yukon where the "International Highway Association of Yukon" was formed in May 1929.[15] The Alaskans, like the U.S. military in 1942, sought the shortest route, but when Alaska's superintendent of highways suggested that the highway run from Whitehorse via Kluane to the Alaska boundary, the Yukon Superintendent of Works replied:

> The Yukon government could not very well approve of the Kluane route. The direction is leading away from that part of the Territory which is considered most promising. I refer to the foothills and height of land which forms the watershed between the Mackenzie and Yukon river tributaries. . . .This range is our White Hope. . .and the Territory needs a better road than we have at present to Whitehorse. . .why not bring the highway via Dawson and in striking distance of our resources?[16]

A highway from Alaska to the "outside" via Dawson and Mayo would meet the needs of Yukoners: improved access to mining areas, local trade, even tourism. These needs seldom coincided with the priorities of outside planners. In order to emphasize the importance of this road, the secretary of the association in Dawson urged local support of its efforts "in putting through a project that means more to Dawson than anything that has happened since gold was discovered."[17]

To a certain extent, Dawson residents succeeded in getting across their concern. The 1933 proposed route, from Vancouver via Hazelton, went through Dawson on its way to Fairbanks.[18] However, nothing resulted from this proposal. Yukon development of any sort was a low priority for the federal government, although B.C.'s premier T. "Duff" Pattullo offered to take the territory out of national hands in order to build the road. Also, during the depression, there was no economic reason for a road to the outside, as long as the White Pass was able to meet the territory's limited needs. Ironically, the introduction of scheduled air service from Dawson to Edmonton and Vancouver via Whitehorse in the late 1930's undermined the rationale for maintaining the old winter road between Dawson and Whitehorse. The mail contracts went from road to air couriers, eliminating the subsidy that had made the overland trail possible.[19]

Through the late 1930's, a number of possible routes for the highway were discussed, most of which included Dawson. Indeed, in July, 1941, it appeared inevitable that the "B" or interior route, which totally by-passed Whitehorse, but went through Dawson, would be the one chosen. The Americans disagreed, preferring the coastal or "A" route via Whitehorse.[20]

Whether either the "A" or the "B" route would have been chosen, given divergent American and Canadian recommendations, is debatable. In the end neither mattered. Ten years of effort almost brought Dawson the external road link it needed so badly, but all came to naught in the face of U.S. military exigencies. In March 1942, George Black suggested to Prime Minister Mackenzie King that a road from Whitehorse to Dawson, then to Alaska, was more efficient than the route proposed, as it could utilize existing routes. But Dawson was irrelevant to American military needs, so the route followed the chain of airports from Fort St. John to Alaska, as the U.S. military demanded.[21]

The construction of the Alaska Highway came at an auspicious moment for the territorial economy. The Yukon was declining slowly in population and economic activity after the Treadwell Company ceased operations at Mayo in November 1941, and the Yukon Consolidated Gold company faced increasing difficulties obtaining labour and materials. The Alaska Highway reversed this decline, but its effects were unevenly distributed. Whitehorse benefited, as the most accessible site along the highway. It had year-round rail connections with the port of Skagway and a modern, first-class airport served by local, national and international airlines and so became the obvious choice as the operational centre for the highway project.[22] In September 1942, its status became official when the Northwest Service Command was established in Whitehorse. The highway, the Canol projects, the Whitehorse refinery in connection with Canol, and other war projects drew thousands of service men and civilians to well paid jobs. Hundreds of others followed to cater to their needs. The transformation of a village of 750 people into a city of several thousand involved massive social dislocations, but these growth problems were more bearable than the stagnation afflicting Dawson.[23]

That sensitive barometer of Yukon prosperity, liquor sales, reveals the highway's contrasting effects on Dawson and Whitehorse. In the month of April 1942, liquor sales in Dawson were $9,000; in Whitehorse they were $7,000. Over the next ten months, until the end of January 1943, peak sales in Dawson were $17,000 in December, and total sales for the period were $111,422. At Whitehorse, on the other hand, sales rose every month until December, when they peaked at $86,900. Sales fell in January 1943 to $54,400 — half of Dawson liquor sales over the ten-month period. Total sales in Whitehorse were $417,000, almost four times those of Dawson. J.E. Gibben, acting controller, recognized the significance of this huge gap:

> It is only in the south end of the Territory that there has been an increase in the purchasing power of the community.... The people in Dawson and Mayo Districts are receiving no pecuniary benefit from war industries or war projects, and increased taxation has brought about a self-imposed liquor rationing. Sales at the Dawson and Mayo stores were never so low as they are now.[24]

The most immediate detrimental effect of highway construction on Dawson resulted from railway congestion as U.S. Army material poured into the Yukon during the late winter of 1942. Unfortunately, the only "funnel" was the White Pass and Yukon Route's antiquated narrow gauge railway from Skagway to Whitehorse. It was barely adequate to carry in the supplies necessary for Yukon's residents; the system could not handle both normal requirements and the thousands of tons necessary for road construction. Priorities determined by American military needs threatened to curtail mining operations and to starve Yukon residents as essential supplies were held up at Skagway. In order to resolve conflicting "priorities" — human survival in Yukon or highway construction — the federal government appointed the territorial controller, G.A. Jeckell, to be "wartime superintendent of transportation."[25] Jeckell was able to ensure that the minimum got through in 1942, but over the winter of 1942-43 congestion on the White Pass was even worse. In the end, Yukon officials got sufficient material in for 1943, but the conflict over transportation priorities was not resolved until the highway was completed that year.

Congestion on the White Pass was eventually solved by negotiations and goodwill between the U.S. military and Canadian officials. Another problem faced by the residents of Dawson, as Gibben noted, was the imposition of wartime taxes, without compensatory "war industries or war projects." Dawson was expensive to live in at the best of times; the new taxes threatened to make it uninhabitable. In July, the *Dawson News* reported that "due in great respect to this new taxation, many are contemplating "evacuating" by fall if at all possible. This is a threat to the community, as with conditions in Dawson as they are, these people likely will not return north, thereby creating a shortage of labour for this camp in the future."[26]

Already that summer, there was a shortage of labour in the district. Many men did not return north in the spring, preferring to seek work elsewhere. Others were drawn off "to construction work on the Alaska Highway, where higher wages were promised," or to such services as restaurant work in Whitehorse "due to continued construction work."[27] By July, there was already "a scarcity of labour in the Dawson district," and the Yukon Consolidated Gold company took the unprecedented step of hiring local native labour for work on its dredges. Unlike whites, natives had little labour mobility, but they were insufficiently integrated into the wage economy to ignore the necessity of hunting for meat in the fall. As a result, they were pronounced good workers, if "undependable."[28]

The exodus from Dawson continued through the fall and winter. In October, the *News* noted as a "Sign of the Times" that the Occidental Hotel would be closing down indefinitely because of the "loss of business generally occasioned by the trek of men to the south."[29] By January, the paper observed that "Dawson City is Very Quiet." Between the close of steamer navigation in October and the end of January, 262 residents had left the district, a massive population loss from a community of little more than 1,000.[30]

Dawson lost more than people to Whitehorse. In July 1942, a locomotive, tender and twenty-two box cars from the old Klondike Mines Railway yards in Klondike City were removed for use on the White Pass.[31] The government also moved its road building equipment to Whitehorse.[32] In October, the proprietor of the Cascade Laundry transferred his dry cleaning plant to the highway centre; his wife stayed in Dawson until November 1943, when she closed the laundry there and joined him.[33] During 1942 and 1943, furniture, machinery, heavy equipment, a sawmill, houses, and even the plate glass windows of a store were moved from Dawson to Whitehorse.[34]

Compared both to what it had been before the war, and what Whitehorse was becoming, Dawson had fallen to a low ebb. In spite of attempts at bravado, the local press reflected the prevailing gloom.[35] Visitors, including the British high commissioner, Malcolm MacDonald, were caught up in the atmosphere.[36] Even the president of the White Pass could offer no more than "while the prospects in the immediate future did not look any too bright for this country, he was optimistic as to the long pull."[37]

But Dawson sustained more serious losses during the war than plate glass windows and more damning assessments of its prospects than those of visitors. Once war projects like the highway and Canol got underway in 1942, the economic centre of the territory shifted south. Mayo was shut down for the duration, and Dawson was barely sustained by a scaled-down Yukon Consolidated Gold Company. Whitehorse, on the other hand, boomed in population, wealth, and problems. Gradually, it exerted its pull on Dawson. In July 1942, it became obvious to the R.C.M.P. inspector that he would have to spend half of his time at Whitehorse. The next year, the force moved its headquarters there and reduced Dawson to the status of a detachment. The editor of the *Dawson News* was fully aware of the significance of the transfer: it was "an historic change for that organization and for Dawson, the capital of the Territory."[38] C.K. LeCapelain, the Canadian officer responsible for liaison with the U.S. military, faced the same problem as the R.C.M.P. The bulk of official government business was in the south. He could not simply transfer the administrative headquarters of the government, but he suggested that the controller spend more time in the south, the same first step the R.C.M.P. inspector had taken in 1942.[39] Significantly, by 1943, the federal departments of labour and transport, plus the Wartime Prices and Trade Board, were located in Whitehorse, not Dawson.[40]

Two further indications of Dawson's decline were the move to Whitehorse by George Black, the Yukon's member of parliament, in 1944, and by the Anglican bishop in 1946.[41] George and Martha Black had been residents of Dawson since the gold rush, but by 1944, George Black's law practice there had dwindled, and he obviously saw little future for the community. The Anglican bishop was, in a sense, following his congregation, removing his episcopal residence to Whitehorse, although St. Paul's in Dawson remained a "Pro-Cathedral" for a number of years. Socially, the removal of Dawson's, and indeed the Yukon's, most prominent couple, and of the Anglican bishop, further emphasized Dawson's decline and Whitehorse's new preeminence.

As early as March 1943, G.A. Jeckell had grasped the implications of the highway for the Yukon and specifically for the two "interior" mining districts around Dawson and Mayo. The road had been built in the wrong place for Yukoners' needs, but an all weather road linking the Alaska Highway with Dawson and Mayo would reduce the costs of mining and living and would provide improved access to mining districts.[42] Jeckell suggested to the federal government that such roads be built as postwar reconstruction projects, but to little effect. In February of 1945, Jeckell made public his views on the necessity of an all-weather road connecting Dawson and Mayo to the outside. In a sense, he was attempting to enlist Dawson and Mayo residents in his campaign to have a road built; recognizing the limitations of bureaucratic pressure, he sought to apply political force.[43] His address had a galvanizing effect on the residents of Dawson, who had been powerless to prevent the rapid decline of Dawson since 1942. Jeckell presented them with a panacea: a road which would offer year-round access to Dawson and Mayo. This would undermine the monopoly of the White Pass (and to a certain extent of Canadian Pacific Airlines), reduce the need for local merchants to carry large inventories, and enable mining companies to remove ore all year. By reducing the cost of living and of mining in the Yukon, it would boost population and production.

The Yukon council submitted a five-year territorial road building programme to the federal government in April 1945. The 382 mile road from Dawson to Whitehorse was identified as the priority.[44] At about the same time, two discordant notes were struck by residents of Whitehorse. One group, the "Whitehorse Men's Council," introduced a resolution to the council which, while supporting the idea of a Dawson-Whitehorse road "in a general way," argued that scarce resources could be better utilized in Whitehorse.

> Having regard to the important part Whitehorse is contributing, and will continue to contribute, to the future development of the Yukon, more especially in the matter of transportation, and as Whitehorse enjoys a daily mail service with the rest of Canada, we submit that the Administrative Offices should now be located in this area.[45]

Another group of Whitehorse residents introduced a petition for "an additional elected member or members of the Yukon Council for the Whitehorse district."[46] This would give Whitehorse political influence commensurate with its economic and demographic advantage and would strengthen its case to move the capital south.

In a sense, these two proposals, for a road to Dawson and Mayo and for the transfer of the capital to Whitehorse, were the opening steps in a race between Dawson and Whitehorse. The former needed a road to protect what little was left, the latter wished to dominate the Yukon totally. Dawson's decline into isolation, and Whitehorse's preeminence on the basis of the highway, appeared to give the latter the advantage, but Dawson still possessed the capital. If its residents could eliminate its isolation, the town could remain the centre of the government.

In the immediate aftermath of the war, there was some complacency in Dawson that it would regain its economic control once gold production resumed, and that Whitehorse would revert to its former subordinate status.

The closing of the Whitehorse refinery and pipeline, and the American pullout in April 1945, do not appear to have been regarded as disasters in Dawson. The *Dawson News* had discussed the 1942 boom in Whitehorse with little excitement; it now looked on the population decline there with similar objectivity.[47] There was probably a belief that Yukon would return to the *status quo ante bellum,* that Dawson and Mayo would carry the territory economically, and that Whitehorse would become again simply the village at the head of navigation. The road from Dawson to the Alaska Highway would reduce the cost of mining and of living, thereby eliminating the community's major disadvantage.

But the Alaska Highway had transformed the Yukon as thoroughly as had the gold rush, to the benefit of Whitehorse and the detriment of Dawson. After the war, Whitehorse deflated somewhat (as had Dawson at the turn of the century), but it did not collapse. As the junction of river, rail, road and air transportation systems, in year-round connection with the rest of Canada, it took over much of Dawson's entrepôt and service functions. It alone was the distribution point for the entire territory and served as a base for economic activities directly related to the highway, including maintaining and supplying the large Canadian military establishment still in the city. The revival of Mayo after 1946 strengthened Whitehorse further and had two serious implications for Dawson: Mayo soon passed Dawson in volume and value of production, so had a stronger claim to road connections than did Dawson; and Mayo was entirely dependent upon Whitehorse for goods, services and transportation. Dawson provided Mayo merely with administration — and even this it had to share with Whitehorse.

Dawson, on the other hand, continued to decline in importance. It took several years for gold production to return to its prewar levels, but wartime increases in the cost of supplies and of labour, in association with a fixed price for gold, undermined profitability. There was no longer a depression to drive workers north to work the dredges so the company had to deal with a formidable union, the Dawson Miners' Union. The firm agreed to substantial pay increases over a three-year contract in 1946, in order to attract workers.[48] In spite of these efforts, it still could not attract sufficient labour to achieve full production. To make matters worse, gold mining after the war was so unprofitable that the federal government had to subsidize it through the "Emergency Gold Mining Assistance Act." This effectively undermined whatever claims Dawson's gold mining had to economic importance.

Dawson was also a drain on territorial revenues. Whitehorse, on the other hand, was a considerable source of revenue through taxes and licences paid there and through its contribution to the territory's profits from liquor sales, the largest territorial source of revenue.[49] Dawson also suffered in contrast to Whitehorse in terms of welfare. It was not a community of young, healthy income earners but had a comparatively large population of indigents, who had to be maintained at territorial expense.[50] It was also saddled with an expensive infrastructure of dilapidated buildings, which could only be maintained at great expense, or which were abandoned, enhancing the impression of a ghost town. The lack of adequate housing[51] and the high cost of living in such an isolated community were vividly demonstrated in the difficulties the territorial government faced in hiring a territorial treasurer in 1947 and 1948.[52] There were no similar problems in hiring staff to fill positions in Whitehorse.

In spite of Dawson's obvious handicaps after the war, its partisans in the local Chamber of Mines defended the city vigorously. The chamber was well organized and ably led by such men as E.O. Envoldsen, H.W. Firth, and Jeckell. It enjoyed strong local support and pursued a consistent programme. The central goal, defined by the secretary-manager, H.W. Firth, in 1947, was

> to reduce the cost of living in this District. With prices and wages increasing, it was felt that unless we could lower our living and operating costs, by obtaining cheaper transportation, and a cheaper fuel for heating and power, the economy of our Mining Industry and the livelihood of our residents would soon suffer, and the future development and future prosperity of the Mayo and Dawson Mining Districts would be retarded.[53]

To this end, in 1945, the chamber gathered a petition with 965 signatures for a road from Dawson and Mayo to Whitehorse and presented it to the Yukon council, which "heartily endorsed this project and memorialized the Federal Government to this effect," and pushed to have air freight and passenger rates reduced.[54] The next year, it continued to push strongly for the road, as well as a connection with the Alaska road system via Sixty-Mile. It also brought the Air Transportation Board to Dawson in May 1946 for a hearing on air rates, worked with Canadian Pacific Airlines and White Pass and Yukon Route officials on freight and tourism needs in Dawson, and got the territorial fuel tax reduced.[55] By 1948, it concentrated upon extending the highway and lowering freight rates.[56]

Of all these projects, a road link with the outside was the priority. The town attempted, with mixed results, to enlist the help of George Black.[57] By the end of 1946, it became obvious that submissions from the controller, endorsement by the Yukon council, and a petition signed by over 900 residents of the Dawson district had not convinced the federal government of the necessity for a road, and Howard Firth wrote the minister of mines and resources directly.[58] In January 1947, the minister replied, referring to limited available resources and the priority of housing and industrial revival over the proposed road, confirming that "construction cannot be undertaken for the time being."[59]

Without a direct road link to eliminate Dawson's isolation and reduce the cost of living in the district, the pressure to remove the capital to Whitehorse would be irresistible. But, as was the case after the First World War, when Yukoners attempted to convince Ottawa of the need for roads in the Mayo district, their lack of control over revenue and expenditure meant that investment and development priorities were determined by the federal not the territorial government.

As early as March 1946, the first hint that the federal government might be considering moving the administration to Whitehorse appeared in the *Dawson News*. Besides its greater population, a direct result of the highway, Whitehorse was considered a more appropriate site for the capital than Dawson "due to its practical situation in regard to being closer to the capital of the nation, and not isolated somewhat, as Dawson is."[60] Residents of Dawson, supported by the Yukon council and the controller, had been trying to overcome that isolation and would continue to do so for several years. However, by now it must have been obvious that the race to get Dawson a road and to keep the capital from moving was on. The outcome of this would determine whether Dawson would remain a significant centre of population or decline even further.

In June, the *Whitehorse Star* reported that the seat of government would be transferred to Whitehorse and that the change would be accompanied by such constitutional changes as the revival of the office of commissioner and the appointment of a judge for the territory.[61] The Yukon's "always afternoon" years were ending, but the expanded government role in the territory could not be carried out in Dawson, which lacked a modern infrastructure and adequate accommodations for an expanded administration.

Over the next four years, the Dawson branch of the B.C.-Yukon Chamber of Mines maintained its pressure for the crucial road connection with the Alaska Highway, while rumours continued to circulate that the capital would move. A *Montreal Star* article, reprinted in the *Dawson News* in July 1948, reported that because Whitehorse did not collapse after the war and had a population of 3,500 to Dawson's 500, it would become the capital.[62] First, however, it would have to be incorporated as a town, and a federal building had to be constructed. For the present, neither was feasible; the Whitehorse federal building was no higher a priority than Dawson's road,[63] and Whitehorse's residents refused to agree to incorporation, so the capital remained in Dawson. As late as 1949, H.L. Keenleyside, the deputy minister of mines and resources, responded ambiguously to a direct question from Firth about "rampant" rumours in the territory that the capital would move. "As far as I am aware," he said, "there is no present intention of transferring the seat of government from Dawson to Whitehorse."[64] He was probably correct. From the time of his visit to Dawson in 1947 until 1949, he had been attempting to acquire or build a more suitable residence there for the controller than the old commissioner's residence.[65]

At the same time, however, the groundwork for the transfer was being laid. By 1949, the federal forestry officer, national employment service manager, Department of Transport airways engineer, and telegraph service manager were all located in Whitehorse, as were three senior territorial officials, the public administrator, liquor controller and sanitary inspector.[66] Each year, the controller and other senior officials spent increasing amounts of time in the south — an expensive and inefficient procedure. The process of what an observer in 1950 called the "infiltration" of Whitehorse was well underway.[67] Additions to the federal and territorial administration were posted to Whitehorse rather than Dawson, leaving a mere shell in the latter. In 1948, another important step was taken when J.E. Gibben, the controller, became the Yukon's first commissioner since George Black. Finally, to overcome the problem of Whitehorse's status, the Yukon council passed a bill in 1949 which provided for civic government in Dawson, Whitehorse and Mayo, once Whitehorse's residents agreed to the incorporation of their city.[68]

In 1950, one interior mining camp was finally connected to the Alaska highway, but it was Mayo, not Dawson. By this time, Mayo was economically far more important than Dawson. The failure of the White Pass to ship all the ore produced in 1947 out to Whitehorse before the winter freeze-up convinced the federal government of the necessity of an all-weather road to Mayo. The first step was a road from Mayo to Carmacks, the site of large quantities of coal. Then, in 1950, the road was extended to join the Alaska Highway near Whitehorse.

The completion of this road did not mean a connection to Dawson, although there was a winter road to Stewart Crossing. The immediate result of the Mayo Road was harmful to Dawson. Mayo tonnage, both inward and outward bound, was far greater than Dawson tonnage, so the White Pass decided to discontinue its Stewart River operations, and to serve Dawson on a reduced basis.[69] In spite of lengthy efforts to obtain road connections, Dawson was more isolated than ever in 1950. Its first road link with the Alaska Highway was, ironically, not via Mayo, but via Alaska, in 1951. The Stewart River-Dawson section of all-weather highway was not completed until 1955, after the battle for the capital had been lost.

In September 1950, the first elected Dawson City Council in nearly fifty years met. Presumably the Whitehorse City Council also met, for it too was incorporated. Once the celebrations over the restoration of municipal institutions ended, however, the new council had to deal with the news that the federal government had finally announced its intention to transfer the territorial capital to Whitehorse.[70] Vigorous protest ensued, but the battle was lost. City council protested, but its arguments were weak, as were those of Aubrey Simmons, the Yukon's M.P., and the Chamber of Mines. Appeals to sentiment, gratitude, the continued importance of mining and tourism to the district, even claims about the damage the move would do to Dawson, were to no avail.[71] As Robert Winters, minister of resources and development, pointed out,

> Whitehorse has good communications with the rest of Canada and with the United States, including airplane and air mail service six days a week, regular and frequent train, bus and truck connections, and telegraph and telephone service. On the other hand, Dawson has scheduled airplane service three times a week, air mail service twice a week, river boat service during the summer months only, no rail connections with the "outside," no all-weather road connections with the "outside," and no long distance telephone. Whitehorse, as the railhead, is the point through which all incoming supplies are distributed and all outgoing concentrates are shipped. Every person and every article of commerce entering the Territory must pass through Whitehorse. Under these circumstances, the result has inevitably been that most of the problems with which administrative officials have to deal can now be handled much more efficiently from Whitehorse than from Dawson.[72]

The irony of Winter's reference to Whitehorse's links with the outside world, which Dawson lacked, was probably not lost on the Dawson City Council or the Chamber of Mines. However, it was too late. Dawson had failed to get its road. The factors in favour of Whitehorse, most importantly its central role in the post-highway economy, were overwhelming. It was already the capital in all but name; with the transfer from Dawson, the changeover from the old, post-gold rush Yukon was complete. Tenders for the Whitehorse federal building were called in June 1952. The Yukon council met for the first time in Whitehorse in April 1953.[73]

The building of the Alaska Highway altered the Yukon as dramatically as had the gold rush. Had the road been built as originally proposed in the 1930's, and had it been designed to meet Yukoners' needs, there would probably not have been the dramatic transformation experienced after 1942. But because it was not built for Yukoners, its effects were unpredictable. The most important consequence was the emergence of Whitehorse as the Yukon's major urban centre. Dawson was already weak before the war, but it lost further strength as the Yukon was transformed by the Alaska Highway and by Whitehorse's postwar growth. Had it obtained the road connection to the outside that its citizens sought, even as late as 1946 or 1947, it might have remained the capital, but even that is doubtful. Dawson was too closely tied, economically, demographically, and politically, to the Yukon as it was before the Second World War to make the radical transformation the Alaska Highway demanded. Whitehorse, the "transportation hub," appeared destined to replace Dawson, the declining "City of Gold."

Notes

1. *Dawson News,* 20 August 1942, p. 2. (Hereafter *DN.*)
2. Figures from F. Duerden, "The Evolution and Nature of the Contemporary Settlement Pattern in a Selected Area of the Yukon Territory," (Winnipeg: University of Manitoba Centre for Settlement Studies, 1971), p. 59.
3. J. Lotz, *Northern Realities,* (Toronto, 1972), p. 80.
4. Ibid., p. 79.
5. *DN,* 25 July 1946, p. 1, 8 June 1950, p. 1.
6. Pattullo Papers, PABC, vol. 71, file 12.
7. B. Gutsell, "Dawson City," Canadian Department of Mines and Technical Surveys, Geographical Branch, *Geographical Bulletin #3,* p. 33.
8. Reports from Yukon Consolidated Gold Co. to controller, PAC, RG 91, vol. 66, file 3525.
9. See *DN,* 29 July to 9 August 1941.
10. PAC, RG 91, vol. 66, file 3525.
11. See *DN,* July to October 1942.
12. Ibid.; see also L. Green, *The Gold Hustlers,* (Anchorage, 1977), pp. 280-87.
13. *DN,* 2 June 1945, p. 4.
14. See G. Bennett, *Yukon Transportation: A History,* Canadian Historic Sites: Occasional Papers in Archaeology and History, No. 19 (Ottawa, 1978), pp. 126-40; R.G. Buckser, "The Alaska Highway: Background to Decision," *Arctic* 21 (1968): 215-22.
15. *DN,* 28 May 1929, p. 4.
16. *DN,* 30 May 1929, p. 1.
17. *DN,* 8 June 1929, p. 4.
18. Buckser, "The Alaska Highway," pp. 217-19.
19. Bennett, *Yukon Transportation,* pp. 122-24, 143.
20. Ibid., pp. 130-31; *DN,* 12 and 15 July 1941, p. 1.
21. *DN,* 20 March 1942, pp. 2, 3.
22. The airport was completed in September 1941; *DN,* 9 September 1941, p. 1.
23. The population figure of 750 came from the 1941 census.
24. Liquor Sales in the Yukon Territory, 1 April 1942 to 31 January 1943, J.E. Gibben to R.A. Gibson, 2 February 1943, PAC, RG 91, vol. 61, file 35405.
25. Bennett, *Yukon Transportation,* p. 138. See also PAC, RG 91, vol. 61, file 35402.
26. *DN,* 11 July 1942, p. 4, see also 8 August 1942, p. 4.
27. M. Macdonald, *Down North,* (Toronto, 1943), p. 106; *DN,* 7 July 1942, p. 4.
28. G.A. Jeckell to Gen. W.M. Hoge, 24 July 1942, PAC, RG 91, vol. 61, file 35402; Yukon Consolidated Gold Co. Report for 1942, p. 2, ibid., vol. 66, file 3525.
29. *DN,* 20 October 1942, p. 4.
30. *DN,* 2 and 26 January 1943, p. 4.
31. C.J. Rogers to G.A. Jeckell, 30 June 1942, PAC, RG 91, vol. 61, file 35402; *DN,* 9 July 1942, p. 4.
32. *DN,* 28 July 1942, p. 4.
33. *DN,* 3 October 1942, p. 4; 2 November 1943, p. 1.
34. *DN,* 13 October 1942; 6 and 30 March 1943; 1 and 22 July 1943; all p. 4.
35. See, for example, *DN,* 18 and 25 May 1943; 1 April 1944; all p. 4.
36. Macdonald, *Down North,* pp. 85, 92. See also G. Taylor, "An Arctic Domesday, 1944" in C.A. Dawson, ed., *The New North-West,* (Toronto, 1947), p. 95.

37. *DN*, 31 July 1945, p. 4.
38. *DN*, 2 July 1942, p. 4; 3 June 1943, p. 1.
39. C.K. LeCapelain to R.A. Gibson, 25 February 1943, PAC, RG 91, vol. 61, file 35402.
40. Canada, Department of Mines and Resources, *The Yukon Territory*, (Ottawa, 1943), p. 6.
41. M.L. Black, *My Ninety Years*, (Anchorage, 1977), p. 147; *DN*, 3 October 1944; 8 May 1945; both p. 4; 29 August 1946, p. 3.
42. G.A. Jeckell to R.A. Gibson, 19 March 1943; 2 August 1943, PAC, RG 91, vol. 61, file 35401.
43. *DN*, 20 February 1945, p. 1. See also 15 February, p. 4; 13 March 1945, p. 4.
44. Deputy minister of mines and natural resources to deputy minister of reconstruction, 14 May 1945, PAC, RG 91, vol. 61, file 35401; Bennett, *Yukon Transportation*, pp. 141-145.
45. *DN*, 9 and 16 May 1946, p. 2.
46. *DN*, 21 April 1945, p. 4.
47. See, for example, *DN*, 31 May 1945; 12 June 1945; and 13 September 1945; all p. 4.
48. See Yukon Consolidated Gold Co. annual reports to the controller; PAC, RG 91, vol. 66, file 3525; *DN*, 6 September 1946, p. 4, for an indication of the unpleasant attitude of the company's president to the workers.
49. Data about territorial and Dawson City revenues taken from "Statements of Revenue and Expenditure, 1943-1948," in the Dawson City Museum.
50. See A.H. Gibson to G.E.B. Sinclair, 31 January and 1 March 1951, PAC, RG 85, vol. 197, file 554-201-1a; annual report of hospitals, RG 91, vol. 66, file 3525. The cost of maintaining hospital and indigent patients in the tiny community of Dawson far exceeded hospital patients in Whitehorse, where there were virtually no indigents.
51. See *DN*, 11 April 1946, p. 2.
52. See PAC, RG 91, vol. 64, file 36198.
53. *DN*, 16 January 1947, p. 1.
54. *DN*, 19 January 1946, p. 2.
55. *DN*, 16 January 1947, p. 1.
56. *DN*, 20 January 1949, p. 1.
57. *DN*, 11 April 1946, p. 2. Ironically, Aubrey Simmons, the Liberal who succeeded Black in 1949, proved more sympathetic to Dawson's need for a road, see *DN*, 16 June 1949, p. 3.
58. *DN*, 12 December 1946, pp. 1-2.
59. *DN*, 16 January 1947, p. 1.
60. *DN*, 16 March 1946, p. 4.
61. *DN*, 13 June 1946, p. 4.
62. *DN*, 22 July 1948, p. 1.
63. *DN*, 24 March 1949, p. 1.
64. *DN*, 2 June 1949, p. 1.
65. Deputy minister of mines and resources to deputy minister of public works, 17 October 1947, 15 March 1948; 10 March 1949, PAC, RG 11, vol. B.3 4260, file 994-2-E.
66. See *DN*, 11 and 18 November 1948, both p. 1; 3 February 1949, p. 4; Canada, Department of Resources and Development, *Yukon Territory*, (Ottawa, 1950), pp. 48-49.
67. *DN*, 5 October 1950, p. 2.
68. *DN*, 17 November 1949, p. 1.
69. *DN*, 12 October 1950, p. 1.
70. *DN*, 14 and 21 September 1950, both p. 1.
71. See, for example, *DN*, 21 September 1950, p. 2; 2 October 1950, p. 2; 8 March 1951, p. 2.
72. *DN*, 22 March 1951, p. 2.
73. *DN*, 5 June 1952, p. 1, 12 March 1953, p. 2.

Index

Active Force Brigade Group, 123, 125
Aishihik, 177
Aklavik, 99
Alaska Ferry System, 142
Alaska Highway Study Commission, 5
Alaska Road Commission, 44
Alaskan International Highway Commission, 4, 6, 19, 44, 48
Alaskan International Rail and Highway Commission, 135
Alyeska Pipeline, 167
Andrews, Frank, 43
Arctic Institute of North America, 85
Armour, Norman, 13
Army Medical Department (U.S.), 65-73
Ashton, General, 5
Attlee, Clement, 87

Baldwin, J.R., 89
Bank of Canada, 89
Bataan Highway, 39
Batelle Memorial Institution, 135, 138, 139, 146
Beattie, Bob, 89, 90
Beaver Creek, 177
Bennett, R.B., 15
Bernier, Joseph E., 102
Better Roads Movement, 55
Big Delta, 40, 41, 63, 176
Big Salmon, 177
Black, George, 188, 192, 193, 196, 199, 201
Bridges, 62, 63
Bright, J.S., 58, 59, 60, 62
B.C.-Yukon Chamber of Mines, 200, 202
British Commonwealth Air Training Plan, 26
British Pacific Properties, Ltd., 10
Brooks Brook, 176
Bureau of Public Roads, 55
Burwash, 160, 176

Cabinet Defence Committee (Canadian), 122, 123
Cabinet War Committee (Canadian), 30, 32, 83, 87, 90, 110
Camsell, Dr. Charles, 86, 96, 104, 107, 109
Canada-United States Basic Security Plan, 121, 123
Canadian Airborne Regiment, 128
Canadian Defence Quarterly, 128
Canadian Highway Commission, 20
Canadian Pacific Airlines, 197, 199
Canadian Rangers, 126, 128
Canol (Canadian Oil) Project, 49, 50, 86, 103, 104, 105, 109, 176, 192, 194
Capes, C.F., 41
Carcross, 160, 174, 179
Carcross Residential School, 165, 166, 181
Carmacks, 176, 177, 201
Cartwright, William, 27
Champagne, 153, 176, 182
Civilian Construction Corps (U.S.A.), 57, 58
Claxton, Brooke, 123
Clifford, Lieut. Col. F. Le P.T., 122, 124
Constantine, Maj.-Gen. C.F., 5
Contractors, civilian, 58
Cook, Les, 44, 58
Corps of Engineers, U.S. Army, 40, 43, 54, 55, 56, 63
Crerar, T.A., 4, 86, 96
Croil, Air-Commodore G.M., 5
Cromie, R.J., 16

Dalton Post, 178
Dawson City, 10, 12, 99, 163, 176, 188-203
Dawson Creek, 33, 42, 50, 60, 63, 65, 68, 71, 72, 75, 76, 108, 135, 146
Dawson Miners' Union, 198
Dawson News, 195, 196, 198, 200
Defense Highway Act (U.S.A.), 55
Dept. of Commerce (U.S.), 45

Dept. of Defence (National Defence), 20, 101, 119-129, 133, 134, 135
Dept. of Energy, Mines & Resources, 132
Dept. of External Affairs, 2, 3, 7, 12, 14, 30, 89, 100, 120
Dept. of Indian Affairs, 160
Dept. of Mines and Resources, 99, 101
Dept. of Transport, 26, 41, 78, 101, 201
Devers, Maj.-Gen. Jacob, 50
Dextrase, Gen. Jacques, 129
Dewdney, B.C. By-election, 5
DeWitt, General, 33
Dickens, Punch, 76
Diefenbaker, Prime Minister John G., 134
Dimond, Anthony J., 2, 14, 26-27
Disease, 65-73, 157-61, 182-83
Dominion Land Survey, 77
Dowell Construction Co., 58
Drummond, Leonard E., 99, 100

E.W. Elliott Co., 58
Edmonton, 57, 58, 62, 68, 76, 89, 96, 99, 100, 103, 128, 193
18th Engineer Regiment, 42, 46, 47
Embick, Lieut.-Gen. S.D., 30
Emergency Gold Mining Assistance Act, 198
Envoldsen, E.O., 199
Exercise Adonis, 124
Exercise Eagle, 124
Exercise North, 124

Fairbanks, 33, 51, 57, 75, 96, 108, 176, 193
Family allowance, 165, 166, 180
Faro, 176
Federal Works Administration, 55
Ferguson, Harley, 50
58th Medical Battalion (Clearing Company), 67
1 Canadian Infantry Brigade Group, 129
1 Canadian Infantry Division, 127
Firth, H.W., 199, 200
Fort Belvoir, 39
Fort Churchill, Manitoba, 120, 128
Fort Nelson, B.C., 26, 40, 41, 45, 48, 61, 77, 78, 85, 122, 139, 141, 142, 175
Fort Norman, 97
Fort Ord, California, 41
Fort St. John, B.C., 26, 39, 40, 41, 45, 51, 58, 65, 67, 68, 76, 77, 78, 85, 109, 122, 124, 135, 139, 141, 175
Fort Selkirk, 177
Fort Simpson, 141
Fort Smith, 97
Foster, Gen. W.W., 90, 91, 104
Foulkes, Lieut.-Gen. Charles, 123

G-4, 27, 28
Gavin, Congressman Leo H., 105
Gibben, J.E., 157, 194, 195, 201
Gibson, Brig. T.G., 127
Grande Prairie, B.C., 26, 77, 85
Gravel, Senator Mike, 145
Great Circle Route, 25, 26, 76
Gruening, Ernest, 2, 4
Gulkana, 45

Haines Cutoff, 110, 111
Haines Junction, 110, 142, 146, 177
Haines Road, 142, 143, 144, 176
Hampton, Ruth, 6
Hay River, 78
Hazelton, 2, 10, 139, 193
Hellyer, Paul, 136
Henry, Maj.-Gen. Guy V., 110, 112
Hickerson, J.D., 112
Hoge, General William (Bill) Morris, 39-51, 54, 57, 59
Honigman, 164
Hoover, President H., 6
House Roads Committee, 28
Howe, C.D., 4, 30
Hutchinson, Bruce, 7, 16-17
Hutshi, 177

Ickes, Harold L., 14, 27
Ilsley, J.L., 4
Imperial Oil, 98, 104
Indians, 151-68, 172-86
Ingalls, Lieut.-Col. Robert D., 41
Interdepartmental Panel on Joint Defence Construction Projects, 109, 110
International Highway Association, 192

Jacquot, Eugene, 156
Japanese threat, 5, 20, 21, 25-33
Jeckell, George A., 190, 194, 196, 197, 199
Johnson, Asst. Secretary of War, Louis, 5, 6
Johnston, R.W., 79

Keenleyside, H.L., 31, 88, 90, 105, 112, 200
Keith, H.P., 41
King, Admiral, 29
King, Prime Minister William Lyon Mackenzie, 2, 3, 4, 10-22, 83-92, 104, 120, 175, 193
Kitching, Brig. George, 125
Klondike Mines Railway, 195
Kloo Lake, 177
Kluane Lake, 47, 79, 108, 156, 174
Kluane National Park, 143, 156, 177
Klukshu, 178, 182
Knox, Secretary of the Navy, 27, 29
Korean War, 126, 127

Ladd Field, 68
Lapointe, Ernest, 15
LeCapelain, C.K., 107, 108, 196
Lend-Lease, 84
Liard River power development, 139, 146
Limited Improvement Programme, 139, 140
Little Salmon, 177
Livingstone, Dr., 99
Lloyd, Trevor, 85, 86
Lord Strathcona's Horse, 127
Lower Laberge, 177
Lower Post, 182
Lytle and Green Construction Co., 58

McCandless, Robert, 156
McCusker, Knox F., 77-78
McDame, 182
MacDonald, Donald, 76
MacDonald, Malcolm, 83-92, 95-101, 103-4, 196
MacDonald, Ramsay, 85
MacDonald, Thomas, 43, 44, 48, 55, 56, 58, 59, 60
MacDonald Memorandum, 95-101
Mackenzie, Ian, 9, 17, 20
Mackenzie, J., 4
McLean, Dan, 76
Magnuson, Congressman Warren, 6, 19, 110
Maintenance, Alaska Highway, 136-37, 141
Marchand, Dr. John, 153, 157
Marshall, General, 27, 29
Mayo, 176, 193, 196, 197, 198, 200, 201
Meek, R.J., 155, 161
Military Co-operation Committee (Can.-U.S.), 121
Mine Access Roads Program, 133
Mobile Striking Force, 123, 124, 125, 126, 127, 128
Moffat, J. Pierrepont, 30, 31, 39
Moosehide, 157
Mueller, Lieut.-Col. E.A., 41
Murray, George, 11
Muskeg, 47

Nabesna, 43
NATO, 125
Navy, United States, 32
Nelles, Commodore Percy W., 5
Nielson, Eric, 138
97th Engineer Company (U.S.), 46
93rd Engineer Company (U.S.), 49
Norman Wells, 86, 96, 97, 103
Northern Nationalists, 85, 86
Northern Roads programme (Dept. of Indian Affairs and Northern Development), 133
Northway, 40, 48, 176

Northwest Highway System, 120, 125, 128, 135, 176
Northwest Service Command, 50, 65, 69, 70, 72, 83, 194
Northwest Staging Route, 26, 42, 77, 85, 91, 103, 105, 175, 192

O'Connor, Colonel James A. "Patsy," 40, 45, 48, 50, 54
Okes Construction Co., 50
Old Age Assistance, 180

Palfreyman, Capt. W.C., 50
Pattullo, Thomas Dufferin, 1-7, 9-22, 193
Pearson, Lester, 106
Pelly Crossing, 177
Penhale, Maj.-Gen. M.H.S., 124, 126
Permanent Joint Board on Defence, 7, 20, 26, 104, 107, 109, 112, 113, 121
Pettit, Maj. Frank, 45
Port Radium, 124
Post Hostilities Problems Committee, 112
Prince Rupert, 57, 58
Princess Patricia's Canadian Light Infantry, 124, 126
Public Health Service (U.S.), 68
Public Roads Administration (U.S.A.), 41, 42, 43, 45, 46, 48, 49, 54-63, 75, 107, 153, 160, 175
Public Works Canada, 132-46

R. Melville Smith Co., Ltd., 50
Ralston, J.L., 22
Reagan, President R., 145
Reid, Escott, 106, 120
Reybold, Maj.-Gen. Eugene, 42
Richardson Highway, 41
Riggs, Thomas, 44, 48
Road Standards, 46, 56, 59, 76, 109
Roads to Resources, 133, 134, 135
Robertson, Norman, 30, 31, 32, 106
Rocky Mountain Trench, 14
Roosevelt, President F.D., 5, 7, 12, 27, 30, 39, 76
Ross River, 182
Routes, 14, 20, 193
Royal Canadian Air Force, 122, 123, 127
Royal Canadian Engineers, 119
Royal Canadian Mounted Police, 102, 123, 163, 183, 184, 196
Royal Commission on Dominion-Provincial Relations, 12
Royal Commission on Government Reorganization, 136
Rust, Ken, 46

St. Lawrence Seaway, 18

Schilsky, Lieut.-Col. Reinder, 45
Seattle, 6
74th Engineer Company (Light Pontoon), 42
73rd Engineer Company (Light Pontoon), 42
Shakwak Project, 144-45, 146
Shakwak Review Committee, 144
Siddall, K.H., 79
Sikanni Chief River, 77, 78
Silverman, Maj. Mendel, 65, 68
Simmons, Aubrey, 202
Simonds, Lieut.-Gen. Guy, 127
Sixty-Mile, 199
Skagway, Alaska, 46, 57, 58, 68, 194
Skelton, Dr. O.D., 2, 3, 5, 14, 16
Slana, 43, 73
Somervall, Lieut.-Gen. Brehon, 42, 48, 49, 50
Soviet Union, 112, 119-29
Special Service Force, 129
Stanford Research Institute, 138, 139, 140, 141, 145
State Department, United States, 7
Stefansson, Vilhjalmur, 102
Stewart, Charles, 19
Stewart Crossing, 201
Stimson, Secretary of War, 27, 29
Sturdevant, Brig.-Gen. C.L., 29, 39, 41, 42, 45, 48, 49, 56
Styer, Maj.-Gen. W.D., 50
Suff, Sir Patrick, 91
Sweetbriar, 124, 125, 126, 129

Telegraph Creek, 182
Territory of Alaska, Dept. of Health, 67
Teslin, 43, 73, 153, 156, 157, 160, 175, 176, 177
35th Engineer Regiment (Combat), 41, 42, 56
340th Engineer Regiment, 42, 45, 46, 47
341st Engineer Regiment, 42
Tolmie, Simon Fraser, 1, 10-11
Topographical Survey of Canada, 78

TransCanada Highway, 17, 134
Treadwell Yukon Company, 190, 191, 193
Truman, Senator Harry S. (Truman Committee), 104, 105
Tully, Colonel Jim
Turner, Frank C., 62
25 Canadian Infantry Brigade Replacement Group, 127

Unemployment, 9, 18
United States Air Force, 122
Upper Laberge, 177
Upper Liard, 160
Urquhart, Dr., 99

Valdez, 57
Vokes, Maj.-Gen. Chris, 126, 127

War Department, United States, 5-7, 16, 25, 27, 28, 42, 75
War Plans Division, United States Army, 26-27, 28, 29
Watson Lake, Yukon Territory, 26, 40, 41, 45, 48, 77, 85, 122, 139, 142, 175, 177
Western Defense Command, United States, 33
White Pass & Yukon Route, 40, 49, 174, 190, 191, 192, 193, 194, 195, 197, 199, 201
Whitehorse, Yukon, 26, 30, 39, 40, 41, 44, 48, 51, 65, 66, 67, 71, 77, 85, 86, 96, 97, 103, 108, 122, 123, 125, 126, 127, 139, 157, 160, 163, 164, 165, 175, 176, 183, 188-203
Whitehorse Star, 200
Wilson, Col. A.R., 28
Wismer, Mr., 41
Works Project Administration (U.S.A.), 57, 58
Wrong, Hume, 106

Yukon Consolidated Gold Company, 190, 191, 193, 195, 196